Praise for Jill Dyché's *e-Data*

"Jill is not afraid to call a spade a spade in this well-written, to-the-point guide on data warehousing. This business-friendly book describes not only the fundamentals of what a data warehouse should be; it describes the fundamentals of why you develop a data warehouse and how to avoid the errors that have caused so many data warehousing projects to fail. While addressed to business professionals, data warehousing staff should read this book. The list of the new top ten data warehousing pitfalls alone is worth more than the price of the book."

> **—Larry P. English, President, Information Impact International, Inc., and author of *Improving Data Warehouse and Business Information Quality***

"This book removes the confusion surrounding the buzz words and backs up the value of data warehousing with real case studies. A must read for organizations embarking on a data warehouse project."

> **—Kevin H. Strange, Vice President and Research Director, Gartner Group**

"Jill Dyché has done the industry a huge favor by writing the definitive 'insider's' guide on data warehousing. Full of practical advice and insights, this easy-to-read book gives business executives all the ammunition they need to make intelligent decisions about if, when, and how they should deploy data warehousing technologies. Humorous and fast-paced, this book was a delight to read."

> **—Wayne Eckerson, Senior Consultant, The Patricia Seybold Group**

"Jill Dyché gives a very readable and understandable account of the value and meaning of data warehousing. I would happily recommend this book to any business person, manager, or executive who has heard the hype but genuinely wants to know the reality."

> **—Barry Devlin, Data Warehouse Executive Consultant, IBM**

"This book is a must-read for any business executive interested in cutting through the hype surrounding data warehousing, business intelligence, and decision support. A plain language, how-to primer that demystifies the process of designing, implementing, and deploying a data warehouse. The ROI for this book will run into the six or seven figure range for most companies."

> **—Michael P. Burwen, President, Palo Alto Management Group, Inc.**

"This is a solid work that hits its mark. I have read, and been bored by, too many management books, but this was a pleasure to read. The book addresses the technical issues without oversimplifying, and maintains a balanced tone that keeps the reader's interest."

> **—Dan Sullivan, Director of Data Warehousing Computer Resource Team, Inc.**

e-Data

Addison-Wesley Information Technology Series
Capers Jones, Series Editor

The information technology (IT) industry is in the public eye now more than ever before because of a number of major issues in which software technology and national policies are closely related. As the use of software expands, there is a continuing need for business and software professionals to stay current with the state of the art in software methodologies and technologies. The goal of the Addison-Wesley Information Technology Series is to cover any and all topics that affect the IT community: These books illustrate and explore how information technology can be aligned with business practices to achieve business goals and support business imperatives. Addison-Wesley has created this innovative series to empower you with the benefits of the industry experts' experience.

For more information point your browser to
http://www.awl.com/cseng/series/it/

Wayne Applehans, Alden Globe, and Greg Laugero, *Managing Knowledge: A Practical Web-Based Approach.* ISBN: 0-201-43315-X

Gregory C. Dennis and James R. Rubin, *Mission-Critical Java™ Project Management: Business Strategies, Applications, and Development.* ISBN: 0-201-32573-X

Kevin Dick, *XML: A Manager's Guide.* ISBN: 0-201-43335-4

Jill Dyché, *e-Data: Turning Data into Information with Data Warehousing.* ISBN: 0-201-65780-5

Capers Jones, *Software Assessments, Benchmarks, and Best Practices.* ISBN: 0-201-48542-7

Capers Jones, *The Year 2000 Software Problem: Quantifying the Costs and Assessing the Consequences.* ISBN: 0-201-30964-5

Ravi Kalakota and Marcia Robinson, *e-Business: Roadmap for Success.* ISBN: 0-201-60480-9

David Linthicum, *Enterprise Application Integration.* ISBN: 0-201-61583-5

Sergio Lozinsky, *Enterprise-Wide Software Solutions: Integration Strategies and Practices.* ISBN: 0-201-30971-8

Patrick O'Beirne, *Managing the Euro in Information Systems: Strategies for Successful Changeover.* ISBN: 0-201-60482-5

Mai-lan Tomsen, *Killer Content: Value Strategies for Web Content and E-Commerce.* ISBN: 0-201-65786-4

Bill Wiley, *Essential System Requirements: A Practical Guide to Event-Driven Methods.* ISBN: 0-201-61606-8

Bill Zoellick, *Web Engagement: Connecting to Customers in e-Business.* ISBN: 0-201-65766-X

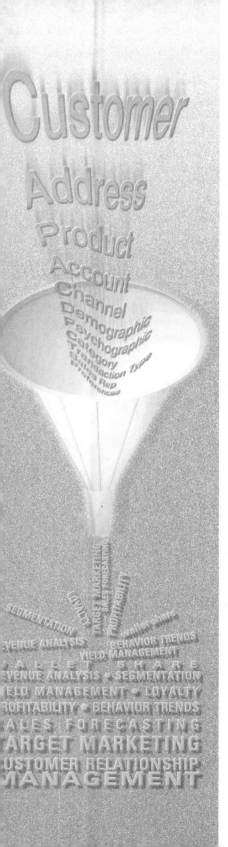

e-Data

Turning Data into Information with Data Warehousing

Jill Dyché

Addison-Wesley

An imprint of Addison Wesley Longman, Inc.
Reading, Massachusetts • Harlow, England • Menlo Park,
California • Berkeley, California • Don Mills, Ontario •
Sydney • Bonn • Amsterdam • Tokyo • Mexico City

The publisher offers discounts on this book when ordered in quantity for special sales. For more information, please contact:

AWL Direct Sales
Addison Wesley Longman, Inc.
One Jacob Way
Reading, Massachusetts 01867
(781) 944-3700

Visit AW on the Web: www.awl.com/cseng/

Library of Congress Cataloging-in-Publication Data

Dyché, Jill
    e-Data: turning data into information with data warehousing/Jill Dyché.
        p.   cm.—(Addison-Wesley information technology series)
    Includes bibliographical references and index.
    ISBN 0-201-65780-5
    1. Data warehousing.   I. Title.   II. Series.
  QA76.9.D37 D93 2000
  658.4'038'0285574—dc21   99–057205

Figures appearing in Chapter 2 and Chapter 6 have been reprinted with the permission of Palo Alto Management Group. The case study appearing in Chapter 3 has been reprinted with the permission of Bank of America. Case studies appearing in Chapter 4 have been reprinted with the permission of U.S. Quality Algorithms, California State Automobile Association, Twentieth Century Fox Film Corporation, Qantas Airways, GTE Corporation, Royal Bank Financial Group, the State of Michigan, and Hallmark Cards, Inc. The case study appearing in Chapter 6 has been reprinted with the permission of Sears, Roebuck and Co. The Data Mining List in Chapter 10 has been reprinted with the permission of Miller Freeman, Inc. Case studies appearing in Chapter 10 have been reprinted with the permission of Allsport Photography USA and Charles Schwab & Co., Inc.

Text printed on recycled and acid-free paper.

ISBN 0201657805

2 3 4 5 6 7 MA 03 02 01 00

2nd Printing   March 2000

To Evan:
As with most things in life,
I couldn't have done it without you.

Contents

CHAPTER 3   DATA WAREHOUSES AND DATABASE MARKETING   43

CHAPTER 4   DATA WAREHOUSING BY INDUSTRY   75

PART II Getting the Technology 133

CHAPTER 5 THE UNDERLYING TECHNOLOGIES: A PRIMER 135

CHAPTER 6 WHAT MANAGERS SHOULD KNOW ABOUT IMPLEMENTATION 165

CHAPTER 7   VALUE OR VAPOR? FINDING THE RIGHT VENDORS   201

PART III Getting Ready   229

Chapter 10   WHAT TO DO NOW   285

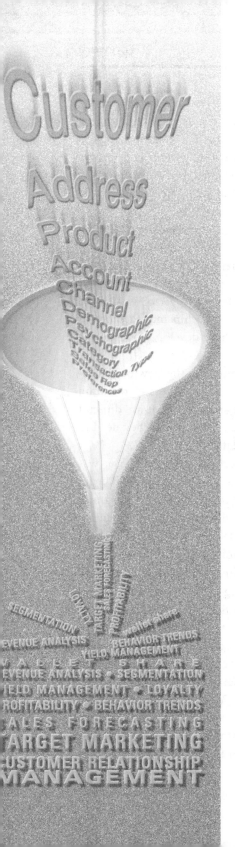

Foreword

When Don Peppers and I wrote *The One to One Future* back in 1993, we knew that our ideas about individual customer differentiation and collaboration would turn some heads. After all, most companies were still extrapolating information about their customers from small samples and relying on mass marketing as their primary means of customer communication. Having a relationship with each individual customer must have seemed like marketing science fiction for most of them.

By the time *Enterprise One to One* was published in 1997, things had changed. Businesses were moving farther away from aggregate market competition and toward one-to-one marketing. Companies had begun collecting information about individual customers, differentiating them from one another, and in the process cementing their loyalty. Moreover, with the onset of the Internet and Web-based marketing, information gathering about customers and their preferences had become easier and cheaper than ever before.

Consumers were cautiously delighted. After decades of anonymity and downright adversarial dealings with merchants and manufacturers, customers were being heard, often for the first time. Companies began to transform their call centers into customer care centers, register each customer interaction, and thereby continually refine the knowledge the company has of each customer. Furthermore, customers began to receive intelligent marketing messages from some companies, and those same companies could send fewer but more precisely targeted messages. Because companies could finally see and understand what customers were doing—and predict what they might do next—they could avoid pestering customers with endless promotions or blanket e-mail circulation. And what customers did receive from the best enterprises was more tailored to their specific preferences, and thus more engaging.

When companies have made it work, many customers have been happy to play ball, sharing their personal data while simultaneously garnering improvements in service, purchase incentives, and other rewards. And because of the Internet, many could reap the rewards without ever leaving home. For many, the relationship has progressed from adversarial to collaborative.

It's clear that some businesses have begun to "get it." One-to-one marketing has resulted in smarter sales campaigns, improved products, better service, and above all increased customer satisfaction. Companies have started measuring this success in terms of share of customer, lifetime value, return on data assets, and retention. Our own business now depends less on trying to get companies to understand one-to-one marketing and customer relationship management as inevitable response strategies and more on helping them develop a one-to-one vision and action plan.

Data warehouses have played an integral part in much of this newfound customer intelligence. Companies realize that it is not good business to maintain many disparate systems scattered throughout the organization that are difficult to access and often contain similar or even duplicate information. They need to redesign these systems to offer integrated customer data.

Although many companies adopted database technology years ago, it was only after their data consolidation had taken place that an enterprise could begin to deliver what Jill Dyché calls "a single version of the truth." Now, once customer data is loaded into a data warehouse and combined with other interesting information—such as product features, purchase history, demographic and household data, and revenues—a company can leverage the combination in innovative ways.

Not only does data warehousing result in refined knowledge about customers, it offers inventive tactics to keep them coming back. In *Enterprise One to One*, we counseled readers that it isn't enough for a business to interact with customers; it needs to render the interactions valuable and interesting enough to motivate customers to initiate contact themselves. Companies such as Qantas Airways, Aetna U.S. Healthcare USQA, and Charles Schwab & Co.—all featured in this book—are using the information on their data warehouses to motivate customers to contact them. These companies are viewed as not only service providers but also information resources. In many cases, a company can now pick up dialogue and service for an individual customer right where the last interaction left off. That's a tough act for a competitor to follow.

Jill Dyché does an expert job of describing the varied uses of data warehouses and data marts, not only in marketing but across lines of business, and not only in the United States but globally. She rightly introduces data warehousing as a tool for business transformation, and the case studies in particular bear out the discovery that data warehousing is less a technology than a business solution. Each of the 12 companies featured in this book represents a best practice, or as Jill calls it, a Data Warehouse Vanguard. And *e-Data: Turning Data into Information with Data Warehousing* deftly outlines how to join their ranks.

The payoff of one-to-one customer relations is a powerful learning relationship with individual customers, a way to build in value and loyalty while at the same time reducing costs of service. Learning relationships can't happen without individual databases and data warehousing. This book will help you with your most basic one-to-one tool.

Martha Rogers
September 1999

Martha Rogers, Ph.D., is the coauthor (with Don Peppers) of *The One to One Future: Building Relationships One Customer at a Time* (Currency/Doubleday, 1993), *Enterprise One to One: Tools for Competing in the Age of Interactivity* (1997), *The One to One Fieldbook* (1999), and *The One to One Manager* (1999). She is a founding partner at Peppers and Rogers Group, based in Stamford, Connecticut, and Adjunct Professor at Duke University.

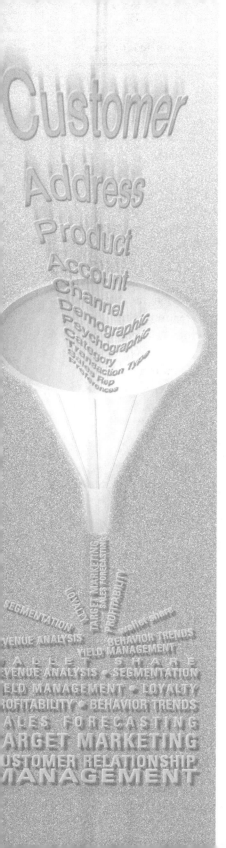

Acknowledgments

As I wrote this book I went through a struggle I imagine most authors endure during the arduous and often debilitating process of book writing: How could I impart knowledge while avoiding well-worn homiletics? How could I share those firsthand experiences and signatory false starts without offending, or at least without hitting too close to home? And how should I describe both state-of-the-art and established technologies and business concepts, tying them together in a fresh new way?

Luckily, I had the support of people with the generosity and authority to say yes. Any effort to describe the business value of data warehousing—the most collaborative of business initiatives—relies on the acumen and experience of its practitioners, many of whom kindly offered interviews for this book.

Sincere thanks go to Philippe Klee, Jay Gurjar, Steve Goudie, and Michael Vodicka from Qantas Airways; Alexandra Morehouse-McReynolds from the California State Automobile Association; David Yamashita from GTE; Kevin Butcher and Pete Rider from Royal Bank of Canada; Chris Kelly from Bank of America; Sue Doby and Rich Burgis from the State of Michigan; Nada Khater from National Bank of Kuwait; Justin Yaros of Twentieth Century Fox; Matt Schoen and Greg Walker of Allsport; Dr. Carol Diamond from Aetna U.S. Healthcare USQA; Tony Marshall of Hallmark Cards; Hank Steermann of Sears, Roebuck; and Nadene Re, Maury Ostroff, Janet Hillier, and Dawn Lepore of Charles Schwab & Co., Inc. These experts have illuminated their journeys into the often murky depths of business intelligence, allowing us all to share their visions.

I'd also like to thank Evan Levy, Bob Newell, Sam Sterling, and Steve Mays of Baseline Consulting Group; Janet Barry and Eileen Doherty of IBM; Bob Doss of Spirit Lake Consulting; Samantha Levy of Twentieth Century Fox; Barbara Britton of BEA Systems, and Linda McHugh at CSAA for opening up their networks as well as providing their own worthy insights.

Morwenna Marshall, editor of *Teradata Review* and *DB2 Magazine,* graciously allowed me to reclaim some valuable text. Also, a heartfelt shout-out to Carrie Ballinger of NCR and Mike Schmitz of DB Assist for providing me with live ammunition on performance benchmarking and database design respectively, and to Bruce Love for revealing his literary war wounds before I went into battle.

The creation of this book was streamlined by Mary O'Brien and Mariann Kourafas at Addison-Wesley. Their patience and support were immutable.

In his notes for *Death of a Salesman,* Arthur Miller wrote, "He who understands everything about his subject cannot write it. I write as much to discover as to explain." Thanks to those mentioned above, I've discovered quite a bit.

I hope you will, too.

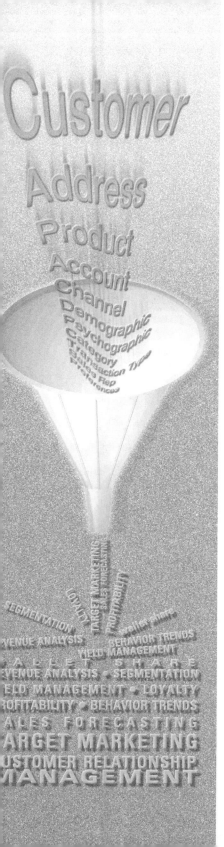

About the Author

Jill Dyché is a partner and cofounder of Baseline Consulting Group, Inc., a firm specializing in the delivery of industry-focused business intelligence solutions. She has worked with data warehouses since 1985 and currently heads up Baseline's Requirements and Audit practice, aligning strategic technology initiatives with corporate business objectives. Jill is a frequent guest speaker at technology and marketing conferences, and her articles have appeared in publications as diverse as *Information Week, DBMS, Oracle* magazine, *Teradata Review, Telephony Magazine,* the *Washington Times,* and the *Chicago Tribune.*

Baseline Consulting Group is based in California, with offices throughout the United States. Information about Baseline's products and services may be obtained on the company's Web site at *www.Baseline-Consulting.com.*

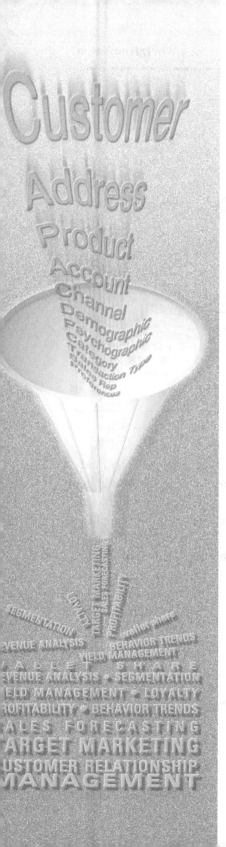

Introduction

E-commerce. Knowledge management. CRM. ERP. Smart cards. Data mining. It's true that in the vast realm of technology, the term *data warehousing* has recently ceded ground to some whiz-bang buzzwords. Even with data warehouse adoption rates steadily increasing by 30 percent a year, the Web and its patois have drowned out discussions of even more advanced technological developments, rendering state-of-the-art technical breakthroughs a second-page story.

At first, I was a bit depressed by all the Web hype. Inasmuch as data delivery was critical to the enterprise, you still needed to store that data someplace, Internet or no. With all the hullaballoo about Y2K and Web portals, had data warehousing simply faded away?

Recent customer experiences quickly shook me awake. Not only have data warehouses not faded away, they've assumed center stage again. While certain terminology might ebb and flow—data warehouses are now synonymous with "decision support" and "business intelligence" and naturally symbiotic with all things Web—the data warehouse is in fact the hub in the wheel when it comes to many companies' most important strategic initiatives.

Attend any conference these days, whether focused on industry, marketing, or technology, and there's bound to be a presentation on customer loyalty programs, retention, or customer relationship management (CRM). Sometimes supply chains and even business process reengineering still rear their heads. The point here is that regardless of what the business initiative is, the data warehouse will likely play a central role in its execution by making key data available to a cross-section of the business.

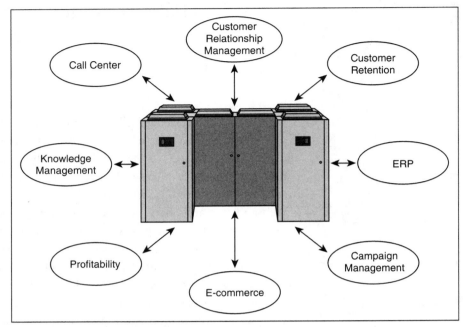

The Data Warehouse = Corporate Information Hub

In this book, the term *e-data* refers to data that has been intelligently modeled, cleansed, and consolidated into a data warehouse so that it's meaningful and useable by business people. The fact is, e-data is more important than ever. Whether you have a data warehouse, a data mart, or a decision support application (chapter 1 defines the differences), or are considering stepping up your CRM, e-commerce, or target marketing programs, having clean, consolidated information is no longer a nice add-on; it's a necessity. This book explains how e-data and a data warehouse can solve a wide range of business problems and provides real-world examples from a diverse set of industries, countries, and companies.

The Book and Its Purpose

A lot has been written about data warehouses. Development methodologies, database design conventions, and system architectures have been surveyed in a myriad of technology books, most of them discerning and clear. These books have pinpointed a market eager for information on data warehousing's technology components and how to integrate them. They are important for practitioners, offering tips on eclectic subspecialties such as data replication, star schema design, concurrency planning, and horizontal database partitioning. They deconstruct the development lifecycle and guide readers through critical processes that are fundamental to data warehouse development.

This is not one of those books.

Rather, it's a book for those of us who aren't interested in lofty technical dissertations but whose work nevertheless touches corporate data in some way. Those who are keen on getting the information the data warehouse can deliver, are hiring staff who will use it, and are interfacing with their technical colleagues in making it all work.

We need to understand what data warehouse technology really does, in common terms, and why it's right for our companies. While we're not interested in implementing it, we'd like to differentiate the well-worn buzzwords. We'd appreciate some implementation scenarios as they pertain to data warehouses and why they're used, and checklists of success criteria. We want to know how e-data can aid in marketing, assist our companies in winning customers—sometimes for the second time—and help us eat our competitors' collective lunch. We want trenchant examples and are hungry for tips from those who've realized the vision. We want to understand what data warehouses will do for us, as well as what they will not.

In short, this is a book for the rest of us.

You the Reader

Readers of this book are most likely business professionals with limited technical expertise or people who have learned a bit about technology in spite of themselves. However, technicians and practitioners might find this book a refreshing review, especially in light of the real-world case studies it presents. The audience for this book thus encompasses a wide range of readers, including those listed below.

Executives and managers will glean a lot of practical information from this book, both in terms of how to tell whether a data warehouse is the right solution for the business problem at hand and how to determine whether an existing data warehouse is living up to its value proposition.

Businesspeople whose thirst for new information alone is often justification for a data warehouse will be interested in how data warehouses are being used in various industry and marketing capacities. The book introduces concepts and terms that managers and end-users alike can learn in order to speak the same language as their information technology (IT) colleagues, ensuring that their business requirements are understood and addressed, and offers several checklists against which to gauge data warehouse readiness.

Marketing experts, including product managers, merchandisers, and strategic planners, can read about key corporate initiatives that directly leverage data warehouses.

IT managers will find this book a practical tool in confirming the requirements for successful data warehouse delivery. The book includes a variety of metrics and success factors with which technology management can measure its efforts or bolster its preparatory activities.

Consultants, too, will find this book useful; they can employ the various checklists and matrices in order to evaluate staff and review delivery success metrics, as well as to prepare their practices for what's on the horizon. Project managers, both administrative and technical, can translate the information for their own implementation strategies, supplementing both their project plans and the methodologies that drive them.

Finally, technical practitioners and implementation team members can use this book for review; in the process they may discover a thing or two about how other companies are implementing their data warehouses and as a result refine existing development activities.

Content Overview

This book provides an evolving look at data warehousing, from its various definitions to its place in the overall corporate infrastructure to its variety of uses. You can either read the chapters linearly or go directly to the areas that interest you most.

Certain readers might surmise that the book focuses on the technology platform, the data warehouse hardware itself. This approach would be like writing a book about television and discussing the electronic circuitry of the television set rather than the actual shows. While the book does explain the underlying technology involved in data warehousing by way of framing the picture, it nevertheless focuses more on "what's inside" the data warehouse, not to mention the prevalent audience. In short, the book is about what data warehouses do for a business.

The book is divided into three parts, which categorize the chapters into high-level areas. Below is a thumbnail sketch of the book's organization and contents.

Part I: Getting the Value

Chapter 1, "What Is a Data Warehouse Anyway?," discusses why data warehouses have seized hold of the corporate *Zeitgeist,* introducing some key concepts and exposing some of the trite aphorisms currently touted by the so-called experts.

Chapter 2, "Decision Support from the Bottom Up," presents an e-data analysis taxonomy for the data warehouse. It describes the four main types of business intelligence that call for data and offers some examples on their usage.

Chapter 3, "Data Warehouses and Database Marketing," outlines both the popular and the emerging database marketing applications that focus on customers while leveraging data, explaining their origins and business benefits.

Chapter 4, "Data Warehousing by Industry," covers the gamut of industry sectors and what they're doing with e-data and data warehouses, using case studies to illustrate various usage scenarios from real-world companies.

Part II: Getting the Technology

Chapter 5, "The Underlying Technologies: A Primer," not only presents some of the baseline technologies and technical concepts involved in data warehousing but also covers some of the technical activities involved in development.

Chapter 6, "What Managers Should Know About Implementation," exposes the often arcane world of data warehouse development, the methodologies it employs, and some of the well-worn staffing mistakes that get development managers into trouble. In addition, it offers some tactical hiring guidelines for you to use when conducting your next round of interviews.

Chapter 7, "Value or Vapor? Finding the Right Vendors," presents metrics for assessing the data warehouse solutions that fit best with your organization and its unique needs, including hardware, database, application, and consulting evaluation criteria.

Part III: Getting Ready

Chapter 8, "Data Warehousing's Business Value Proposition," explains how to justify your data warehouse in terms of both "hard" and "soft" benefits and offers ways to continue justifying the warehouse over time.

Chapter 9, "The Perils and Pitfalls," presents several sets of metrics in order to outline why some customer data warehouses succeed while others fail. Not content with offering the negatives, this chapter concludes with a list of what the "vanguards of data warehousing"—those companies attributing improvements of several orders of magnitude to their data warehouses—have in common when it comes to successful decision support delivery.

Chapter 10, "What to Do Now," provides some advice from the trenches on how to continue your data warehousing journey, whether you're a seasoned traveler or are just breaking in your boots.

The appendix of supplementary reading material provides a guide to other recent works for those readers who want to learn more about either the business or the technology side of e-data.

A Case Study Sneak Preview

This book is replete with both real-world case studies of companies that use data warehouses and profiles of staff members and their roles in data warehouse development teams. For example, you'll see the following processes in action.

- By using customer segmentation, **Bank of America** is getting to know its customers even better.
- **Charles Schwab & Co., Inc.** is applying the same customer satisfaction principles on which it has built its leading brokerage business to its data warehouse end-users.
- **Qantas Airways** was able to predict the Asian economic crisis with the data warehouse, and is gearing up for an encore.
- **GTE** is socializing e-data across the enterprise and across the country.
- The **California State Automobile Association** is doing more than delivering new marketing programs with its data warehouse, it's motivating cultural change.
- Canada's largest bank, **Royal Bank of Canada,** doesn't let different vendors get in the way of delivering best-of-breed e-data across its business.
- The **State of Michigan's** Family Independence Agency uses its data warehouse to behave more like a cutting-edge commercial business than a government bureau.
- **Twentieth Century Fox** may well change the face of the entertainment industry with its data mart.

These case studies and others should at a minimum serve as examples by which you can measure your own progress with e-data, and at best provide you with some great role models.

Requisite Caveats

This book is replete with examples of both successes and failures. It takes on some of data warehousing's sacred cows, including exalted methodologies, big consulting companies, venerated data models, and empire-building managers. Of course, there are exceptions to these and other evils portrayed in the book.

Most technology books abstain from discussions of specific vendors for valid and practical reasons. However, because of this book's heavy emphasis on real-world examples, specific vendors pop up here and there, particularly in chapter 4, where most of the case studies mention the company's chosen data warehouse platform.

New companies and technologies are emerging every day, and I apologize to those vendors that may have slipped through the cracks. The technologies discussed in the book are those of particular interest to the primary audience, that is, businesspeople, and thus a mere nod of the head to the many worthy data warehouse software companies that target—and are of greater interest to—the IT side of the house.

From time to time the vendor discussion will be updated and supplemented. For an updated discussion of emerging data warehouse topics, keep an eye on this book's corresponding Web site: *http://www.baseline-consulting.com/e-data.*

PART I

Getting the Value

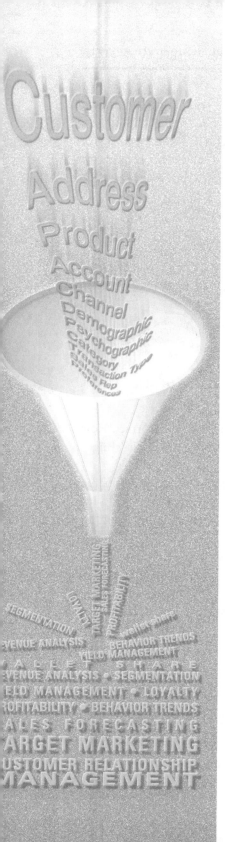

CHAPTER ONE

What Is a Data Warehouse Anyway?

O ne of the first customers I ever worked with had an extremely pressing need for a data warehouse.

My client, Jeff, invited me to his office to give me the lowdown on his business problems. When I arrived, Jeff looked at me as if I were a divine messenger sent to redeem him from paperwork hell. His desk was piled high with stacks of computer printouts and binders accentuated with yellow sticky notes. As he stood to greet me, he appeared tired and rumpled.

"All-nighter?" I asked tentatively.

"A few," he replied wearily.

As the director of marketing for a large bank's retail division, Jeff was responsible for briefing executive management on new and current marketing programs, reporting on net customer losses and acquisitions, and explaining fluctuations in revenue. The research Jeff's staff performed in order to create new marketing campaigns—not to mention deploy them—was staggering. Jeff himself had been working through the night poring over protracted printouts, trying to map new customers to the products they'd purchased.

Flash forward ten years. Jeff, now the bank's executive vice president of sales and marketing, still answers to executive staff regarding the Marketing Department's progress. And the customer churn and market differentiation challenges still exist.

The difference now lies in *how* Jeff gathers and analyzes that information. Whereas before, Jeff and his staff would request voluminous paper-based reports, studying and combining details from numerous production systems across the bank's organizations that culminated in the creation of complicated spreadsheets, now they click a mouse button.

The true benefit, however, is not so much in the time and effort saved as it is in the way the bank is leveraging technology to help its business thrive. At the center of this new technology is the data warehouse.

The Data Warehouse Defined

The definition of data warehousing has evolved since its origins in the early 1980s. Before we clarify an acceptable definition, let's look at some of the more common definitions:

- A data warehouse is a repository of subject-oriented, historical data.[1]
- The data warehouse is a collection of smaller "data marts."
- Any separate hardware platform—be it a mainframe computer or a PC—that enables a businessperson to make a decision can be considered a data warehouse.

Depending on your environment, all of these definitions can be correct. However, the most important components of a data warehouse in today's highly charged business world are as follows.

The data warehouse is indeed a separate platform—a computer different from the other computers in your IT environment. For example, figure 1-1 illustrates some of the different computers your company might be using for different functions:

Of course, different companies will have different versions of these technologies. Many small to midsize firms have never had mainframes, relying instead on larger versions of the server described. Part II of the book discusses how these different computers relate to the data warehouse. For now, let's just note that depending on the analysis being done, each of them could be considered an analysis platform in its own right.

---

1. This definition is actually a subset of the formal definition of a data warehouse as described by Bill Inmon. Dr. Inmon is considered by many to have identified the data-warehousing trend. His complete definition explains that the data warehouse is subject-oriented, integrated, time-variant, and nonvolatile (although most modern data warehouses break at least one of these four rules).

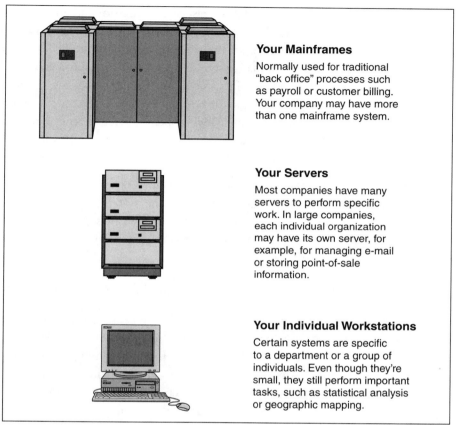

Your Mainframes

Normally used for traditional "back office" processes such as payroll or customer billing. Your company may have more than one mainframe system.

Your Servers

Most companies have many servers to perform specific work. In large companies, each individual organization may have its own server, for example, for managing e-mail or storing point-of-sale information.

Your Individual Workstations

Certain systems are specific to a department or a group of individuals. Even though they're small, they still perform important tasks, such as statistical analysis or geographic mapping.

Figure 1-1: Your Company's Different Computers

Let's forget the complex definitions about historical data, time granularity, and interconnecting servers and focus on the four general principles of data warehousing listed below. These hold true regardless of the platform, amount of data, and software being used, and they should be enough for you to form your own mental picture of a data warehouse.

1. A data warehouse is usually—but not necessarily—a separate computer, or "hardware platform." This platform may be large (a mainframe computer) or small (a workstation). In some cases it might be a collection of distributed platforms. In others, it could exist on a set of "nodes" on a larger computer platform.

2. The data on the data warehouse is used for decision making.
3. Data warehouses duplicate data that already exists elsewhere in the business (probably on one or all of the three types of computers described above). While this data redundancy sounds wasteful, it's actually a very good thing.
4. A data warehouse is not just a computer sitting someplace in the bowels of your company's data center. It's a combination of the hardware, specialized software, and data. Normally, when people refer to "our data warehouse," they're talking about a hardware box, a collection of software products and tools, and lots and lots of data.

In short, a data warehouse is a repository of information extracted from other corporate systems—be they transactional systems, departmental databases, or the company's Intranet—and accessible to business users. So, now that we know what a data warehouse comprises, what does it DO?

Data Warehousing, Decision Support, and Business Intelligence

Decision support, commonly denoted as DSS for "decision support systems," is a broad area of analysis that enables people to look at data in order to make decisions—be they large or small—about how their companies do business.

Even before adopting data warehousing, my client Jeff was a specialist in DSS. He had to be. At least once a day, his phone would ring and some executive's assistant would be requesting revenues for a certain product or inquiring about the success rate of a recent marketing campaign.

At first, Jeff wanted to quit. "How do they expect me to turn on a dime to give them these answers?" he'd grumble. The turnaround time just to access product revenue data—calling the IT people, lodging his request, and waiting for delivery of the paper printouts—normally took over a week, never mind the analysis.

Before they could simply log onto their desktop PCs and run queries—a query is a question asked of a database—most businesspeople were forced to wait days, weeks, and sometimes even months for answers to simple business questions. One department I know used to request month-end financial results and would receive a binder full of sales and revenue figures *six months later!* Figure 1-2 illustrates an all-too-typical lifecycle for acquiring valuable business information.

The analysis phase of this cycle could be considered decision support, however manual. The flaw in this cycle—which has been simplified for discussion, believe it or not!—is not only the amount of time it takes but also the resources involved. "Behind the scenes" staff—those who receive the report, interpret the

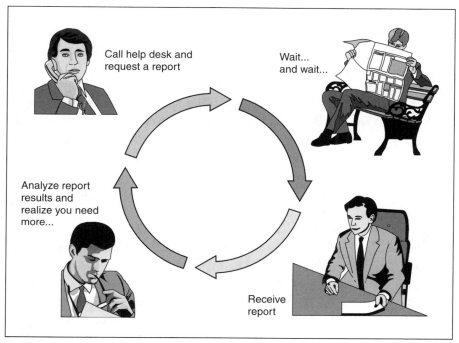

Figure 1-2: The Historical Process of Retrieving Information

necessary data, and wade through the company's operational systems to gather the appropriate information and return it—can be numerous. This type of process requires not only time, but staff resources.

Furthermore, the cycle in figure 1-2 merely represents one guy's DSS query. Multiply that by the number of staff needing similar information, but perhaps in slightly different ways, and you've got a data-gathering bonanza. In other words:

Number of Users * Number of Report Requests Per User

=

A Huge Query Backlog!

It's important here to understand the difference between data and information. The data warehouse synthesizes some very important data, but only when this data is combined into meaningful answers or reports that can aid in the interpretation of business events can it be considered information. While data has been difficult enough for companies to find and process, information has been next to impossible to obtain. And e-data, data that is cleansed and consolidated for access by a variety of business users for a variety of purposes, is the holy grail.

For example, a billing system can tell a company that a customer spent $100. An order and provisioning system can provide data that says the customer has a long-distance service. And a switch can tell a customer service manager where the customer may have called. But the data warehouse is by far the best way of collecting and storing the data necessary to tell the manager that the customer spent $100 on long-distance calls to Hawaii. Now that's information!

Where e-data comes into play is when that information is provided to customer service representatives who, though geographically dispersed, can use this customer information to tailor their responses to service requests and new orders. This not only prevents the customer service rep from having to gather information about the customer from different sources, it also ensures that the customer receives consistent service, irrespective of which call center or service representative handles the request.

The "old way" of communicating with the company's varied and disparate data sources is represented in figure 1-3:

Figure 1-3: The Old Way of Information Gathering

Imagine what our friend in figure 1-3 will need to go through to combine product information with sales, revenues, and campaign success measurements. Like my client Jeff, he has a range of information sources to consult—from servers to paper reports—and, worse, a limited time in which to generate the right information.

The real value of a data warehouse is that it makes new business knowledge available literally at the touch of a button. Finding, collecting, and synchronizing data is all performed electronically—hence the *e* in e-data—not manually by the end-user. Thus, the e-data way of information retrieval dispenses with tracking down the right data—which, by the way, takes most of the time—and provides the needed information in a direct, rapid, and meaningful way, as in figure 1-4.

Chapter 2 will discuss what these two savvy employees just did. Hint: It's even easier than calling the help desk, and the data warehouse is never cranky!

Besides understanding that decision support helps people take certain business actions, there's the newer term *business intelligence*. Business intelligence is one of those monikers that encompass the set of products and services for accessing and analyzing data and turning it into information. It's another one of those terms that defines the superset of data analysis products, from spreadsheets to

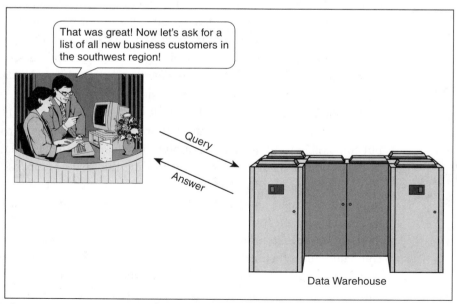

Figure 1-4: Gathering e-Data from the Data Warehouse

enterprise resource planning (ERP) to data mining. In short, business intelligence is a broad term that companies—especially vendors—are using to position new products and services, and it is frequently synonymous with decision support.

When the data-warehousing marketplace is discussed in industry journals and trade publications, it's increasingly referred to in terms of business intelligence. Companies like IBM have defined business intelligence as a major corporate initiative, and diverse data-warehousing components such as hardware, software, application tools, and data mining all wind up under the business intelligence umbrella.

The Data-Warehousing Bandwagon and Why Everyone Jumped on It

Data warehousing expanded dramatically in the late 1980s, when businesses began realizing the value of their data. Back then, the focus was more on how to integrate data warehouses into a company's existing IT infrastructure than it was about business value.

In these early days data warehousing was motivated by a number of separate factors.

- Mainframe offload. Frequently, a company's mainframe system was busy enough already, and upgrades—adding more hardware and processing power—could be just as expensive as buying a brand-new data warehouse. These mainframes were often "transactional" systems performing mission-critical functions such as customer billing or banking deposits. Companies were loath to tax their mainframes any further, and the data redundancy and separate processing data warehouses provided were enticing.
- Dirty data. Different data from all over the enterprise, from accounts payable to compensation to customer information, was often not only hard to find but impossible to understand, and often just plain wrong. The data warehouse provided a single platform for loading this "heterogeneous" data. It also offered a pretext for data cleansing—checking it for quality and accuracy, and reformatting it so that it was comprehensive and useful before it was loaded into the warehouse.
- Security. In order to protect their mission-critical operational systems, most companies limit their access to a few experts. When data from these operational systems was requested, those experts spooned out data to those who needed it rather than making it available to the business at large. Data

warehouses offered a more generally accessible environment for frequently sought-after information.

Before data warehousing, retailers like Wal-Mart and banks such as Citibank couldn't buy large enough computers to track their inventories. Telephone companies couldn't store all their customers' numbers in one location. Hospitals had nowhere to put patient records. Data warehouses made it both functionally plausible and technically possible for businesses to store large amounts of disparate data in one location. The economics of microprocessors, disk drives, and general computing made this increasingly feasible.

As pioneering companies began leveraging decision support analysis and computing power became cheaper, the business value of data warehousing became clearer, and companies outside the *Fortune* 100 began clamoring for new ways of looking at their data.

Companies began to recognize that their executives weren't the only decision makers, and that there was some sound basis for the demand for e-data. The logic went something like the representation in figure 1-5.

Everyone in our business is a decision maker.

Decisions are based on both "hard" and "soft" facts.

Our business has an enormous data inventory.

Figure 1-5: Justifying a Data Warehouse

While the old justifications for data warehousing described in figure 1-5 are still very real, new benefits pertain more to running the business than to aligning data with technology. For example:

- The truth! No more conflicting numbers, or multiple answers to the same question! The consolidation of heterogeneous data has enabled companies to answer different questions with the same information, in effect linking the manufacturing floor with the executive boardroom. This does not imply that the data warehouse must always be a single physical platform. What it does mean is that the data warehouse is the corporate authority when it comes to defining and explaining a customer, a product, or a business event, in effect eliminating wrong answers.
- Simpler implementation. Although most companies can no longer live without data warehouses, the technology is rarely considered mission-critical. Because data warehouses are "informational" and not "operational," they don't abide by the stringent security, design, and technology restrictions of their operational cousins. (Later, we'll talk about why these points are still very important to consider when implementing a data warehouse.)
- Customer intimacy. This is by far and away the most common reason businesses give when responding to why they need a data warehouse in the first place. Moreover, it encompasses each of the points described above. Chapter 3 is dedicated to the topic of understanding customers better.

Who uses data warehouses? Companies in a range of industries, including the following:

- retail
- consumer packaged goods
- telecommunications
- financial services
- transportation
- health care
- government
- utility companies
- manufacturing

And who within these companies benefits from the e-data analysis a data warehouse provides? Anyone who makes decisions! Below, a few of the more common job titles sported by data warehouse users:

- product manager
- financial analyst
- buyer
- strategic planner
- marketing analyst
- salesperson
- sales manager
- merchandiser
- store or branch manager
- corporate executive
- executive assistant

Just as the Chrysler Corporation improved efficiency by colocating different workers in a product team, data warehouses improve efficiency by colocating data. A data warehouse consolidates many types of data from many data sources in order to facilitate data analysis for fact-based decision making (see figure 1-6).

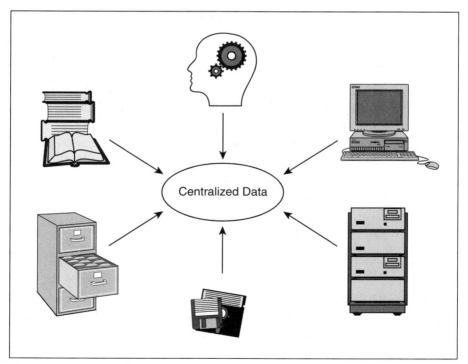

Figure 1-6: e-Data Originates from Many Places

So why did companies decide to move forward with data warehousing, and how are they using decision support? Here are some of the reasons companies have spent the time and money necessary to implement a data warehouse.

Data-Warehousing Objectives

- To provide a single view of our customers across the enterprise.
- To put as much business information as possible into the hands of as many different users as possible.
- To improve turnaround time for common reports.
- To monitor customer behavior.
- To predict product purchases.
- To perform statistical analysis on data from one location instead of many.
- To compensate for the recent downsizing of our IT department.
- To improve responsiveness to business issues.
- To increase the accuracy of measurements.
- To improve productivity.
- To increase and distribute responsibilities.

Here is a partial list of how data warehouses are helping companies in different industries:

- A pharmaceutical company increases its revenues by 20 percent by both analyzing competitive behavior and cross-selling products to its existing customer base.
- A major long-distance company reduces its product development cycle time by 40 percent by understanding which specific features it should combine to create new and innovative products.
- A manufacturer monitors the movement of specific products in order to predict restocking requirements for its various retail merchants.
- An Internet service provider offers customer usage information and network outage reports via the Web to its service providers in twenty-seven different countries.

We'll see lots of examples of data warehouse successes—and failures—throughout the remainder of the book. But for now, it's helpful to know that companies are using their data warehouses not just to look at customers but also to monitor a host of different business factors.

Some Trite Data-Warehousing Aphorisms

Be it in politics or in technology, look for the bandwagon and the sound bite's not far behind. As data warehousing left the realm of the IT department and began pervading business, people rushed to redefine it. Sometimes this resulted in *reductio ad absurdum,* contorting the concept of data warehousing into brief, often painfully simplistic statements in an attempt to characterize it concisely.

Below we list a few of the classic data-warehousing aphorisms you will hear, if you haven't already, and explain why they're dangerous—and sometimes downright wrong!

- *"If you build it, they will come."*
  It was the baseball movie *Field of Dreams* that begat this alarming phrase, which then shot through data-warehousing seminars and presentations like a line drive off a curve ball. Except, it's wrong. The claim implies that if you simply acquire data warehouse technology and begin loading data from your transaction systems, users will eventually catch on and begin rallying round. In fact, these very users should be the ones defining the need for the data warehouse in the first place. In reality, if you build it, they probably won't even know.

- *"The hardest part about data warehousing is sourcing and loading the data."*
  This explanation is often proffered by well-meaning experts who have spent time in the development trenches. Extracting data from source systems, "transforming" it—improving the quality of the data and unifying data formats so that the data in the warehouse is understandable—and loading it into the data warehouse is indeed difficult, cumbersome, and time-consuming, but it is not the most difficult part. The most difficult part of implementing a data warehouse is getting everyone to agree on its objectives and defining the deliverables and implementation priorities correctly the first time out.

- *"The data warehouse can't be all things to all people."*
  Yes and no. The key to a successful and usable data warehouse is its ability to meet business objectives. Can you serve all of the people all of the time? If you understand their requirements, can provide the appropriate data, and can build a technology architecture to deliver on them, then the answer is a hearty yes! Will somebody always want more? Absolutely.

- *The data warehouse is the only remedy for being "data rich and information poor."*

   While this is the ideal, some data warehouses—particularly those that have mistakenly been populated by "dirty data"—can actually compound the problem of too much disparate corporate data by representing yet one more corporate server with information that no one trusts.

- *"Data warehousing is not a technology, it's a process."*

   It's true that a successful data warehouse represents a series of evolving informational needs being realized over time, and the more it's used, the more the business will rely on it. But many people take it too literally, hence delaying decisions about large hardware purchases or expensive application software by instigating cumbersome custom development projects or commissioning endless studies. While this aphorism means well—implying that good data warehouses are never finished—it can be misinterpreted with disastrous results. We'll refer to it again in the book to mean that successful data warehouses provide incremental and ongoing value.

It is tempting to listen for the maxims and clichés that will elucidate the complex and often arcane truisms of data warehousing. Beware the "expert" who leaves you with a glib motto and a pie chart. It's never that simple.

Venus and Mars: How IT and Businesspeople Communicate

You may have seen some version of the following joke on the Internet:

> A man is flying in a hot air balloon and realizes he is lost. He reduces altitude and spots a passerby on the ground below. He lowers the balloon further and shouts, "Excuse me, can you tell me where I am?"
>
> The passerby says, "Yes, you're in a hot air balloon, hovering 30 feet above this field."
>
> "You must work in information technology!" says the balloonist.
>
> "I do," replies the man on the ground. "How did you know?"
>
> "Well" says the balloonist, "everything you've told me is technically correct, but it's of no use to me."
>
> The man below responds, "You must work in management."
>
> "I do," replies the balloonist, "but how did you know?"
>
> "Well," replies the man below, "you don't know where you are, nor

Figure 1-7: Can We Talk?

where you're going, but you expect me to help. You're in the same position as you were before we met, but now it's my fault."

This joke captures the classic tensions between IT and businesspeople. Nowhere are these tensions more apparent, and more disruptive, than in implementing strategic technologies.

Common myth has it that the IT department comprises a bunch of nerdy wise guys who work in cubicles strewn with foam footballs and high-tech gadgets. IT "techies" are believed to wear sweaters because of their proximity to the computer room and Birkenstock sandals because they're a reliable fashion statement. They're thought to be supercilious, work strange hours, and sometimes appear unwashed.

Likewise, the stereotype of end-users is of a bunch of demanding businesspeople who don't care how anything works and just want their reports on the double. These people have "real" careers, dress for success, and drink iced tea at lunch (though they'd prefer scotch). Their impeccably clean foreign cars disappear en masse from the corporate parking lot at 5 P.M. sharp, radios locked onto "easy listening" music as they run successive red lights to get home. And drink scotch.

Like all modern myths, these two contain a grain of truth even though they have become a bit overblown. But try telling that to the programmer who's just received her fifth emergency change request in a day. Or to the merchandiser who doesn't understand what MOLAP[2] is but knows he needs a product sales report before he places his monthly order with a supplier.

The fact is, the disparity between IT and the end-user community is not merely one of communication or knowledge, but one of culture. And it is this disparity more than any other that accounts for the failure of strategic technology programs, or at the very least missed expectations, in companies large and small.

As we've seen in this chapter, data warehouses began as solutions to technology problems. Mainframe offload and dirty data were enough justification to implement this new technology, which often ended up saving thousands of dollars.

But data warehouses have quickly become much more: They've transcended the "nice to have" and become a competitive advantage. Businesspeople who until recently never had a workstation on their desktops are now using e-data to make decisions that are saving their company money. As we'll see in chapter 8, data warehouses deliver not only cost savings, but revenue. And no one's looking back.

What this means for businesspeople is that they can get more information than ever before in less time. And quicker decisions are just the tip of the iceberg. Data warehouses are resulting in process improvements, faster time to market, enhanced customer loyalty, and even the ability to predict future trends and patterns. Once businesspeople taste the sweet fruit of business information, they simply want more.

What this means for technology workers is that it's no longer enough to be intimate with state-of-the-art databases and hardware platforms. Technologists need to become closer to the business their companies are in. And this means getting to know what users want to do and how that fits with the larger corporate objectives.

---

2. MOLAP stands for multidimensional online analytical processing, and we'll describe it in chapter 3.

Previously, many IT professionals were accustomed to translating business requests into technical queries and delivering the answer via paper reports. Now users retrieve their own reports. This change has redefined the role of the IT professional from one of data provider to one of partner in crime. IT can no longer be content to provide enabling technologies: Those technologies have to meet specifically defined requirements.

And what if the resulting technology doesn't cut the mustard? Pity the IT department that misinterprets a user's requirements. Users are getting smarter, and they are more likely to go it alone.

Some Other Buzzwords and What They Mean

This chapter has already introduced several new terms, and the book will continue to discuss terminology used in conjunction with data warehouses and their corresponding business uses. Let's look at some other basic terms in context.

You should be familiar with the terms *database* and *database management system*. Data warehouses run sophisticated database software that organizes and manages the actual data. A database is a logical definition of where the data is stored. Most data warehouses on the market represent data in *relational databases*, meaning that the data is stored in *tables*, consisting of rows and columns. The database management system (DBMS, or RDBMS for relational database management system) is the actual product that operates the databases.

The DBMS constitutes the core of the data warehouse, and most data warehouse vendors are really database vendors that recognize the unique requirements of storing large amounts of data for the purposes of decision support. Without a database, the data warehouse would simply be a hardware platform with lots of data on disks, but no way for users to access that data.

Another term that's already come up is *data mart*. A data mart is a data warehouse, only smaller; in other words, it's a subject-specific data warehouse. Data marts are normally used by one department or group of users in a company for a defined set of tasks.

For example, one telephone company I know has a data mart specific to network planning. This data mart helps the company's networking staff determine its technology assets, optimal network routing, and capacities. It gets its data from a larger "enterprise data warehouse" that the company maintains in a separate location.

The data mart's relationship with the enterprise data warehouse and with the end-users is illustrated in figure 1-8.

Note that this data mart is considered a "dependent data mart," since it receives data from a data warehouse. Stand-alone data marts, those that get their data directly from transaction systems and don't rely on other data warehouses, are called "independent data marts."

While we're on the subject of transaction systems (the systems that run the business operations for a company), we should also explain what we mean by *online transaction processing* (*OLTP*). OLTP systems are transaction systems that are highly tuned to perform their work quickly, often in real time, and often using mainframes or other large servers. For example, an OLTP system processes a bank's ATM transactions. OLTP systems are often "source systems," systems whose data is loaded onto the warehouse. Established OLTP systems are also

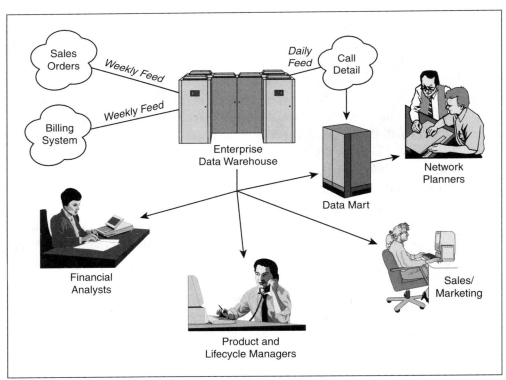

Figure 1-8: A Telephone Company's Data Mart

known as "legacy systems." Technically, a source system can be anything that provides the data warehouse with its data, be it an OLTP system or a spreadsheet on someone's PC.

You should also be familiar with the term *application*. Though applications can run anywhere—on mainframes, servers, PCs, or anything in between—when you're looking at data in a data warehouse, you're looking at it via an application. As complex as data warehouses are, it's the application software that runs on the end-user's workstation that is the unit of delivery. To access all that data, the user normally has a tool on her PC that allows her to log on, query the data warehouse's database(s), and inspect the results. Applications are also referred to as end-user interfaces.

You've probably heard about different types of analysis in conjunction with data warehousing. *OnLine Analytical Processing* (OLAP), multidimensional analysis, and data mining are all different types of applications that deliver e-data. We'll talk about them all in the next chapter.

Some Lingering Questions

In the following section we answered some frequently asked questions to further elucidate some of the topics discussed.

We know we need a data warehouse. How do we know whether we should start by implementing a data mart or an enterprise warehouse?

That depends on who you are. You could be an IT director who's frustrated with the volume of data requests that are piling up from different business units, which, irrespective of their differing responsibilities, have eerily similar data needs.

Or you could be a vice president of marketing, worn out from your salespeople's requests for automated compensation reporting or customer profiling. You might even have requested that these functions be developed for you, only to be admonished by your boss that your people should be out in the field selling, not in the office playing Who's Who on the company nickel.

Either way, the question can really be answered only with another question, namely:

How pervasive is the perceived need for decision support functionality?

If two or more organizations across the company are clamoring for data and share the need for common data—for example, unified customer billing reports—then an enterprise data warehouse that stores heterogeneous data and can make a multitude of different information available might be the ticket for you.

If the answer focuses on a department, and a clear number of users require similar functionality, such as monitoring room occupancy rates across hotel properties, a data mart might be the answer. Just be careful: Once a few people get access to the data, more people will want it. Careful planning is key!

Chapter 5 will show examples of both data marts and enterprisewide data warehouses.

I keep hearing that data warehousing is a strategic tool for companies, but every case study I come across describes some tactical improvements. How are data warehouses really strategic?

There's a fundamental distinction between what companies DO with their data warehouses and what they DECIDE based on the decision support analysis being performed. There are some fantastic and well-planned data warehouses being used in business today, but no one is actually ACTING on the results of the analysis. So in these cases, the data warehouse is simply being used to confirm already held beliefs.

If this meets the end-users' requirements, then fine. One of the main benefits of data warehouses is that they help people do things better and faster. But true strategic use of the data warehouse results in business improvements that may help the company beat its competitors. These improvements can be anything from faster product time to market—thanks to the eradication of endless product service and feature pairings in favor of definitive answers to what customers will buy—to mass customization, that is, developing and marketing certain products to a certain customer or group of customers, to enabling analysis of clickstreams from its e-commerce Web site.

Moreover, data warehouses are surprising their users with information they didn't know to expect. This is what data mining is really all about, and we'll talk more about it in the next chapter.

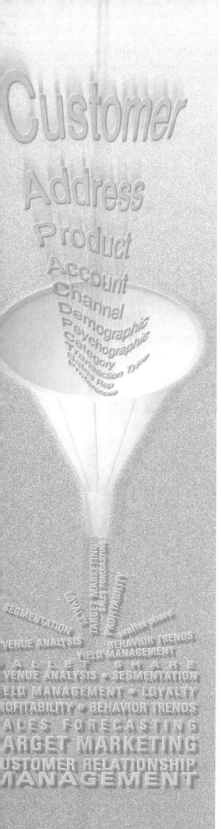

CHAPTER TWO

Decision Support
from the Bottom Up

The following scene is a reenactment based on a meeting I had with a prospective client who asked me to pay a visit to talk about data analysis. While any resemblance to actual persons is purely coincidental, you might recognize some of the characters.

FADE IN:

INT. CONFERENCE ROOM OF MAJOR BANK'S HEADQUARTERS—DAY.

Dressed in business attire and seated around a large mahogany table are MARIANNE, a product manager, SHANE, a marketing analyst, CHARLIE, a database administrator swigging a soft drink, and JILL, a data-warehousing consultant. In strides MR. B, vice president of marketing. Hastily shaking Jill's hand, he deposits himself at the head of the table and leans forward.

MR. B: Jill, nice of you to be here, how was your flight?

JILL: Oh, it . . .

MR. B: Good. The reason you're here today is because we need some tips from you. I just read a magazine article that has kept me awake for two solid nights. One of our competitors has begun doing some type of data analysis that has me concerned.

JILL: What sort of analysis?

MR. B: What was that they were doing, Shane?

SHANE: Data mining.

MR. B: That's it. Data mining! We want to do data mining. And we want you to tell us how to start.

JILL: Great. What sort of data mining were they doing?

MR. B: What sort of data mining, Marianne?

MARIANNE: They were able to predict which of their customers would buy a new product. Then they'd generate lists of names and base their mailings on them.

JILL: Intelligent target marketing! Great! Tell me about the target marketing you're currently doing.

They all look at each other.

JILL: OK, let's look at it another way: where do you keep your customer data?

They all look at Charlie.

CHARLIE: Uh, which customer data?

JILL: You know, your company's customers. How do you access their information?

CHARLIE: Well, some of it's on our billing system. And some of it's on our marketing analysis system. And customers less than a month old are on our order and provisioning system until we can get them over. . . . And then we have some ex-customers in an Access database on Craig's laptop . . .

JILL: And which of those customers do you want to market your new products to?

They all look at each other.

MARIANNE: Well, ideally, all of them.

MR. B: Absolutely! All of them!

JILL: So, when you need information on a certain customer's purchases, or how a product is selling in a geographic area, what do you do?

SHANE: (sheepishly) We call Charlie.

They all look at Charlie again. Charlie takes a swig of his soda and spills it all over the table.

JILL: (removing her jacket) How much time do we have?

FADE OUT . . .

This company had a legitimate business need: targeting the right product to the right customer. However, the existing technology didn't offer an easy solution. Customer data was decentralized, and the company relied on one human resource, Charlie, instead of leveraging a data warehouse in order to consolidate and interpret customer information intelligently.

Put another way, the bank wanted to run before it could even walk.

The lack of appropriate technology wasn't the only problem. The business processes themselves were maddening. Marketing personnel had to call or e-mail Charlie every time they wanted information (in both cases, praying he would answer), explain the problem, wait for the response, inspect the result, and in most cases then refine the question and resubmit it.

And even if these users had been able to log on to a data warehouse and retrieve customer data, most of them wouldn't have known what to do with it.

The Evolution of Decision Support

This section describes the various categories of decision support analysis, beginning with simple queries and ending up with some of the most advanced analysis techniques ever. These categories suggest an evolutionary approach to building and using a data warehouse, particularly when the data warehouse is enterprisewide, that is, represents various business functions across the company, but also for functionally specific data marts.

Standard Query: The Workhorse of DSS

In chapter 1 we introduced the concept of a query, a question you ask of the database. So what's the big deal?

The big deal about queries is that despite the newest advanced algorithms and innovative visualization tools, queries are by far the most pervasive analysis method. In fact, more businesspeople submit queries to data warehouses on a daily basis than perform the other three types of analysis combined.

The irony here is that many companies new to data warehousing want to bypass querying a data warehouse and jump right to advanced analysis. Our friends at the bank are typical of the company that wants to use decision support for "strategic" purposes.

But what's more strategic than putting detailed and meaningful information about customers, products, and behavior right on the desktops of business people across the company? The ability to submit simple queries alone can provide many companies with fresh and meaningful facts that can feed the most strategic decisions. Furthermore, users who can analyze data returned from simple queries are more apt to support funding for more advanced types of decision support, since they've already witnessed its benefits.

The following query can provide an enlightening set of data to the businessperson who previously had no data access at all:

Display all customers who purchased Product X last year.

Queries are often "canned," meaning that they're predefined, just like a standard business report you might see on your desk at the end of every month. Canned queries are represented as an icon or picture on the screen of your desktop PC. While the underlying data can change from day to day or hour to hour, the canned query need not be rewritten each time.

One company I worked with required financial analysts to wait for a tape mount—a process in which a tape is put on a tape drive in the data center in order to read its contents—to access product revenue information that was over a year old. Depending on the request backlog, this procedure could take weeks. Once the financial analysts were provided with a set of canned queries, they could access revenue history with the click of a mouse button. These users weren't experienced data analysts, just businesspeople who required the data in order to do their jobs.

Another type of query is submitted without preparation, often as soon as the user dreams it up. These ad hoc queries are often unique to a particular user and a specific problem, whereas canned reports, conversely, are usually widely deployed. Figure 2-1 illustrates both kinds of queries. Ad hoc queries are original or detailed enough to make "canning" them impractical and thus are created anew each time they are run. Ad hoc queries are often specific to a product, distribution channel, or customer account.

Aside from providing faster turnaround time, queries empower employees to think—and act—for themselves. Because answers to questions can now be found virtually immediately, businesses can take swift action to respond to a competitor's marketing blitz, change a customer's address, answer a question in real time, or encourage an unhappy customer to stay.

"I think we get about 20 percent of our value from canned reports," says Tony Marshall of Hallmark Cards, Inc. "The other 80 percent comes from our end-users' ability to ask new questions with ad hoc queries. It is with this type of analysis that our business partners can identify emerging trends in the marketplace and support the process of innovative decision making."

Figure 2-1: Canned Queries versus Ad-Hoc in Practice

Indeed, ad hoc queries can furnish the on-demand information necessary to enable the business to become more nimble and responsive. Underestimating the value of submitting simple queries, or waiting until more advanced analysis levels can be attained, can in fact be a fatal competitive error.

Multidimensional Analysis: The Power of Slice 'n' Dice

Multidimensional analysis is the next rung on the analysis ladder. While some users will be happy submitting standard queries, others—particularly those who need to perform research or dig deeper into specific data—need a more powerful analysis technique with which to investigate and compare information.

Multidimensional analysis provides different perspectives on the data via "dimensions," or vantage points from which to look at data. "Time," "location," and "product" are examples of common dimensions.

The giveaway for multidimensional analysis is that the user normally wants to see information *by* a certain dimension. For example, customers *by* geographic region, sales *by* city, or calls *by* time of day. Often, that user retrieves an answer set and examines that information several times using different dimensions. For example:

Show me all new business customers for each sales region.

The dimension used to categorize new customer sales in this query—sales region—is geographic. Once the user retrieves this answer, she can request additional detail, for example:

Show me all new business customers for each sales district.

This multidimensional report will "drill down" from summarized regional data to specific districts.

The tools used for multidimensional analysis are similar and are in many cases the very same tools used to perform standard queries. In fact, both standard queries and multidimensional analysis can be canned for repeated use and are normally submitted with user-friendly software tools. The difference is that while standard queries normally retrieve a large cross-section of different data, multidimensional analysis is used to look at the same data in different ways.

While the users of multidimensional analysis are most often the same people submitting standard queries, they are normally more comfortable with both the data they are analyzing and the analysis tool they are using. Nevertheless, multidimensional analysis has been a boon to the average businessperson looking to plumb the well of corporate data.

Modeling and Segmentation: Analysis for Knowledge Workers

As the user community for the DSS analysis grows, user sophistication likewise matures. The average business user will probably remain content with canned reports and some multidimensional analysis for the long term. However, as the data becomes more voluminous and detailed, and new business perspectives evolve, "knowledge workers" such as marketing analysts and statisticians require more highly evolved analytical capabilities in order to gather new information.

Using existing data on the data warehouse, chiefly historical data, can aid analysts in actually predicting future events. Predictive work can be performed against large volumes of detailed data using specific analysis tools that extract data from the warehouse and analyze it to populate "models." A model is simply a collection of patterns for a given characteristic and as such is represented either graphically or through a set of rules or notations. Although many modeling "algorithms"—logical analysis techniques—have existed for a dozen years or more, only since the advent of decision support have they been able to exploit the rich detail and historical information—the e-data—that is centralized in the data warehouse.

Segmentation isn't new either. Indeed, this marketing discipline has been around since the introduction of demographic studies in the 1960s and 1970s.

Segmentation divides customers or other data areas into certain bands or segments, in which common characteristics may define behavior, and thus dictates sales and marketing strategies.

Once customer segmentation is performed, the segments themselves can be analyzed as dimensions with multidimensional analysis tools. This gives less technical users the opportunity to examine the models that were created using advanced analysis without having to perform the analysis themselves.

This book classifies modeling and segmentation together, because although they involve different underlying techniques, they fall under the rubric of classical marketing analysis and require similar skill levels. In most cases, modeling and segmentation use specialized software. This means that the data analyst performing them has most likely been trained to operate specially developed tools and understands the data at a more detailed level.

Knowledge Discovery: The Power of the Unknown

Companies have spent millions of dollars trying to understand the best customers for given marketing campaigns, many of them resorting to the least complicated, albeit least reliable, tactic of mass-marketing to every known prospect. Knowledge discovery is represented by any number of high-powered algorithms that search for patterns in large databases. Unlike modeling, these patterns are not specified beforehand, so in fact the user is searching for answers to questions he or she did not know to ask. The result is that *the data warehouse can tell the business* where the interesting patterns, relationships, and "hot spots" are.

If detailed data is available, however, significant behaviors, patterns, and sequences can be pinpointed without requiring a data analyst to look for them. Since knowledge discovery tools locate specific patterns and relationships that are unspecified by the user, examples of them focus not on what is being searched for, but on what is found.

While true knowledge discovery activities eliminate an already held hypothesis, many are nevertheless bound by a particular business objective or data subject area. This means that a given knowledge discovery project will most likely focus on an area of the business—say, customers and what they might do next—irrespective of what it might find there.

The promise of data warehousing, as our banker friend knew, is the ability to find the "unknown answer" in the data and use it for new and innovative ways of increasing revenues.

Some Real-Life Examples

Now that we've introduced the four levels of analysis, let's look at some examples that characterize the use of each one.

The pyramid in figure 2-2 represents a straightforward "evolution" for decision support analysis. It's sort of a decision support taxonomy. You'll see this pyramid again later in the book as we pivot it to look at the various tools used for each type of analysis.

Following the pyramid from the bottom up allows the company's prowess in analysis to evolve along with its data warehouse infrastructure. In other words, as analysis methods and technologies grow and mature, so do the data warehouse hardware, software, and data. Just as a child learns more with each successive grade in school, a company gets more value from its data warehouse by steadily adding supplemental technologies and growing its user community over time.

This is not to say that you must absolutely begin with standard queries. However, a good measure of your data warehouse's quality and usability is that if you can't perform standard queries, you're probably not ready for multidimensional analysis. Likewise, if you can't seem to deploy multidimensional analysis, you're probably ill equipped to begin modeling.

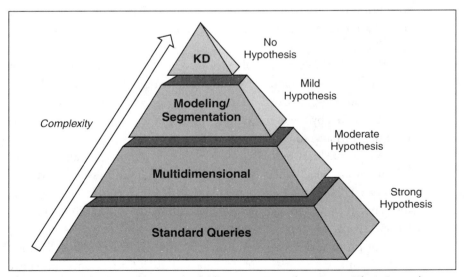

Figure 2-2: The Baseline Pyramid (Source: Baseline Consulting Group)

Just as the data in the warehouse evolves and matures, its users grow in their data analysis skills, as well as in their comfort with the technology. The more often an end-user logs on to a data warehouse and retrieves meaningful e-data, the more the data warehouse becomes a business staple. And an end-user whose use of that e-data has resulted in business improvements—be they time or cost savings, or process consolidation—is probably the person who will sponsor the next project, and perhaps even fund it.

If our friends at the bank had taken a "bottom up" approach, slowly implementing vertical subject areas and acquiring different tools, they'd be well on their way to the sophisticated modeling they so badly want to do. As it is, they need to spend time and money building their data infrastructure before they can truly hope to capitalize on the promise of predictive models. In the meantime, the bank's main competitor is getting smarter about its customers.

The following sections depict how real users have carved out uses for different levels of the pyramid. You can measure them against what your company is doing, or what you want to be doing.

Standard Queries

Figure 2-3 shows how a small telephone company classifies the types of queries its users submitted.

This telephone company delivers sales reporting, product cost information, usage and revenue reports and month-end profitability reports—all by using standard queries. These queries have enabled its staff, who include salespeople, product managers, and marketing analysts, to examine e-data and make on-the-spot decisions.

For example, certain users have access to a canned report enabling them to ask the following query on a regular basis:

*List all customers whose peak-hour usage revenues
have decreased by 20 percent or more.*[1]

The result of this query can trigger a host of different business decisions, from offering discounts on products and time bands to discontinuing a product whose sales are sliding.

---

1. Although this query is canned, the user can dynamically modify the percentage amount, so that 20 percent becomes 35 percent, depending on the business circumstance. This is known as a "parameterized" query.

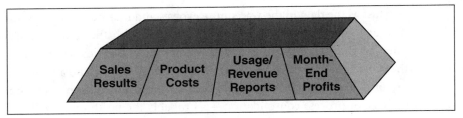

Figure 2-3: A Sample Query Breakdown

Most standard queries have fairly strong hypotheses. The following query from a mortgage company, for example, presumes that Customer X has paid his bill late, perhaps repeatedly:

> *Show all of Customer X's loan numbers and*
> *payment dates in cases where payments were*
> *over two weeks late.*

We may even know when those bills were paid. The user submitting this query may simply be following up on a lead or verifying a widely held suspicion in order to write Customer X a collections letter. Since this query is confirming a suspicion, it has a strong hypothesis.

The simple query can have far-reaching benefits across the business, for example:

> *Display all cellular customers whose inbound*
> *calls were incomplete more than 20 percent each week.*

The answer to this question can identify high-usage customers who might need additional equipment; probable market competitors; candidates for upgraded products; suspicions about fraud; potentially dissatisfied customers; and more. In short, it can help the company retain and add customers.

Multidimensional Analysis

Let's now suppose that the above query response triggers another question. For example, now we may want to know:

> *Of those customers (whose inbound calls were*
> *incomplete more than 20 percent of the time), which of*
> *them roam outside the network?*

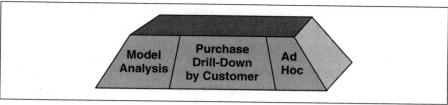

Figure 2-4: A Sample Multidimensional Analysis Breakdown

This question "drills down" into a greater level of detail, providing important information about origin and destination patterns that might spur additional sales to high-value customers and even dictate new product or service programs. A sample multidimensional analysis breakdown is shown in figure 2-4.

Let's look at an example of drill-down with OLAP. The following standard decision support query serves as a foundation for follow-on multidimensional analysis:

Show me quarterly booked revenue
for large business customers in the northern, northwest,
and southwest regions for 1997 and 1998.

The answer to this query would appear in tabular form similar to that of table 2-1:

Table 2-1: A Basic Decision Support Report

	1997				1998	
	Q1	Q2	Q3	Q4	Q1	Q2
North	50	35	44	95	45	33
Northwest	38	43	43	50	38	45
Southwest	34	23	46	72	30	28
Booked Revenue (in 1000's)						

It turns out that the revenue amounts in the northwest region are lower than expected. A product manager may choose to examine another level of detail:

Show me the same data by district
within the northwest region.

The response would appear similar to the data in table 2-2:

Table 2-2: OLAP Output

		1997				1998	
		Q1	Q2	Q3	Q4	Q1	Q2
North		50	35	44	95	45	33
Northwest	District A	13	15	14	18	11	14
	District B	10	12	12	13	8	16
	District C	15	16	17	19	19	15
Southwest		34	23	46	72	30	28
		Booked Revenue (in 1000's)					

Since the northwest region's District B has the lowest revenues, the user would want to examine the area's geographic breakdown to identify the root problem:

Show me the same data for District B in the northwest region.

Table 2-3 clearly shows that the Cleveland revenues are lagging behind the rest of the district. By drilling down to more detail, the user can quickly track a revenue problem to a specific location rather than assuming that the problem was company- or territorywide.

Table 2-3: Drill-Down

		1997				1998	
		Q1	Q2	Q3	Q4	Q1	Q2
North		50	35	44	95	45	33
Northwest	District B	2	3	4	4	2	4
	Toledo	6	7	6	6	4	9
	Columbus	2	2	2	3	2	3
	Cleveland	2	2	2	3	2	3
Southwest		34	23	46	72	30	28
		Booked Revenue (in 1000's)					

You may have heard the term "slicing and dicing," which describes the ability to mold the answer set to the end-user's liking. OLAP tools are unique in that they make it easy for users to ask for the same data in different ways. After all, a list of products and their sales dates doesn't help a lifecycle manager who wants that information by geographic region, by area code, or by demographic segment.

Modeling and Segmentation

Models can offer a company a fixed and easy way to determine future customer behavior, as well as long-term viability, while segmentation can classify and re-classify customers according to demographic characteristics, purchase patterns, propensity to buy, and other categories.

Here are some possible sample segments:

- customers who respond to new promotions
- customers who respond to discounts
- customers who respond to new product offers
- customers who do not respond to promotions

Segmentation offers insight into how a company should treat a discrete band of customers and illuminates answers to questions such as the following:

- To which initial group of customers should we target a particular new service?
- Who will most likely call with a service request once a new service is deployed?
- Which customers are most likely to commit fraud?
- Which customers are most likely to respond to rebates?

A regional bank uses both attrition and lifetime value modeling (see figure 2-5), both of which access historical data from the bank's data warehouse.

Modeling examples include the following:

- *Lifetime customer value.* What are the attributes that affect a customer's long-term value/profitability to the business?
- *Customer attrition.* How likely is a specific customer to leave? How soon will the customer leave? Are there other characteristics that should be considered when examining customer attrition (e.g., purchase patterns, service slow-downs, etc.)?
- *Predictive modeling.* How will product sales be affected by bad weather this spring? What effect will the economy have on sales?

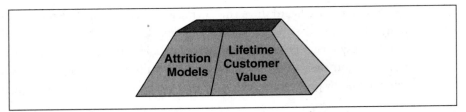

Figure 2-5: Sample Modeling/Segmentation Breakdown

Chapters 3 and 4 feature case studies illustrating the actual use of modeling and segmentation.

The modeling and segmentation category falls between multidimensional analysis and knowledge discovery for a very good reason: Once segments and models have been created, they can be further explored with multidimensional tools. More captivating still, segments and models can be redefined in new and unforeseen ways using knowledge discovery.

Knowledge Discovery

Unlike the other types of analysis, knowledge discovery is "zero hypothesis" analysis. Since we don't know what questions to ask, we have no idea of the answers we'll be getting back. Knowledge discovery, also known as *undirected knowledge discovery,* finds hidden patterns in the data reflecting customer behavior, product sales, cancellations, future purchases, and other events. These patterns are too specific and seemingly arbitrary to specify, and the analyst would be playing a perpetual guessing-game trying to figure out all of the possible patterns in the database. Instead, the special knowledge discovery software tools find the patterns and tell the analyst what—and where—they are.

Of course, few companies can justify a random fishing expedition with their e-data, especially considering the cost of the tools and the extent of the data preparation required. Thus, some sort of business objective should be defined prior to embarking on knowledge discovery.

A pharmaceutical firm uses knowledge discovery to examine what happens when certain drugs are taken together, identifying unknown patterns of product affinities. The company also looks at sequential product purchases in order to determine whether certain medications are triggering the need for others (see figure 2-6).

Affinity analysis is one of many types of knowledge discovery. A powerful affinity algorithm reads all the data elements in the data warehouse and matches each attribute with every other data item without regard to meaning. While this

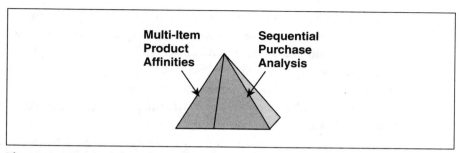

Figure 2-6: A Sample Knowledge Discovery Breakdown

may at first glance seem like "brute force" analysis, the value comes with the output. The result is a set of rules that describe certain relationships between data. These rules can yield some interesting surprises.

Consider the value of this affinity analysis finding:

Of the customers who purchase potato chips,
63 percent also buy candy bars.

This is a very interesting finding, especially as the business had no way of proving its truth prior to knowledge discovery. But because of the data relationships and the power required to exponentially match every attribute with every other attribute, an analyst could never have confirmed it conclusively.

However, the power of affinity analysis is really showcased when multi-item affinities are revealed:

Of the customers who buy potato chips and candy bars,
74 percent also buy red wine.

With this type of knowledge, which could never have been found with a query or multidimensional analysis but which lies like a golden nugget within the data warehouse, a grocery store can take a host of actions, from sending coupons to frequent buyers who buy one of these three products to removing discounts on red wine to placing products more effectively within a store.

Other examples of "aha!" data that can be uncovered through knowledge discovery are listed below:

• Certain "trigger" products affect other purchases. For example, the likelihood of a brokerage firm's successfully marketing a debit card to customers who already have checking accounts is relatively high.

- The "next likely purchase" can be uncovered. This type of sequential event analysis combines customer behavior and product sales history to establish purchase patterns in order to predict certain purchases for a given customer or customer segment before they occur.
- Recognizable patterns in the slowdown of purchases or service cancellation can be discerned. In other words, what happens before cancellation? What are the factors that identify slowdown or cancellation? This type of analysis can help a cable television company prevent service cancellation more effectively than standard attrition models.
- Which customer characteristics affect a product's life span? In one situation, families whose children had recently graduated from college were found to be more likely to trade in an old car for a new one.

With knowledge discovery the data never lies; it's only the interpretation of the data that is in question. As with modeling and segmentation, the results of knowledge discovery come in many forms and should be analyzed by specialists familiar with both the relevant tools and the data residing in the data warehouse.

Wherefore Data Mining?

Notice that we haven't mentioned the term "data mining" yet. There's a good reason. Data mining isn't so much a type of analysis as it is a classification of a variety of analysis types.

Many software vendors, eager to taste the sweet fruit of increased sales, have in fact tainted the entire repast by declaring their products data-mining tools. Some ambitious vendors—particularly those fond of replacing the term "decision support" with "data mining"—would go so far as to consider each level of the pyramid to be data mining!

Here data mining is viewed as encompassing modeling/segmentation and knowledge discovery (see figure 2-7).

Data mining has historically been synonymous with statistical analysis, performed by Ph.D.s in order to develop a more accurate understanding of detailed data. Increasingly, data-mining tool vendors have made it easier for nonstatisticians to use their tools not only to detect interesting patterns in data but also to apply the results.

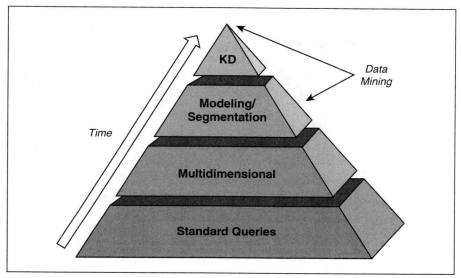

Figure 2-7: Where Data Mining Fits

Throughout the book we'll be looking at how data mining is being leveraged in different companies and industries, as well as what the payback has been so far. Where it makes sense, we'll use the term "data mining" to mean the practice of advanced data analysis, but we will specify whether that analysis is modeling, segmentation, or knowledge discovery.

Data Warehousing in the Real World

This book features examples and case studies of customers who may well be considered data-warehousing pioneers. Most of them have moved beyond just querying the data and have succeeded in delivering actionable decision support to their business users.

However, many of the data warehouses installed today are still being used to perform basic operational functions. Far from being a criticism, we view this use of operational data warehouses as extremely worthwhile. While operational functions such as revenue reporting and sales analysis might not be as complex or as glamorous as, say, customer lifetime value analysis, they are nevertheless pervasive. Indeed, many of the early adopter companies featured in this book embarked

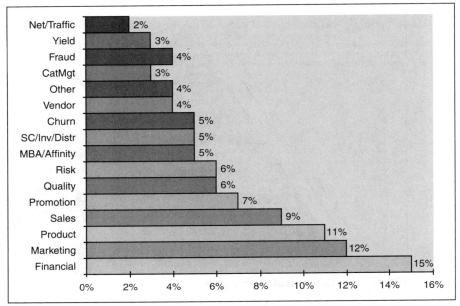

**Figure 2-8: Current Application Share (Source: Palo Alto Management
Group)**

on their data-warehousing journeys with simple reports indicating monthly revenues or customer addresses. As simple as these reports were, they often represented a business user's first look at the data. They heralded major change.

A 1999 report by the Palo Alto Management Group confirms that this basic
reporting is still very much the norm. The report found that financial analysis
and general reporting were the two most popular applications. Figure 2-8 ranks
the types of decision support being done in order of popularity.

The report also cites the trend of business intelligence reporting gradually
surpassing the boundaries of "knowledge workers" and entering the hands of
employees across the enterprise.[2] In other words, the bottom of the pyramid—
queries performed by average business users—is still very much the mainstream
when it comes to data warehouse and data mart usage.

Chapters 3 and 4 explain the application areas listed in the figure above and
present some real-life examples of their usage.

---

2. Palo Alto Management Group, *Business Intelligence and Data Warehousing: Crossing the
Millennium,* 1999, 12. For a summary of the report, see *www.pamg.com.*

What It Takes to Get to the Top

Back to our friends at the bank. As we have already observed, although they couldn't even submit standard queries, they wanted to skip right to modeling—and probably all the way to knowledge discovery—without establishing the proper building blocks.

If they had been ready to do predictive modeling, what would they have needed? Most of the companies that have made it to the top of the pyramid share the following traits:

- The data they have targeted for analysis exists on as few different platforms as possible, ideally on a centralized data warehouse or data mart. This saves the time and effort necessary to consolidate and match data elements.
- Their business users are accustomed to accessing the data warehouse directly in order to obtain information.
- They have staff users of varied skill sets, from nontechnical neophytes to power users.
- They have a "toolbox" of varied application tools with which to query the data. One tool cannot possibly be all things to all people. A variety of tools enables different user categories to employ the most appropriate tool, as well as demonstrating the company's commitment to heterogeneous usage of its data warehouse.
- They believe strongly in the business value of the data warehouse and available funding for ongoing projects.
- One or more executive sponsors from the business side advocates current and future decision support activity.
- They are willing to change their business processes and practices. Data warehousing can result in productivity improvements, cultural transformations, and profitability enhancements. The company must be able to support and adapt to these new improvements.

These are some of the fundamentals that should be in place before your company bites off advanced analysis. But don't despair if you're still doing standard queries. You may still be way ahead of your competitors. As the old Chinese proverb goes, "The journey of a thousand miles begins with a single step."

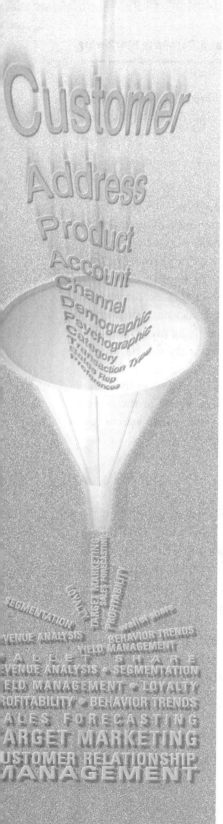

CHAPTER THREE

Data Warehouses and Database Marketing

Knowing one's customer has been a goal for corporations since the middle of the century, way before databases were a gleam in the eye of marketing executives. Back in those days, companies spent lots of time asking the question, "Who is buying our products?" In the 1960s, retailers and advertising agencies slowly lifted their heads and began asking instead, "Why are people buying the products they do?" Thus emerged the study of motivational research.

Motivational research encompassed an eclectic collection of practices that helped companies figure out what made people tick. It employed information-gathering techniques ranging from surveys to hypnosis to Rorschach tests to an interesting device called the "Lazarsfeld-Stanton Program Analyzer," which recorded a research subject's emotional reactions to an array of inquiries based on the pressing of buttons. Focus groups have remained a staple in motivational research and are still used by various industries to gauge consumer reactions and feelings. They remain the preferred method of consumer testing in the entertainment industry and in some consumer packaged goods companies.

As technology evolved and more customer information slowly became available, companies realized that they could review that information in the form of hard data, most of which was simply a by-product of their day-to-day operations. In doing so they could now monitor, track, and understand the panoply of customer behaviors without bothering actual customers—and moreover, delight them with new and innovative products.

Remember the trite aphorisms we introduced in chapter 1? Recently, another trite aphorism began circulating in corporate marketing departments. Paraphrased, it goes something like this:

> "Companies should be shifting their focus from products to customers, and if they don't all hell will break loose."

The point here was that companies—and marketing departments in particular—should begin looking not at *how* they were researching, building, deploying, and selling their products, but *to whom*. Like motivational research before it, this change was embraced as a revelation, particularly to companies who had been selling commodity products and concentrating on their business processes.

In a recent *Information Week* research survey of over 300 IT executives, over half the respondents cited using customer data to increase sales per customer as a management priority, while over 70 percent focused on raising overall customer satisfaction levels.[1] Customer data, along with other key data subject areas, is integral to the way companies are now doing business.

This chapter explains how this data is being used by companies in the "kill or be killed" territory of competitive strategy; it also covers several of the current marketing concepts that are not only being implemented using data warehouses, but often justify their acquisition in the first place.

Customer Relationship Management

Recently, my car's requisite 5000-mile service checkup prompted my first trip to the dealer since I'd bought the car some months before. Rather than just dropping the car off for this routine maintenance, though, I decided to wait it out with my laptop and installed myself in the service department's empty waiting room.

Three minutes into my e-mail, Joel, the salesman who had sold me the car, entered the waiting room and greeted me by name. I hadn't seen Joel for several months and couldn't believe he'd recognized me. He inquired about my family and remembered that I had bought this particular model in part because I needed to transport my dogs—whose names he'd also remembered. To top it all off, as he proffered me a piping-hot foamy hazelnut latte (my beverage of choice, but how had he remembered?), he offered me a loaner car. I was dumbstruck.

---

1. Sweat, Jeff, "Customer Centricity in the Post-Y2K Era," *Information Week*, May 17, 1999, 50. See also *www.informationweek.com/734/customer.htm*.

My bafflement was short-lived. As I sipped my latte, it slowly dawned on me that Joel knew I was coming. When I'd made my service appointment several days earlier, the service department's system had somehow alerted the sales department, which then looked up my customer profile. Joel hadn't emblazoned my dogs' names into his memory—he probably didn't even remember I had pets—it was the company's database that recalled my favorite coffee and impressed the heck out of me.

Call it what you will. Relationship marketing. Continuous customer management. CRM. It's the concept *du jour* to describe the new customer focus in business. The trend advocates "customer intimacy": establishing improved knowledge of customers, who they are, what they might buy, their contacts with your company, and how they've evolved. The subtext here is that the better you know your customers and their behaviors, the more likely you are to keep them and sell them additional products. Irrespective of Joel's actual powers of recollection, I'd buy another car from him.

CRM is more than customer knowledge; it's the process of understanding discrete customer activities and modifying business processes around them. While e-data is crucial to successful CRM, the true measure of success is in higher sales, promotion response, and customer satisfaction rates. It's about understanding, and thereby ultimately owning, the customer experience.[2]

Interpretations of CRM vary, from instructing staff in a call center to say "thank you for calling" to training bank tellers in proactive selling to studying detailed data about purchase behaviors in order to predict what customers will buy next. The former two are easily implemented but often yield unreliable results. But understanding what drives customers—what motivates them to buy, their preferred sales channel, even their pet peeves—can bestow valuable and often unforeseen business knowledge. Companies that up to now weren't sure how they could glean payback from a data warehouse are now giving the technology a second look.

CRM means that a hotel knows that a regular guest goes to movies in the theater across the street, and provides him with discount coupons upon check-in. It means that when a company calls a help desk and complains about a product defect, the telemarketing people don't try and sell more of that product two

---

2. "Owning the customer experience" is an emerging slogan that many companies and marketing organizations have embraced. Variations on this are "reinventing the customer experience" and "refreshing the customer experience."

hours later. It means that when a shopper researches a product on the Web, the Web site can direct him to his preferred non-Web sales channel. It means that when a customer calls a company's headquarters and requests that her name be removed from all mailing lists, her sales rep in the field isn't still busy licking stamps.

Before discussing individual marketing tactics, let's spend a few pages distinguishing between analysis of customer segments, which we briefly introduced in chapter 2, and individual customer records. Both are critical to the success of customer marketing efforts, both are best leveraged with data warehousing; but each has its own specific uses and strengths.

Customer Segmentation

In chapter 2 we talked about segmentation from an analysis standpoint. It's second from the top on the pyramid, since it's more difficult to segment and model customer data than it is to query it, but it's not as complex as knowledge discovery, where the hypothesis is conclusive only once data-mining tools have been run and their results interpreted.

Customer segmentation has its roots in some basic marketing principles. Most companies with marketing departments categorize their customers in some way, usually by geography or demographic indicators. In principle, a data warehouse isn't required in order to segment customers.

Segmentation has helped companies separate their good customers from their bad ones by revealing which customer categories warrant the most time and expense. Customer segmentation avoids the "throw it at the wall and see if it sticks" approach to marketing, historically represented in the form of mass mailings and blanket telemarketing campaigns.

For example, segmentation can allow a general merchandiser to target fine jewelry to a couple who both work and whose kids have left home, rather than to a family with four young children. The empty-nester couple—represented by a customer segment containing customers with similar attributes—is more likely to have the disposable income and lifestyle that would warrant such a luxury purchase. Simpler yet, a segment can be defined that assembles all customers—regardless of behavior or demographics—who have purchased jewelry more than once during the past twelve months.

More than ever before, retailers are honing in on their best customers: those who spend the most money on the most profitable products. Customer segmentation plays a key role in helping retailers pinpoint customer niches. For example, Radio Shack has developed catalogues featuring products of specific interest to niche segments, resulting in reduced store inventories and increased purchase rates.[3]

Historically, companies have not had the necessary data to segment their customers. Furthermore the technologies that have traditionally performed segmentation were limited in the number of data attributes they could process at one time. This forced companies either to summarize or to limit the data that they were segmenting, often dropping important details.

Segmentation was traditionally user-driven, meaning the data analyst would decide what to look for, select data summaries to segment, and subjectively evaluate the results. The factors used to define segments and their relative weightings were thus left up to the knowledge worker, who often knew more about statistics than about the way the business worked. Segmentation results ended up being of questionable accuracy and value.

Even when the results were accurate and yielded valuable information, segmentation didn't denote specific actions to take. Just because a grocery store identified a customer as "desirable" didn't mean it knew whether to sell that customer motor oil or bran muffins.

Things have changed. As they began collecting data and storing it on their data warehouses, companies became alert to the variety of segmentation possibilities. Some have become quite sophisticated, segmenting customers into small groups with very specific attribute combinations. When a home-decorating Web site can recognize that shoppers in different geographic areas prefer different colors of indoor paint, the company can craft specific campaigns for shopper neighborhoods. Different customer types should ultimately drive different marketing strategies.

And the old ways of customer segmentation have given way to a more advanced means of segmentation, or "clustering" (see figure 3-1). Clustering tools allow companies to perform customer segmentation against lower-level details such as product category or individual product, creating not only new customer groupings but also groupings relative to other business factors. Moreover, the data-mining tools performing this clustering define the clusters for the knowledge worker, not the other way around.

Grouping customers according to suspicions or to prove theories is valuable, especially when technology is leveraged to aid in those groupings. Customer

3. Fleischer, Jo, "Radio Shack Has Questions, Its Data Warehouse Has Answers," *RT Magazine*, March 1998.

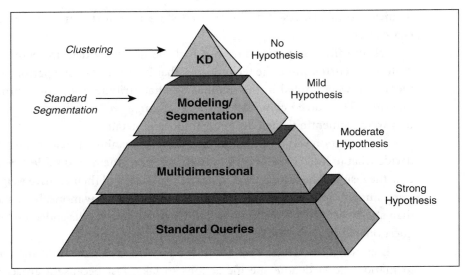

Figure 3-1: Segmentation and Clustering

segmentation has allowed companies across industries to change the way they treat various customer sets, ultimately saving time and money while improving customer satisfaction.

In short, segmentation has been a boon to companies that previously treated their clientele like one massive populace. And some of these customer groups are making way for even smaller segments: segments of one.

Individual Customer Analysis

It wasn't enough for Joel, my car dealer, to segment me merely as a caffeine-dependent pet lover. That data alone wouldn't have enabled him to distinguish me enough from other customers to impress me and secure my loyalty as he did. In fact, relying only on the knowledge that I was a member of such a segment—"Hi, ma'am, how is your ferret? How's about an espresso shot?"—might actually have backfired.

Even companies that concentrate mainly on segmenting customers must have the corresponding customer detail to be able to drill down into specific attributes and behaviors. These companies can often apply CRM practices to the detail itself, targeting individual customers. Marketing departments that have traditionally relied on segmentation and event summaries to dictate new selling strategies are now realizing that deploying customized campaigns and driving measurably successful target-marketing programs often call for the ability to know exactly who's who in the vast customer array.

While the concept of one-to-one marketing has been around for less time than customer segmentation, it is not new. Pioneering companies saw the advantages of storing and analyzing individual customer records in the late 1970s and began practicing it soon thereafter. Citicorp, Bank of America, Sears, and Liberty Mutual were just some of the early adopters of detailed customer record storage.

Individual customer analysis is particularly useful to companies with commercial clients. Since a company's best customers are more often than not its corporate customers, segmenting them may not provide the level of detail necessary to create differentiated relationships.

Many companies are using customer details to create "top n" customer lists. A telephone company that knows its top 20 customers can tailor product packages for each one, assign each a dedicated sales and support staff, and create individual sales plans and forecasts. The more detail a company has about its high-value customers, the more customized its contacts with those customers can be. For example:

List contact names and telephone numbers of
top 20 customers whose sales revenues
have decreased more than 30 percent from a year ago.

This query does more than generate a customer list; it offers a tactical contact plan. In addition to providing the company with sales comparisons, the results of this query can enlighten field sales staff about which customers may have problems regarding satisfaction or product usage and can lead to proactive problem resolution, preventing attrition.

Companies are using individual customer information to reformulate their products, often adapting and packaging them not for a given customer segment, but for an individual. In their book *Enterprise One to One*, Don Peppers and Martha Rogers refer to this individualized approach as "mass customization" and cite examples of companies that have justified the approach.

. . . many businesses today can routinely produce customized products or services tailored to the specific needs of an individual business or consumer rather than to the general needs of a "segment" of customers."[4]

---

4. Peppers, Don and Martha Rogers, *Enterprise One to One: Tools for Competing in the Interactive Age,* New York: Currency/Doubleday, 1997, 12.

Indeed, one-to-one marketing has taken root, as large customer segments traditionally used for product-marketing campaigns have given way to targeted segments of one.

Companies are also updating their data warehouses each time a customer-specific "event" takes place. Not only does this provide a graduated level of detail about customers, it allows for point-in-time analysis. Event-driven marketing allows companies to examine a customer's place in the supply chain in order to predict the next logical purchase. Similarly, life-stage marketing tracks life events—graduation from college, marriage, birth of first child, etc.—in order to proactively market new products and services. For example, the recent college graduate may be interested in a new credit card, whereas the newly married couple may be scouting for a home loan. The fact that over 50 percent of college students have at least one credit card indicates that banks are recruiting new customers as early as high school.

The problem with one-to-one marketing is that it is sometimes not worth the effort and expense for companies that sell commodity products or have millions of customers to store individual customer records. It's not realistic to send a custom mailing to each traveler in a frequent-flier database or to everyone holding a phone card; segmentation is still a much more efficient and less costly approach in such instances. Ironically, it is usually just those companies that have acquired data warehouses in order to efficiently store and manage customer detail.

Of course, some industries are better equipped to adopt CRM than others. Those data-warehousing early adopters are especially ahead of the curve.

Case Study: Bank of America

From an imposing office tower in the heart of downtown San Francisco, Christopher Kelly considers the last three years at Bank of America. That his title is "senior vice president of affluent and consumer database marketing" is a testimonial to the bank's belief in the potential magnitude of database marketing's business impact. That his organization has already saved the bank millions of dollars is a fact not lost on its new parent company, NationsBank.

Kelly manages a group of marketing analysts responsible for poring over Bank of America's two-terabyte customer database. The varied analysis methods and advanced technologies his department employs are proof that Kelly's group is as much a strategy center as it is an analysis organization.

"Our job is to execute marketing strategies that create relevance with our customers," he explains. With 30 million households resulting in 300 million banking transactions monthly, Kelly's staff wisely combines a state-of-the-art data warehouse with a variety of analysis techniques in order to understand customer behavior better.

Among a variety of analysis strategies is the segmentation Bank of America's massive customer database, the results of which are leveraged by the bank's retail division. Typical customer segments include the following:

- demographic segments
- geographic segments (regions, states, etc.)
- behavioral segments, including product ownership and channel usage
- customer value segmentation
- customer tenure
- needs-based segmentation

The resulting business activities involve everything from reallocating marketing and sales resources around segments to designing unique, segment-based customer communication strategies. The bank also evaluates product development and pricing against certain segments. "We use a 'Rubik's cube' approach to segmentation," says Kelly. "We slice and dice data in different ways to identify homogeneous customer niches."

Chris Kelly is proudest of his group's accomplishments in CRM (see figure 3-2). The bank is using CRM to identify customer behavior "triggers," such as what prompts customers to purchase new products or close accounts. Life-stage marketing is the exemplar of the group's analysis skills. "We're tracking certain customer life events," Kelly explains, "in order to know what a customer might buy next, and to be able to offer such a product in a proactive way."

The intent of Kelly's organization is not only to provide retail banking staff with the data and findings they need in order to come up with new marketing programs, but to ensure that the findings ultimately result in valuable business actions. To this end, the bank regularly updates its data warehouse with the results of its marketing programs.

What's singular about Chris Kelly and his team of marketing analysts is that they aren't just hacking away at data in order to arrive at "neat to know" findings that are never deployed beyond the desk of the knowledge worker—an all too common phenomenon in advanced analysis organizations. "The idea is to create a perpetual marketing process," he claims. "We certainly have the customer and behavioral trigger data to do just that."

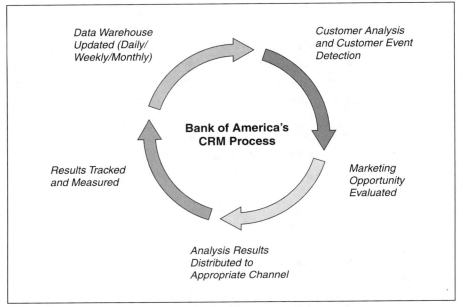

Figure 3-2: Bank of America's CRM Process (Source: Bank of America)

Bank of America's recent acquisition by NationsBank has involved pre-dictable reorganizations and departmental mergers. Nevertheless, Kelly's group has remained largely intact. They will continue to mine the two banks' combined customer base for interesting and actionable marketing knowledge. Says Kelly, "We're trying to create a unique experience for the customer, and with it, a unique value proposition: one that only BofA can offer."

A Word About CRM Technology

The database-marketing activities covered in the remainder of this chapter can all be classified under the general CRM rubric. It's important to note, however, that the technologies used to perform CRM vary in their functionality and usage. While customer segmentation using statistical analysis tools might solve one problem—and can rightly be called CRM—another problem might call for a specialized CRM software package.

When they discuss CRM, most vendors are talking about any technology that helps a company monitor its customer interactions. Each time a customer "event" takes place, whether it is ordering a product from a Web site or checking in for a flight, the customer leaves a footprint. CRM technologies aim to track these footprints in order to guide the customer on the most profitable journey possible. Often, CRM is coupled with "campaign management," the ability to validate, create, launch, and monitor a new marketing campaign with the best customer intelligence possible.

A recent AMR Research report estimates that the CRM technology market will surpass $7 billion by 2002. CRM tools cover a range of capabilities, from sales force automation to closed-loop customer care processing to basic ad hoc reporting. Some CRM tools leverage data-mining technologies and can go so far as to justify why certain customers are worthiest of a new campaign. Some support analysis of where marketing dollars are being misused. Others simply generate customer lists with little logic to corroborate the selections made.

With the assorted functionality offered in the CRM market, it's no wonder that the pricing of CRM technologies is likewise broad. CRM tools can cost anywhere from $50,000 for a reporting-cum-campaign-analysis tool all the way to $1 million for a marketing-automation package.

As I write this, most of my customers are in the throes of evaluating CRM tools. Several are attending analyst conferences hoping for the answer to their CRM questions, and a handful have CRM pilot projects underway. But different CRM tools solve different business problems. For example, some CRM packages offer a "front-office" solution, helping companies to manage their sales forces and mailing lists, while others are oriented more toward the "back office," supporting advanced customer-behavior analysis and prompting the resulting business actions. Not all of them begin with the assumption that clean, consolidated e-data on a data warehouse is a mandatory starting point.

What does this mean for your company? That it should identify the gaps in its customer management strategy prior to choosing a CRM product. Most CRM tools support the Internet, but if your customers routinely contact you via your help desk, will a CRM tool's Web support functions really help? Certain off-the-shelf CRM "suite" products may turn out to be overkill, while industry-specific or functionally oriented CRM tools might not do enough. Many CRM vendors are naively pushing the technology as an alternative to data warehousing. It should instead be considered the point of integration.

So proceed cautiously! Like the larger data-warehouse marketplace, when it comes to CRM, one size doesn't fit all.

Popular Database-Marketing Initiatives and What They Mean

It's important to note here that most companies begin using their data warehouses not for marketing purposes, but for tactical reasons such as supply-chain or basic revenue reporting. The data warehouse evolves over time, enabling the company to provide answers to basic business questions, as well as leverage its data for more strategic purposes.

Once customer data is available online, marketing use is the natural evolution of the data warehouse. But marketing is a broad discipline that encompasses a diverse set of activities. This section briefly introduces some of the most pervasive marketing activities exploiting data warehouses and decision support.

It should be noted here that while many of these concepts are "cutting edge," they often require no more than simple canned reports or ad hoc analysis in order to find significant information that can enhance the corporate bottom line. Although software vendors are increasingly automating functions such as churn prediction and customer profitability calculation, these types of data can be generated "manually" using "brute force" queries and homegrown applications. The real challenge is getting the data on the data warehouse in the first place!

Target Marketing

We've already touched a bit on target marketing: marketing a particular product to a specific customer or customer group. Marketing high-end products to high-income customers as in the jewelry example above is just one of many cases where target marketing can result in payback. The concept of target marketing has been around for a while, but only recently have companies become sophisticated in its practice.

Years ago, J. C. Penney sent its catalogues to most households in the United States, even though the company understood all too well just how costly it was to produce, print, and mail millions of catalogues to customers who might never even open them, let alone buy something. But back then, it was impossible to actually measure the ratio of mailings to sales.

Such mass-mailing strategies amounted to little more than guesswork and blind faith. In the current competitive environment, growth demands and business requirements dictate that companies have to find other indicators for marketing—and respond to them more quickly.

The advent of specialty retailers has changed the face of marketing across industries. Retailers now specialize in selling specific niche products such as children's clothing, women's underwear, red meat, and auto parts. And since specialty products attract distinct customers, it would be impractical for these retailers to market to everyone everywhere. Instead, they identify only those customers for whom their merchandise was developed.

While target marketing can involve simple decision support queries resulting in characteristics of targeted customer segments, data-mining tools can define many of these characteristics for a company. Predictive models can indicate the customers most likely to buy a certain product or service.

A nascent application of target marketing is the examination of the prior purchase. A customer buys building supplies at a hardware superstore. As it tracks individual purchases, the store then mails that customer a discount coupon on landscaping products. When combined with the data in the data warehouse, predictive modeling tools can help companies not only indicate which customers are most likely to purchase a given product but also pinpoint the next product that customer is likely to buy. Retailers that participate in multiple lines of business, such as Amazon.com and The Limited, can leverage predictive purchase data to attract customers back into a store or Web site, or steer them to a sister location.

The simple graph portrayed in figure 3-3 comes from a "visualization tool" that graphically depicts potential sales for a brokerage house's new mutual fund.

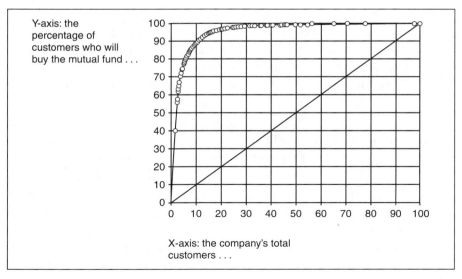

Figure 3-3: Predictive Target Marketing

The x-axis represents the percentage of the company's total customer base, while the y-axis represents the percentage of customers who are likely to purchase the product. The diagonal line down the middle indicates a random response rate; if every customer was mailed a brochure about the new product, the response rate would rise proportionally.

Figure 3-3, the result of the brokerage firm's predictive modeling against its data warehouse, shows that 10 percent of all the firm's customers represent 90 percent of the sales opportunity for this mutual fund. The firm can now go back to its data warehouse to find out who those customers are and market exclusively to them.

As a company's customer population increases and it learns more about its individual customers, target-marketing indicators can grow from a few specific customer attributes to hundreds. Data from address information to date of birth to last item purchased can spawn a host of new target-marketing programs. And as the number of customers and attributes grows, the data warehouse becomes more necessary than ever.

Cross-Selling

Companies are using their data warehouses to increase an individual customer's propensity to buy a product, either during the same shopping trip (or telephone order, or branch visit), or on a subsequent trip. The goal is to increase an individual customer's overall purchase.

Cross-selling helps companies hone in on existing customers who might buy new or additional products or services at a particular time of contact, be it during the purchase of another product, a service visit, or even a complaint call. While more of a sales activity than a pure marketing tactic, effective cross-selling means that the customer has been qualified as a desirable buyer of a product or service and is solicited to buy that product while in contact with the vendor.

The classic cross-selling example, illustrated in figure 3-4, is in banking: A customer interacts with a branch teller to perform a transaction. While processing the transaction, the teller calls up the customer's profile on his computer. The profile indicates that the customer might be a good candidate for home refinance.

How did this happen? In creating customer profiles, many financial institutions are not only including basic information such as name and address and average balance, they are also using data-mining tools in order to generate more intricate figures, such as the customer's overall profitability and her next likely purchase. When such a profile is called up during the customer's visit, the teller

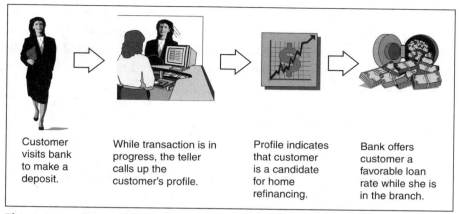

Customer visits bank to make a deposit.

While transaction is in progress, the teller calls up the customer's profile.

Profile indicates that customer is a candidate for home refinancing.

Bank offers customer a favorable loan rate while she is in the branch.

Figure 3-4:   Cross-Selling in the Bank Branch

can offer her the product she is likely to buy, and the customer can take advantage of being in the branch in order to buy it. Both parties win.

Another common example of cross-selling is the last time you made an air travel reservation. When you called the airline's reservation number, the representative—who may actually work for a third-party reservation agency—asked whether you needed a car rental when you reached your destination. If your answer was yes, you were then connected to a car rental agency, and the reservation agency most likely took a commission on your car rental.

Likewise, home shopping and e-tailing companies are working to stimulate add-on sales. The more information the site or call center has about a buyer, the more likely it is that the company can propose an add-on product that the captive customer might buy. Catalogue companies are currently using cross-selling techniques to offer discounts to buyers after they have placed their orders. The logic here is that if the customer bought Product A today, she is also a likely candidate for Product H.

Companies are increasingly tuning in to "up-selling" opportunities: persuading their customers to trade up to more profitable products. The adolescent voice blaring through the fast-food drive-thru asking, "You wanna supersize that?" is the most glaring example of up-selling.

While cross-selling and up-selling are widely used in the retail industry, they're even more ubiquitous in industries that maintain a lot of data about individual customers. Banks, telecommunications companies, and utilities are all relying on purchase incentives to stimulate growth. Recently, a cable company performed an analysis of customers who were active buyers of pay-per-view sporting events. By analyzing e-data on past pay-per-view orders, including day of the week and time of day, the company could offer a discounted pay-per-view wrestling match to residential and business customers calling in new orders.

Ineffective cross-selling can, however, result in "cannibalization," whereby the customer buys the marketed product but in the process displaces an existing one. The next-to-last thing a company wants to do is to replace a prior revenue stream that might have been more profitable than the new one (not to mention torpedoing its marketing return rate). The last thing a company wants to do is to wear a customer out with too many attempts at cross-selling.

Thus, the more data available to the business, the more effective the cross-selling effort. And it's critical for your cross-selling and up-selling to be effective the first time, since you might not get a second chance.

Sales Analysis and Forecasting

Sales analysis is one of the foremost uses of data warehouses and data marts. The ability of a company's executives, financial staff, and the salespeople themselves to monitor sales has become crucial to a company's planning, staffing, and resource allocation activities.

Sales analysis involves a degree of subjectivity. Some consider it revenue analysis, while others concentrate on sales productivity. Here are typical queries:

Show me this quarter's sales for everyone in Territory 4 compared with sales for the same period last year.

Display commissions for salespeople in the southwest region.

List revenues for Product X so far this month by sales manager.

Retailers may simply want to understand what's being sold in certain stores or locations and whether sales for specific products or categories are rising or falling. This information can aid in a variety of business actions, from price changes to advertising campaigns to coupon releases.

Traditionally, businesses have forecast sales by comparing last year's sales with generally available economic indicators to extrapolate future sales. In short, sales forecasting has relied on guesswork. Such simplistic means of sales prediction and subsequent planning is no longer realistic because competition in all business sectors is rampant. Monopolies being relatively rare, similar businesses compete for the same consumer dollar. Companies must be more exact than ever about where their revenues originate.

The fine art of sales forecasting now relies on a number of factors: Floor layout, store location, weather, and economic conditions are merely a handful of indicators that can ordain whether a customer purchases a product. Moreover, those indicators may differ by store, Web site, region, geography, or company.

Sales forecasting should not be done in a vacuum, which is why a data warehouse plays a key role (see figure 3-5). The goal isn't merely to forecast revenues, but to respond adequately to consumer demand, be it for more earmuffs, a newly approved drug, or a new home equity line of credit. Sales forecasting means knowing how to supply sales channels, affect prices, and promote specific products and services.

The ability to forecast sales companywide, market by market, and channel by channel assists merchants in planning future orders and working with their suppliers to schedule promotions and determine optimal replenishment strategies. The greater the accuracy of sales forecasts, the less inventory the retailer must store, thus decreasing capital costs and increasing supply-chain efficiency.

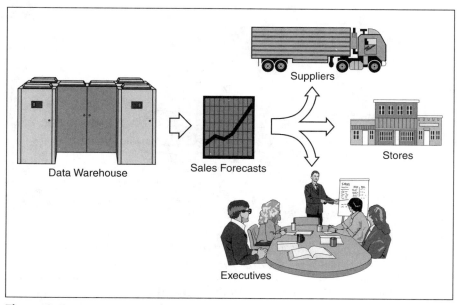

Figure 3-5: Sales Forecasting

Last Fourth of July weekend, an East Coast grocery chain sold three times more beer than the year before, running out in most of its stores and thus forfeiting significant revenue. This year, beer sales were down. By analyzing data on its data warehouse, the grocery chain can examine historical price points on beer and determine not only how much to stock this year but also whether or not to advertise it, and at what price.

The ability to forecast sales accurately doesn't just affect revenues, it can have repercussions on customer satisfaction. A thirsty beer drinker can be an unhappy camper, so it's wise to have plenty of stock on hand.

Market Basket Analysis

There are different names for it: association analysis, product affinities, and the ever-popular market basket analysis. The collection of products in a customer's market basket—whether they be groceries, bank accounts, or telephone services—can tell a company a lot about that customer, and a lot more about future sales opportunities.

"Into every shopping cart a little mysterious Mediterranean product must fall."

Figure 3-6: Market Basket Analysis in Action

The most famous example of market basket analysis is the "beer and diapers" anecdote, in which a retailer reportedly discovered that when men went to buy diapers, the likelihood of them also buying beer was extremely high. Despite an article in *Forbes* magazine (April 6, 1998) debunking the story as mere myth, retailers are still taking market basket analysis very seriously.

Companies increasingly want to know the combination of items in a customer's "basket," and more specifically which products might be "pulling" others—triggering the purchases of other products. While there are some obvious product adjacencies—peanut butter with jelly, for example—it is those that are less obvious that are the most interesting.

Market basket analysis facilitates the study of purchase trends as well as the pricing and promotion of certain products. It can elucidate how purchase patterns change over time and help a retailer understand timing dependencies, such as seasonal or holiday purchase trends. Businesses can also model market baskets that simulate expected purchasing patterns and calculate the profitability of those baskets.

Some grocers are now using market basket data to generate real-time coupons for products that are deemed "affinities" to other items a customer might have in his basket. See chapter 4 for an example of market basket analysis at a grocery store.

Promotions Analysis

Promotions analysis tells companies across industries whether and how new advertising or marketing campaigns will work. As with other types of analysis, promotions analysis can occur either before or after the promotion, and either to predict or to measure its effectiveness.

For example, once a promotion is complete, a business can determine whether it did indeed attract new customers, and moreover, if existing customers responded to the promotion. Did the promotion result in net new sales, or in cannibalization of existing products? Was the loss on a promoted product regained in the form of other purchases?

Retailers in particular want to understand the optimal products to advertise in order to maximize the number of items found in the market basket. And they want to accomplish this while preventing profit erosion.

Sears, Roebuck, & Co. uses its data warehouse to track product performance in advertising circulars, enabling the company to compare results based on the placement and size of an item in the ad. "Analysts in our Marketing area can determine how an ad performed," says Sears's Hank Steermann, "and make decisions about how better to feature that product during the next promotion."

Several software vendors have developed campaign-management products that not only track sales spurred by certain sales campaigns but also measure their effectiveness. Such software tools allow a company to define campaign execution metrics prior to launching the campaign, as well as providing a campaign-tracking process to measure the program's success. Smart companies then register the tracking data by loading it into the data warehouse. Thus, in the case of a successful campaign, similar measurements can be leveraged in future marketing initiatives, whereas unsuccessful campaign attributes can be avoided.

Advanced companies use the e-data in the data warehouse to predict how well a marketing campaign will do and then revise their sales strategies accordingly. Some are integrating their campaign-management strategies with their promotions. Thus, event-driven marketing is further enabled by the deployment of customized campaigns and their subsequent measurement.

Customer Retention and Churn Analysis

In the quest to optimize revenues, many businesses have found that keeping a good customer is far less costly—three to ten times cheaper—than finding a new one. Companies in all industries are developing ways not only to analyze customer attrition but also to predict it.

Churn analysis involves examining the behavior patterns of customers who have left for competitors, with a view to prevent remaining customers from leaving. This type of analysis is especially important to businesses that can track individual customer relationships and have acknowledged competitive pressures. For this reason, banks and telecommunications companies perform extensive churn analysis activities, whereas grocery stores and, until recently, utility companies do not.

Where the term "attrition" implies a customer who has left, "churn" implies a customer who has left but may possibly come back. The greater the percentage of customers who leave, the greater the

- loss of overall revenue
- loss of the initial investment to attract new customers
- potential for lost profitability from high-value customers
- loss of future revenue
- additional costs of customer support
- loss of a stable market base for new services

Churn solutions are varied, and many businesses have developed their own churn analysis and predictive tools unique to their industries. Packaged churn detection software that uses historical data from the data warehouse is emerging from a variety of vendors, and many standard data-mining software vendors have added "propensity to churn" models to their technology repertoires.

Basically, two different types of churn are of concern to businesses:

1. *Customer-initiated churn.* The customer disconnects service, closes an account, or ceases to shop at a given store, and the company does not know why.
2. *Competitor-initiated churn.* A competitor "steals" the customer from an existing product or service provider.

Since the former type of churn is far more common, companies need tracking indicators to predict such actions. With this information in hand, they can then induce good customers whose behavior displays these indicators to stay by way of customer retention programs. These programs might include providing free products and services, establishing discounts for customers likely to churn, removing service charges, or elevating service levels.

A good example of a customer retention program at work is the airline industry's frequent-flier programs. Because of my reduced travel schedule, my airline of choice recently demoted me from "gold elite" status to "silver" status, in effect limiting some of my frequent-flier perks. However, the airline's letter notifying me of my downgraded status was accompanied by several first-class upgrade coupons. Having most likely performed the necessary analysis to know that such demotion makes customers more likely to churn to another carrier the airline motivated me with additional upgrades. It worked, and I stayed.

Businesses employ various churn analysis techniques. It is in fact very simple to predict churn with standard decision support queries that indicate the events leading up to a service cancellation. With further queries, a company can discover which of these events have occurred with other customers and take steps to induce those customers to stay. Segments of customers likely to churn can be established and tracked over time. A key point is that even a small rise in the customer retention rate often can result in a significant profitability increase.

Thus, a company can surmise who *might* leave, and why. Indeed, the answer to this question may dictate that certain customers with a propensity to churn should be allowed to do so based on their accompanying profitability or customer value scores (see below).

Industry-specific churn and attrition analysis tools that can access data on a data warehouse are the preferred method of detecting churn for most businesses. Thus, a credit card company can examine customer churn or card churn, while a telecommunications company can look at product churn.

But don't presume that only financial services and telecommunications companies are hard hit by churn. The Gartner Group recently projected that top Internet service providers could each lose more than $6 billion annually as a result of customer churn.

Profitability Analysis

Companies are quickly realizing that not every customer is necessarily a profitable one. Many companies are shifting their strategies from increasing the number of their customers to increasing the profitability of existing customers. Thus, increased customer profitability is a staple on the menu of most corporate marketing strategies.

Profitability calculation can either be a matter of simple addition or a complex maneuver combining detailed cost information with sales figures, rolling up to the desired profitability level. But there is actually more than one type of profitability analysis. Profitability can be determined at multiple levels, for example:

- Product profitability—examining individual and combined product sets to determine whether they make or lose money, and how much.
- Channel profitability—calculating the profitability of various delivery channels. In the case of a bank, those delivery channels can range from the branch to the grocery store kiosk to the individual ATM.
- Account profitability—considering an account, which may be owned by one or more customers and include one or more products.
- Customer profitability—examining combined sets of customer products and services, along with customer behaviors, to determine each customer's overall profitability. Customer profitability can be ascertained for individual customers as well as customer segments.

Understanding whether a product is profitable or not can result in a range of decisions, from promoting the product as part of an advertising campaign to packaging that product with more or less profitable products to discontinuing the product altogether. Prior to understanding and storing detailed product cost information on their data warehouses, many businesses were unwittingly losing money on certain products.

Channel profitability is increasingly practiced in this age of mergers and acquisitions, in which merging companies want to leave their most profitable stores or branches alone and eliminate the costs of less profitable sales channels by closing them altogether. In addition, entire channels can be introduced or phased out based on their profitability. Some firms are able to use existing channel and cost data from their data warehouses to predict the likely profitability of new or emerging sales channels such as their Web sites.

The goal for many companies is to calculate the profitability of each individual customer. In order to do this, they must first understand which products and services the customer has purchased, which products the customer might buy over time, and the costs of new and future products, as well as of ancillary services that the customer might be using, such as a call center. Because of the quantities of data and processing required, a data warehouse is virtually indispensable in order for large companies to calculate customer profitability.

Once customer profitability is understood, a business can combine profitability information with other value metrics in order to decide whether a customer is "valuable" and worthy of continued expense. In some cases profitability information can help a company pinpoint unprofitable customers who should be profitable or identify others who should just be allowed to churn.

Customer Value Measurement

Customer value modeling is an emerging analysis technique, especially in cases where the company can track who individual customers are and what they have bought. Banks, telephone companies, and health care providers have been researching customer value analysis with mixed results.

The principle behind customer value analysis, also known as lifetime customer value (LCV), is that a given customer is assigned a certain value score based on a variety of factors for a designated span of time. The calculation for LCV indicates the relative value of customers over the course of their relationship with the company. The value score—typically derived by assigning weights to each factor and combining them—helps determine precisely how individual customers should be treated—for instance, whether the cost of providing them with a private banker will be offset by their overall value to the bank. Some companies are using customer value modeling to create "perfect client" profiles and are even attempting to mold less than perfect clients into perfect ones through various programs.

In the vast majority of cases, customer value is contingent on customer profitability information, which is painstaking to calculate and maintain. However, profitability might not be the sole value metric in determining whether a customer is worth retaining. In some cases, an unprofitable customer may nevertheless act as a wonderful reference or as a channel for more profitable customers.

The traditional benefit of customer value analysis has been to weed out customers worth the cost and effort of customer retention and other marketing programs. After all, why spend money to keep customers who don't bring in revenues?

The temptation is simply to deposit customers into one of two buckets: "good" and "bad." However, the best way to perform customer value measurement is by segmenting customers using relative value weightings.

The challenge here is that customer value measurement cannot occur in a vacuum but must leverage detailed product, cost, and customer information that is often integrated only in the data warehouse. Historical behavior information is key for this, which means that a company must keep comprehensive information about every customer in order to calculate customer value reliably. Most customer value models leverage a company's internal metrics, as opposed to standard measurement sources such as profitability or revenues. Thus the definition of customer value can be dramatically different from one organization to another, between companies, or even within the same company.

In addition, the more diverse a company's products and organizations, the more difficult it is to establish a total customer value. A small business might have a highly profitable T1 line, while that business's owner might also have a standard telephone line at home. Unless the telephone company recognizes that the small business owner is also the residential consumer—an unwieldly maneuver without a data warehouse—the customer's total value can never be accurately calculated and thus can never provide accurate customer knowledge.

Product Packaging

Many companies adopted the philosophy of managing each product as if it were their only product. Nevertheless, a collection of products and services has allowed companies across industries to "bundle" those products together in new and unique ways. The name of the game with custom product packaging is to combine a set of products and services into one fixed-price unit. The aim is to combine highly profitable products into the mix to ensure net profit and motivate customers to buy the set.

But how do companies know which products and services should be combined? Certainly, product profitability information is critical. But so is data pertaining to product sales history, customer purchases, and product usage. The company that cannot match a customer to a product or set of products is not yet ready for new product packaging.

Product packaging often uses the same type of analysis as market basket analysis: the ability to look at product affinities in order to see which products might "pull" others, and which customers buy them. While the logic of combining products often depends on the type of industry, figure 3-7 shows how a company might choose to bundle three different products together into one package.

By combining Products D and E (which together represent a per-unit revenue shortfall of $500) with Product C (which represents $600 in per-unit profit), the product vendor can make a net profit of $100 per sale. Furthermore, the vendor might choose to price the product at a premium, further boosting its overall revenues. Price elasticity modeling and what-if analysis can help the company determine the best price.

The goal of any retailer is to sell the consumer as much product as possible when he walks in the door, McDonald's being the avatar of this philosophy. Recognizing the downward price pressures inherent in its market space, along with increased competition, the company introduced its "extra value meal" combining several products: a hamburger, fries, and a drink.

The "extra value meal" not only provided more product and thus fueled additional sales, it freed McDonald's customers from having to calculate prices, while at the same time getting the customer who might have bought only a sandwich and a drink to add fries to his order. The meals also simplified inventory management

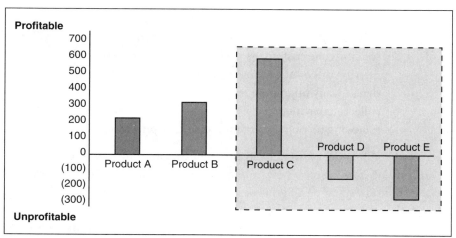

Figure 3-7: Product Packaging

and preparation. Ultimately, the packaging technique helped McDonald's up-sell to the consumer, increase revenues, and improve price perception.

Call Centers

Data warehouses often contain historical data about customer interactions, including customer-initiated contacts such as complaints. While they belong in the domain of operations rather than marketing, call centers can produce dramatic consequences for customer relationships. After all, with industries like banking downsizing their brick and mortar operations and thereby minimizing actual physical customer contact, a call center—also known as a help desk or customer care center—is often the only way a customer can communicate with the company.

Most of the current literature on call centers revolves around the telecommunications systems and automated support technologies necessary to operate them. While historically considered one of many infrastructure expenses, call centers are rapidly becoming profit centers for their businesses. Corporations have spent hundreds of millions of dollars adopting new interactive voice response (IVR) systems, reengineering their call center processes, and retraining their staff to be more friendly.

Because call centers are sometimes the only contact point through which companies can solicit customer feedback, the customer service representatives (CSRs) who staff them are increasingly being charged with a variety of unrelated tasks, for example:

- conducting ad hoc customer satisfaction surveys
- cross-selling or up-selling new products while the customer is on the phone
- soliciting the customer's feedback on an unrelated product or service
- offering discounts or purchase incentives on upcoming products
- dynamically upgrading service
- collecting payment
- following up on service requests or new purchases

When the customer calls in, the CSR can punch up the customer's account number or customer ID, immediately accessing the customer record or profile. But how does the CSR know whether to pitch a new product, or instead transfer the customer to the collections department?

By combining a variety of information—from outstanding balance information to lifetime value to propensity-to-buy scores—that the call center system has neither the power nor the capacity to process, the data warehouse can offer a CSR a variety of valuable information about a customer. The call center system can generate a query to the data warehouse, asking for a customer profile or for specific customer information. This allows the CSR not only to take the appropriate action but also to personalize the service. For example:

> While I have you on the line, Mr. McIntire, can I send you a frequent-buyer card that will automatically give you a 10 percent discount on the remainder of this year's purchases?

> or

> I see here that you recently ordered an additional phone line in your home office, Mr. Newell. Were you happy with the service you received? How's the new line working out?

> or

> Hmmm. It seems you've hit your credit limit several times during the last year, but your payments have been on time, Ms. Smith. I'm going to go ahead and raise your credit limit an additional $5,000 . . .

Any of the above responses can transform a complaint call into a customer loyalty victory.

Often, call center systems will in turn populate a data warehouse with historical information about a customer's contacts, including how often the customer called, when the call was made, and whether it ultimately cost or earned the company money. This data can be used when calculating a customer's profitability; the key here is whether, despite having bought profitable products, the customer cost the company money in *time*. Few companies have integrated this advanced level of customer information into their profitability calculations.

Of course, call centers also accommodate faxes, e-mails, and service-center visits. The point is that each customer "touch point" represents a renewed opportunity to retain a customer, be it through additional sales or a simple thank you. Either way, the data warehouse is the key to knowing exactly which tactic to take for each customer, in effect fueling the "one to one" flame.

Sales Contract Analysis

Many businesses with commercial customers habitually draw up contracts that span products, prices, service levels, and time frames. By examining either existing or expired contracts, these companies gain yet another window into customer behavior.

Not only does contract analysis help companies better understand products and services that have been purchased together, it can trigger customer retention programs ahead of a contract's expiration, the point at which many customers are likely to change suppliers.

A telephone company client of mine used to wait until a few weeks prior to a large business client's contract expiration and then e-mail a reminder to the account representatives. The account team would then scramble to find the contract, draw up a new one—normally identical to the old one—and arrange a meeting with the customer to renew. Often the customer had already been researching alternative carriers and discounted rates.

Once their data warehouse allowed them to store this information centrally, they became proactive about renewing contracts. Figure 3-8 shows their updated contract renewal process:

Step 1:
Find contracts
soon to expire.

Step 2:
Examine customer
profitability/value.

Step 3:
Devise list of "work to
renew" customers.

Step 4:
Rewrite and
present new
contracts.

Figure 3-8: The New Contract Analysis

The company was now able to locate contracts months in advance of their expiration and then perform some statistical modeling in order to assign the customer a value score. The contract renewal terms would be based on this score, and the higher the score, the more favorable the new contract terms. Account teams with low-value customers could wait for those customers to contact them. The company's analysts could spend time researching high-value customer usage patterns and behaviors; the more detailed the data about each customer, the greater the degree to which the new contract could be tailored to each customer.

With data on the data warehouse aiding every step of the process, the business contract renewal program was elegant in its execution, and it measurably reduced the standard attrition rate of business customers.

Database Marketing Lessons Learned

The aim of database marketing is to sell the right product to the right set of customers, replacing mass marketing with a highly differentiated approach to customer sales. Indeed, relationship marketing experts warn that the greater the degree of standardization in the marketing process, the greater the likelihood that customer relations could in fact be jeopardized.

"The fact is that *any* policy applied across the board to all customers, intended to benefit the enterprise in all situations, is likely to *harm* relations with at least *some* customers," explain Peppers and Rogers.[5] These days, few companies can afford to imperil customer relationships, and most are spending significant sums to secure them.

Owning the customer experience means applying these one-to-one principles to treat customers better *at the time of the sale*, as well as understand their future buying behaviors.

For instance, Furniture.com offers its customers online design consultants who can monitor the firm's Web site and offer real-time assistance to online shoppers via live chat. Such a customer service strategy can leverage both product purchase history and detailed customer profiles to optimize the shopping experience and maximize the shopping cart at the time the customer is buying. It can also elevate customer loyalty into the stratosphere.

While the pendulum has thus swung firmly in the direction of increased customer knowledge through data, it is swinging back again toward product knowledge. For as critical as it is, detailed customer data in and of itself means nothing without product data. Though Greater Customer Knowledge has become the latest corporate incantation, insight into customer behavior cannot be gained without supplementary business data. In other words, customer data is only part of the story.

Contrary to all the hullabaloo, the goal is *not* just to sell more products to more customers. It is in fact to sell the *right* products to the *right* customers at the *first* attempt, and in all subsequent attempts.

---

5. Peppers, Don and Martha Rogers, *Enterprise One to One*, 319.

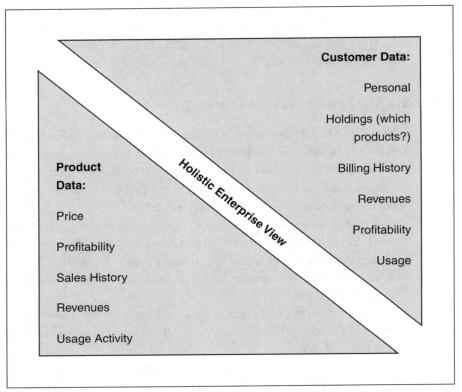

Figure 3-9: Minimum Data for a Holistic Enterprise View

To employ customer relationship marketing effectively, companies should establish the minimum data subject areas pertaining to customers and products, as shown in figure 3-9, in order to achieve a holistic view of the business.

This information can be equally effective on a marketing data mart or on an enterprise data warehouse. The point is knowing what customers are buying in order to be able to both understand current behaviors and predict future activities. Since customer data alone won't permit this level of analysis, it has a lower chance of resulting in data warehouse payback than more integrated data does.

In the next chapter we shall see how companies in specific industries *are* seeing such a payback. It's not simply about selling more or about building up market share. It's wallet share—the degree of the customer's business a company maintains—that's the new brass ring.

Some Lingering Questions

I work for a large retailing company. We've had a data warehouse for over ten years, but we can't seem to deal with "one to one." Why not?

Retailing is a sticky business. While you guys are arguably ahead of the technology curve, it's difficult for you to perform the level of detailed customer analysis that other industries are doing, because you don't have the same level of customer information. For example, when I apply for a checking account, I have to fill out an application that includes a variety of details that sooner or later end up in a data warehouse and can therefore be used by the bank to get to know me better.

Conversely, I don't have to provide any information at all to pop into my local supermarket for some hair mousse and a candy bar. This is why retailers are resorting to frequent-shopper programs: They require customers to supply their name, address, income, and brand preference information when applying for the program—and then store that information, along with each customer's subsequent purchase transactions, in return for coupons and other discounts.

If your company has such a program, you're in good shape. You can monitor what a frequent shopper purchases, examine the purchases over time, and even model that shopper's typical market basket, creating purchase incentives and customer loyalty in the bargain. If you haven't gone the frequent-buyer or store-specific credit card route, you'll be relying on the more traditional analysis techniques of product purchase reporting and supply-chain analysis, *sans* specific customer information. While this is not the ideal scenario, you can still perform some interesting analysis without detailed customer data. And an e-commerce Web site where shoppers must enter personal information prior to making a purchase is the emerging solution to this problem for a range of retailing firms.

This chapter depressed me. My company's not doing any of the marketing activities you've described. Are we hopelessly behind?

Not necessarily. There's a danger to some of these activities, namely, that companies find them much more seductive than the day-to-day reporting functions that can literally run the business.

To use another retail example, market basket analysis is a very hot item in retailing. I know several retailers that have launched market basket analysis programs but nevertheless can't report on stock levels in their stores. These retailers can't tell a store manager what products to reorder, or whether revenues are better than at the same time last year.

I recently spoke at a marketing conference where I presented a case study from an HMO that was using data mining to forecast care patterns in different geographic areas. An audience member taking copious notes raised his hand and earnestly asked, "But how did you find all the patient records and get them into one place to begin with???" Imagine considering predictive modeling without knowing where the data is!

The fact is, you have to walk before you can run. So take heart! Your company's slow and steady approach to data acquisition and analysis may mean you're doing things the right way!

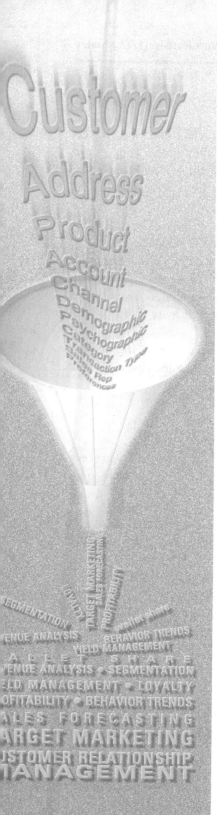

CHAPTER FOUR

Data Warehousing by Industry

I know what you're thinking. You've read the title of this chapter and are immediately flipping through it to find the section on the industry you work in. Or you may be muttering *sotto voce*, "My industry's not in this book. None of the books ever talks about my industry. . . ."

Hold on! It may seem unlikely, but understanding other industries can help you better understand your own. Indeed, consultant and futurist Watts Wacker advises his clients to read trade magazines from other industries. He explains it this way:

> Let's say I'm working with a bunch of computer executives. Once a week for six weeks, I'll send them a different trade magazine—*Progressive Grocer, Automotive News,* something from the corrugated-box industry. . . . Their assignment is to find two things in every issue that relate to their business or provoke their thinking. Everyone comes in with at least ten. It's a remarkably broadening exercise.[1]

So reading this chapter will not only open your eyes to how a range of industries uses data warehousing, it will probably highlight some common themes. After all, everyone's trying to get more customers. And everyone's trying to maximize

1. Diamond, David, "What Comes After What Comes Next." *Fast Company New Rules of Business,* volume 1 (supplement to *Fast Company* magazine), 35.

profits while growing market share. In a sense, every industry is in retailing, inducing customers to buy products and services.

Although each industry is doing things a little differently, they all have a lot to learn from one another. Specialty retailers could certainly learn a thing or two from banks about storing and analyzing detailed transactions. Health care companies could learn a lot about creatively deploying data from government agencies. (Yes, government!) And utility companies and telephone companies operate in the same deregulated, information-starved boat.

Most industries are at least experimenting with the database-marketing techniques described in chapter 3. In addition, a cross-section is also attempting more general forms of analysis such as profitability calculation and yield management. To avoid duplication, I've categorized the various analysis types by the industries in which they are prevalent, but there's no exclusivity in any of the business efforts described here.

So read the whole chapter. At worst, you'll pick up some terminology in case you happen to change jobs someday. At best, you could get some new ideas that embolden you to make some changes in your current company.

Retail

Pardon the pun, but there are lots of eggs in the retail basket. After all, a grocery store is different from a general merchandiser. In reality, the retail industry comprises many types of businesses, each sharing issues common to retailers while tackling challenges specific to their niches. The following list includes some of these businesses:

- drugstore
- grocery
- specialty retail
- mail order/catalogues
- general merchandise
- food service
- Internet store front (a.k.a.: "E-tailing")
- consumer packaged goods

Arguably, data warehousing's early adopters, retailers—most of them general merchandisers—made huge strides in the 1980s gathering data from their point-of-sale (POS) systems and storing those transactions on data warehouses. Each time an item, be it a refrigerator or a jar of cashews, was scanned, it was consigned to the store's POS server. This server is among hundreds or even thousands of in-store servers that ultimately source the data in the warehouse.

There is currently an onslaught of retailing innovation, with e-commerce being a top-of-mind strategy for many companies across industries—not to mention technology vendors—as new retailers emerge to transform the very nature of consumerism. For instance, Mercata (*www.mercata.com*) prenegotiates volume discounts with its vendor-partners, giving shoppers—who aren't paying for the overhead of a physical storefront—ever lower prices corresponding with demand. And Netgrocer.com invites consumers to buy their groceries online, while it maintains a running tally of the shopper's virtual market basket and ships the merchandise via FedEx. Moreover, the company allows regular shoppers to prearrange scheduled purchases and keeps customers' purchase history for easy return "trips."

Industry analysts predict that brick-and-mortar retailers will see a slowdown in sales growth over the next several years.[2] Hence, brick and mortar is hastily moving to "click and mortar," and the process of engaging, acquiring, and retaining customers is likewise evolving. Less foot traffic, combined with the e-tailing invasion, means that retailers are staging an epic battle to compete for every consumer dollar. And the data warehouse has become a key weapon in their collective arsenal. Companies like Wal-Mart, Kmart, and Dayton-Hudson, the grizzled veterans of retail data warehousing, no longer have a hold on the technology as a strategic weapon. Upstarts like Amazon.com, Costco Wholesale, and The Limited have adopted data warehouses of their own and are sharpening their skills as well as their swords.

Uses of Data Warehousing in Retail

Retailing businesspeople are combining transaction-level POS data with other types of data and performing analyses that can aid in a range of business activities. Since, as we've mentioned, selling the right products to the right customers is a key goal across industries, you'll be seeing variations on retailing strategies throughout this chapter.

---

2. Silverman, Dick, "Retail's Big Bang Facing Big Bust." *Daily News Record*, October 27, 1998.

A retail company includes a number of typical data warehouse users:

- merchandisers
- buyers
- store managers
- product managers
- warehouse and distribution staff
- marketing analysts
- executives

People in these jobs are frequently unaware of the data warehouse—often located hundreds or thousands of miles away from the actual user—that delivers the data to support their information needs. But most large and midmarket retailers have a data warehouse somewhere supporting one or more of the business initiatives discussed below.

Market Basket Analysis

As discussed in chapter 3, market basket analysis isn't exclusively for retailers, but it was invented by them. Understanding the number and combination of products in a customer's basket can tell a retailer a great deal about that customer, as well as why he purchases particular products or groups of products. This information in turn can drive critical business decisions that may increase profits.

Market basket analysis can actually become very complex, addressing not just "two-item affinities"—as in the hackneyed beer-and-diapers fable—but three, four, and "n-way" product affinities. By being able to predict which products are likely to be purchased together, retailers can influence everything from prices to store layouts to the entire supply chain. Market basket analysis in fact enables retailers to cross-sell their merchandise; through these various tactics they can encourage customers to purchase more in one shopping trip.

Table 4-1 shows three affinity rules that a grocery store identified by analyzing its sales for a 24-hour period: The first rule shows that cold medicine was bought with bottled juice, and that this combination was purchased together in 1.4 percent of actual shopping trips. The average revenue for all of the shopping trips involving this purchased pair was $29.52, and the profit was $3.94. The affinity value indicates that when cold medicine was purchased, bottled juice was also purchased 56 percent of the time. The "inverse affinity" represents the percentage of time—in this case 8 percent—when bottled juice was purchased and the customer also bought cold medicine.

Table 4-1: Sample Product Affinities

Product	Product	Freq %	Avg $	Avg Margin	Affinity	Inv Affinity
Cold Medicine	Bottled Juice	1.4%	29.52	3.94	0.56	0.80
Cold Medicine	Aspirin	0.7%	28.79	3.76	0.27	0.18
Cold Medicine/ Bottled Juice	Aspirin	0.40%	30.75	4.64	0.87	0.01

This kind of data illustrates which product sets customers buy, enabling the retailer to reevaluate placing juices on sale during cold season, since they're likely to be purchased anyway. After all, the more cold medicine the store sells, the more bottled juice it might also sell. A comparison of the first and second affinities in the table indicates that while shoppers buy cold medicine with aspirin, they don't purchase them together often. In fact, shoppers are more likely to purchase cold medicine with juice than with aspirin (56 percent versus 27 percent).

The third row illustrates a "three-item affinity," showing the likelihood of cold medicine, bottled juice, and aspirin being purchased together. There is an 87 percent likelihood that a shopper who buys both cold medicine and juice will also buy aspirin. With this information, a grocery merchant is not likely to add an aspirin discount to a cold medicine or juice coupon, since the shopper will probably buy aspirin at the retail price.

In-Store Product Placement

Stores won't admit it, but stocking shelves with the optimal product volume is a fine art, as is placing products in the correct relative locations. Detailed purchase analysis shows conclusively that these decisions pay off. Moreover, certain products have a finite shelf life, so encouraging their purchase without lowering the price so much as to lose money turns out to be a delicate task for retailers, especially those selling perishable goods.

You probably know why grocery stores place milk at one end of the store and bread at the other. By placing these staples far apart, the shopper must traverse the entire store, making unplanned purchases along the way. Retailers thus use decision support to understand which items are being purchased, figure out where they belong, and even modify store configurations in order to maximize the number of items in the market basket. In addition, retailers are able to negotiate more effectively with their suppliers, often charging premiums for end-caps—end of the aisle product displays—or high-profile product placement. A manufacturer will often pay the retailer a premium to ensure that its baby wipes end up at eye level on the shelf.

Product Pricing

Retailers are constantly monitoring revenues and profits on specific items, changing prices accordingly. Price elasticity models manipulate detailed data to determine not only the best price for a product, but often different prices for the same product according to different variables.

Data warehousing has also made the practice known as "differential pricing" much easier by allowing companies to price certain products according to different customer demographics or segments. Since retailers that can access customer data can become ever more specific in defining their customer segments, they can establish prices with even more precision.

For example, a video store may promote a "dollar off" all children's video rentals, relying on the pull of the accompanying grownup videos, or it may offer discounts to frequent renters or film school students.

Product Movement and the Supply Chain

Due to the finite shelf life of some products, particularly in the grocery sector, and the fact that some products fly off shelves while others languish for weeks or months, product replenishment is a high priority. Analyzing the movement of specific products and the quantity of products sold helps retailers in all market segments predict when they will need to order more stock.

Product sales history is an indicator of future product movement, and as we've already seen, the data warehouse is the de facto location of sales history data. By tapping into this history, merchandisers can define which products to order, the optimal number of units (that is, not overbuying, but at the same time avoiding being caught short), and the frequency of reorders.

Technology has come a long way in allowing retailers to reorder merchandise automatically as it moves out of the store. Some retailers have large warehouses that stock additional products and distribute them to stores when supplies get low. Others rely on automated replenishment or business-to-business e-commerce, that is, interconnecting their order systems with those of their suppliers in order to enable "just in time" delivery.

Indeed, the supplier relationship is a key business driver for data warehouses. The consumer packaged goods industry is a large data warehouse user in its own right that can provide retailers with important data about orders and replenishment. Packaged goods manufacturers can also provide general sales and movement data on a single brand, or on an entire product category. And making this information available to retailers gives consumer packaged goods firms increased bargaining clout. In turn, retailers can provide manufacturers with frequent-buyer information to enlighten them on the types of consumers buying their merchandise.

The above business drivers are only a sampling of how retailers are using their data warehouses. They transcend simple decision support, involving OLAP and even knowledge discovery. Applying the pyramid we first saw in chapter 2 provides an idea of the complexity involved in some of the key retailing business drivers (see figure 4-1).

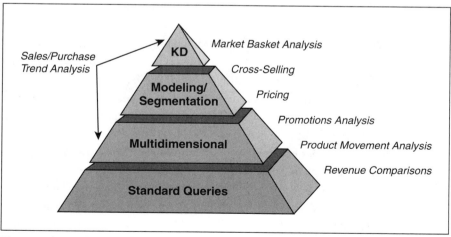

Figure 4-1: Types of Analysis in Retail

The Good News and Bad News in Retailing

The good news about how retailers are using their data warehouses is that, of all the industries, retailers are the most open to trying out new analysis techniques and adopting state-of-the-art tools to enable the discovery of new information about customers, their purchases, and the most likely avenues to maximize profitability. Retailers have been very effective at combining simple, online DSS queries with more sophisticated software—including knowledge discovery tools—in order to leverage their e-data, turning it into knowledge.

Many retailers are spending millions on their data warehouses, data marts, and associated tools. The most forward-thinking of them have graduated all the way to knowledge discovery analysis and thus understand cross-selling opportunities and future customer purchases. Retailers, having mastered the integral basics of sales and revenue reporting, have made great strides in actually using the results of their decision support analysis.

The problem in retailing lies in the lack of success measurement. Advanced analysis techniques being practiced by many retailers have failed to influence the magnitude of business change that would offset its cost. Many retailers use their data warehouses simply to produce targeted mailing lists, while neglecting to track success and subsequently refine their strategies. In such cases, the data warehouse may pay for itself, but it will probably not be profitable and definitely won't be viewed as a strategic asset.

The point here is that with data warehouses and indeed most strategic technologies, at some point risk reduction should give way to value creation. The retailers doing it right are those who are willing both to make changes as a result of their analysis and to incorporate those changes into their regular business processes.

A large general merchandiser client of mine holds a monthly analysis review meeting. These meetings are led by a business analyst who shares new findings on everything from promotion uplift results to coupon usage.

The result of this meeting is a list of business instructions that is communicated to various departments and individuals. "Make tortilla chips an end-cap across the aisle from the tequila" is a typical example of an item on the list. Once the change has been made, the retailer monitors the purchases of the products in question and presents the results at the next month's review meeting. The participants then determine whether the change was effective, note the sales changes, and enter the results into the data warehouse to register actions and monitor improvements.

The evolution represented by the pyramid is key here. In order to maximize the benefits of advanced analysis, companies should ideally be able to start with basic profit and loss, expense, and revenue data in order to determine the potential degree of improvement. Retailers, like all industries, need to walk before they can run.

Case Study: Hallmark

Few retailers in today's marketplace have the singular brand recognition of Hallmark Cards, Inc. In fact, the company is the world leader in greeting card sales. Preferring the moniker of Personal Expressions Company, Hallmark traverses the general merchandise, specialty retailing, and consumer packaged goods niches, even showing up entertainment powerhouses with its breakthrough Hallmark Hall of Fame and Hallmark Entertainment, Inc., television specials.

Lest you think it's easy for a card company to enter multiple merchandising milieus, consider that Hallmark tackles seasonality and product deployment issues that transcend the average retailer's shipping and stocking cycles. Hallmark boasts a complex and evolving product line, which includes not only greeting cards but also party supplies, ornaments, flowers, music, and paper goods. The company distributes its products, which can amount to 40,000 SKUs at any given moment, to a range of merchants. A retail chain without cards in time for Mother's Day could lose thousands of dollars in revenue, not to mention disappointing many customers.

"We really do partner with our vendors and chains," explains Tony Marshall, Hallmark decision support specialist. Straddling business drivers and technology solutions with equal ease, Marshall describes how Hallmark justified its foray into data warehousing. "Hallmark's business is based on its ability to help people worldwide communicate their feelings," he says. "In this kind of business, you need information systems to keep the company in touch with its customer base."

With these goals in mind, Hallmark began storing POS data on its Teradata platform as far back as 1990. By 1992, the company had over 200 users analyzing sales by product type, store, and time frame, among other dimensions. Today, the company has deployed its Teradata data warehouse on an NCR 5100 platform storing data from 17 major retail chains as well as 2,500 specialty stores. The POS database alone houses 4.25 billion rows of data.

Rich with detailed data and heedful of its partnership philosophy, Hallmark is providing value-added business information to its vendors. The company distributes sales reports detailing the performance of certain product lines and individual products. These reports yield assorted information about which types of products are performing best, breaking down 21 different product characteristics from editorial theme to recipient to price to "attitude."

Sales information also loops back to Hallmark's marketing and creative staff. Data analysts in these areas examine sales and revenue data across product lines and drill down to specifics to help determine which product features should be incorporated into next year's product lines.

Hallmark now has thousands of analysts and managers using decision support to recount high-level management data, wholesale shipments, manufacturing quality, and other key aspects of the business. The fact that most of this reporting is done on an ad hoc basis, with users free to drill down to the detail they need, is a testimonial to the empowerment of Hallmark's business community, not to mention the company's solid technology choices.

Hallmark has certainly given the term "early adopter" new meaning, even in the retailing sector. So how will it stay ahead of the curve? "Utilizing Internet technologies is a big drive for us now," says Marshall. "Our data volumes are exploding, and we're looking at ways to deliver information to even more people."

With all that data for all those users, it's a safe bet, as far as corporate data goes, that for Hallmark's end-users every day's a holiday.

Financial Services

If retailers were data warehousing's early adopters, then banks were its pioneers. Companies such as Citibank and Bank of America had ventured into the data-warehousing frontier before the term had even been coined, investing in large database platforms to house detailed transaction data when hardware prices were still astronomical.

In 1996, Gartner Group surveyed 144 financial institutions and discovered that their goals of customer service and marketing effectiveness, together with cost reduction and operational effectiveness, justified data warehousing.[3] Despite their widespread acceptance of data warehouse technologies, though, banks were clearly still straddling the fence between cost reduction and value creation.

---

3. Gartner Group presentation, "Breakthrough Banking Applications," delivered at the Profitable Data Warehousing Strategies for Financial Institutions seminar, Atlanta, Georgia, February 12–13, 1996.

Only a few years later, financial services companies had moved to the cutting edge of decision support. Regulatory and market developments resulted in a torrid competitive climate, and the Internet is now increasing the temperature by allowing new players to enter the market without the burden of existing branches and aging infrastructures.

Contrary to the image of financial services as equivalent to banking, the industry actually comprises a range of companies, such as banks, savings and loans companies (S&Ls), credit card companies, brokerage and securities firms, and investment banks.

The line, however, is beginning to blur. "Relationship banking" means that financial institutions are looking less like product purveyors and more like financial consultants, selling everything from passbook savings accounts to life insurance to mutual funds. As with other industries, financial services companies are focusing on optimizing customer retention by combining original marketing programs with upgraded service.

In the last several years, most banks have embraced the notion of "retail banking," which applies some of the retail concepts described above and in chapter 3 to the consumer banking world. "Wholesale" banking, on the other hand, concentrates on commercial clients, who are usually the bank's highest-impact, highest-revenue customers. While retail banking may sound like an obvious evolution in financial services, many banks were slow to move in that direction and focused more on their internal processes than on their customers. The widespread rush toward retail banking has changed all that.

Retail banking is forcing many banks to state clearly, or at least identify, their desired market sectors. Banks are honing in on their consumer customers, the segment in which the volume of customers and optimal product sales can result in significant profits.

For banks, business intelligence has become a business mandate as well as a competitive weapon. Federal regulatory agencies have come down hard on financial institutions, and new rules such as "know your customer" directive that financial institutions are able to discern which customer is which in order to qualify them for appropriate products and potentially avoid fraud. The 1999 Financial Services Modernization Act freed financial services and insurance companies to sell each other's products, but also required them to disclose how they will use data collected from their customers. Thus, customer information is no longer just a marketing luxury, it's an operational necessity.

While most banks are active in both commercial and consumer banking, they are also trying to pinpoint specific high-value customer sectors and dominate that market. To this end, Dutch bank ABN AMRO is attempting to attract affluent international consumers,[4] California's First Federal Bank has tried to attract more conservative consumers, and Harris Bank of Chicago has created a separate organization focused on small businesses.[5] Many banks are instituting private banking, in which a consumer or household has its own personal bank representative, leveraging the perceived prestige to attract high-balance customers.

As in retail, the major banking players no longer have a lock on data warehousing. Many smaller regional and midmarket financial services firms have been lauded as data warehousing success stories.

Uses of Data Warehousing in Financial Services

Financial services firms are combining transaction detail—originating from ATM machines, Web sites, and teller transactions—product information, and data on customers and their account histories to perform the following types of analysis.

Profitability Analysis

Every financial services firm out there is talking about profitability, and most say they're achieving it. While most banks have performed the rigorous activity-based costing programs necessary to resolve individual product costs and thus ensure product profitability, many are still working on the complex "roll-up" programs, or buying expensive software products to determine customer and household profitability.

Customer profitability is the most highly coveted form of profitability information for a very good reason: A company cannot know the true *value* of a customer without understanding how *profitable* that customer is. And without knowing its customers' value, the bank is forced to guess how to treat them. In other words, the goal is to allow the less valuable customers to leave and avoid the expense of bringing them back. Without knowing how valuable a customer is, customer retention is a shot in the dark.

---

4. *ABN AMRO Bank Matters,* March–April 1999.
5. Keltner, Brent and David Finegold, "Adding Value in Banking: Human Resource Innovations for Service Firms," *Sloan Management Review,* fall 1996, 59.

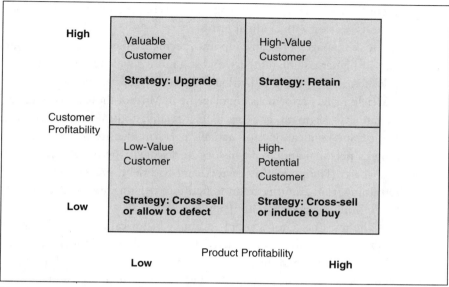

Figure 4-2: Customer Profitability Analysis

The combination of different types of profitability can aid a financial services firm in making informed decisions about how to treat its customers.

Figure 4-2 suggests possible new customer segments, each with its own marketing strategy. Banks can map the results of customer profitability analyses back to their channels to determine high-value branches, or to specific geographical areas to extrapolate high-value cities or neighborhoods to target. Changes in a customer's profitability over time can also uncover previously unknown customer behavior patterns. Many banks also use profitability analysis to help dictate the creation of new products, or the expunging of old ones.

Risk Management and Fraud Prevention

It's been said that while some banks manage risks, others seek to avoid them altogether.[6] In the age of record-breaking bankruptcy rates and stolen identities, banks and S&Ls can't be too careful about which customers they approve for loans and credit cards. A data warehouse provides a banking company with a

---

6. Oldfield, George S. and Richard S. Reynolds, "Risk Management in Financial Institutions," *Sloan Management Review,* fall 1997, 33.

scientific approach to risk management, as opposed to the traditional guessing-game associated with credit approval.

Risk management can pinpoint specific market or customer segments that may be higher risk than others, and at a more detailed level, it can determine the risk factors of specific individuals. There are several specialized software tools that help firms perform risk management. Most of these tools assign a score to a customer or segment, gauging its risk relative to other customers or segments. Some fraud verification tools actually perform identity verification, rating a customer's personal and credit history to discover whether she is indeed who she says she is. The possibility of reducing bad debt, preventing foreclosures, and refraining from granting credit to fictitious persons promises to save some banks tens of millions of dollars annually.

The most basic tools simply examine historical customer behavior to verify that no past defaults have occurred. Others analyze delinquent accounts to identify trends in payment history. More advanced predictive tools provide a recommendation (yes or no) on approval of a specific loan type and can even suggest alternative credit products or payment schedules, effectively increasing the odds of a successful deal.

Have you ever received a call from your credit card company verifying a recent purchase? This is fraud prevention at work. Hand in hand with risk management, this strategy actually helps firms detect fraud before it happens, usually by examining fraud that has already occurred and mapping similar events to customer behavior patterns. By identifying these "event triggers," financial firms can nip fraud in the bud. Figure 4-3 is an example of a sophisticated model used by some firms, against which they regularly analyze credit card usage.

The most advanced types of risk management and fraud detection support continuous remeasurement of behavior. By evaluating how fraud and delinquency patterns change over time, as well as determining which types of customers and accounts are worthy of proactive credit solicitations, banks can both prevent lost income and fine-tune their marketing activities.

In cases where a financial institution has already incurred fraud or delinquency, data analysis can indicate whether the existing risk might be transferred to another institution such as a collections agency or another bank.

It should be noted that while fraud verification and detection capability saves companies millions, it remains an expensive undertaking, particularly if the company tries bypassing data warehousing in an attempt to save money.

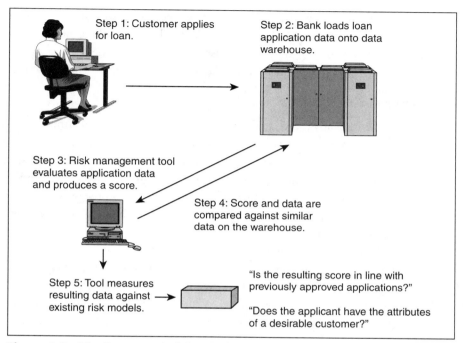

Figure 4-3: The Process of Risk Management

Propensity Analysis and Event-Driven Marketing

Chapter 3 discussed churn propensity, the likelihood that a customer will leave an institution for a competitor. The previous section revealed that it's possible to predict a customer's propensity to commit fraud. This type of predictive analysis is not limited to addressing customers who cost the bank money; it can also be used to generate significant additional revenue.

Common wisdom has it that it is three to ten times less expensive to sell a given product or service to an existing customer than it is to find a new one. Propensity-to-buy analysis helps banks recognize whether a customer is likely to purchase a given product and service, and even when such a purchase might occur. By understanding which products attract which customers, banks can reduce their marketing costs substantially and also prevent customer defections to other banks for similar products.

For example, when parents need a loan for their daughter's college education, the bank can use its data to surmise that a graduation gift or wedding might be next. Given that there are potentially thousands of different lifecycle events that might trigger new banking needs, banks are working hard to store event information in their data warehouses and to acquire the appropriate predictive tools to pinpoint optimal new marketing opportunities.

Response and Duration Modeling

This type of advanced analysis can tell a bank which customers are likely to respond to a given promotion and purchase the advertised product or service. In the case of duration modeling, the firm can predict how long a customer will actually keep the promoted product. Duration modeling can also aid a bank in predicting how long a new customer responding to a promotion is likely to stay with the bank or, based on historical account activity, how long an existing customer is likely to remain.

Duration modeling is particularly useful for credit card companies marketing affinity cards to specific customers or segments. These firms use duration modeling to determine not only how long a customer might keep a card but also how often the card will be used. They can also model duration based on different interest rates in order to offer a given customer segment the best rate for the optimal duration.

When combined with profitability information, response and duration models can result in well-informed decisions about individual customers and can trigger decisions about product upgrades or replacements.

Distribution Analysis and Planning

With the advent of Web banking, mini-branches, and banking by phone, banking customers have lots of options when it comes to how to manage their money. Service delivery preferences differ among individual customers, customer segments, and customer demographics. By understanding how and where customers perform their transactions, banks can tailor certain locations to specific customer groups, not to mention specific products and services. Moreover, using careful analysis of the various delivery channels allows banks to make decisions about branch layouts, staff increases or reductions, new technology additions, or even closing or consolidating low-traffic branches.

By combining channel activity with channel profitability data from the data warehouse, financial services firms can induce their customers to change to lower-cost distribution channels by lowering fees or providing additional services. The introduction of Internet banking has eased the in-branch bottleneck and resulting staffing headaches for many banks and has resulted in significant savings.

As in retail, the business problems just described are some of the higher-profile ones that rely on data in the data warehouse. While most can be performed manually, some require more cross-functional data and complex algorithms than others, as figure 4-4 illustrates.

The Good News and Bad News in Financial Services

Financial services firms have an industry edge in that they began to use data analysts—statistical analysis experts who employ concepts like linear regression to find or support data-corroborated business findings—before other industries did. Long before data warehousing, banks employed statisticians to monitor trends and examine various fluctuations in data, albeit using more archaic and cumbersome tools.

For this reason, banks that adopted data warehouses underwent less of a training curve. They also understood earlier how to apply key learnings and integrate them into their business processes.

Although decision support has been deployed to businesspeople unaccustomed to performing their own analysis—branch personnel and bank executives are regular users of decision support—financial services firms have retained their data analyst groups, which in many cases have been using data warehouses to perform the most cutting-edge analysis techniques.

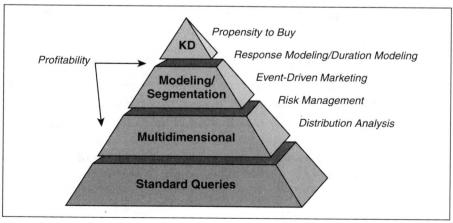

Figure 4-4: Types of Analysis in Financial Services

Visionary banks have recently positioned insurance and investment products alongside more traditional financial offerings in order to target the right customer the first time out. The latest development in retail banking is tapping into the profile of a customer who is in the branch. The teller's workstation not only executes the customer's requested transaction, it alerts the teller to possible new products the customer might buy. This type of cross-selling dispenses with costly marketing campaigns and mailings, in essence transforming the bank teller from service provider to personal sales associate.

The same banks have adopted informed target marketing, gearing their marketing campaigns not to haphazardly gathered customer segments but rather to particular consumers. Incorporating knowledge about an individual's behavior, such campaigns promise much higher success rates. In fact, one bank recently realized a 6 percent response rate to a targeted direct mail campaign—triple its normal response.[7]

Deregulation, mergers, changing demographics, and nontraditional competitors are forcing a paradigm shift, and financial services firms must be nimble in order to respond. As in most industries, the smaller firms are slower to adopt the expensive technology required for a data warehouse, but ultimately quick to experience its value.

The laggards are those financial services firms, usually well established, that are unable to overcome entrenched business processes and cumbersome legacy systems and insist on maintaining hierarchical organizations and cultures (in other words, outdated management styles). Cringing at the thought of giving businesspeople direct access to customer data, such firms are unable to deploy decision support successfully, and this inability is usually an indicator of more deeply rooted problems.

Case Study: Royal Bank of Canada

Royal Bank of Canada's status as the country's number-one bank hasn't rendered Kevin Butcher complacent for a minute. As the bank's vice-president of management and marketing information, Butcher has implemented a complex and dynamic technology infrastructure to support multiple organizations and business objectives. To say that data warehousing is a staple of his strategy would be putting it mildly.

---

7. Graham, Ann and John W. Geyer, "All for One and One for All: How KeyCorp Reacquainted Itself with Its Customers," *Forbes Competitive Edge*, September 1998, 24–28.

Royal Bank's customer information exists in a combination of an enterprise data warehouse and various data marts, all built around a sophisticated process that simultaneously extracts, cleanses, and redirects data. Butcher is justifiably proud of its establishment. "Not a lot of companies have implemented a centralized process for feeding all their data marts," says Butcher. "To be scalable you really do need to establish an infrastructure first for both data and metadata."

The "infrastructure" not only links the bank's source systems with data marts for marketing, card services, trust, and commercial banking data marts, to name a few, it is beginning to provide the batch interface infrastructure for the bank's legacy systems. This visionary approach to establishing the processes for furnishing data up front has allowed Royal Bank to sustain a wide and evolving range of technologies and analysis methods.

Royal's enterprise data warehouse uses IBM SP2 hardware running the DB2 UDB RDBMS. Its data mart technologies run the gamut from Teradata for marketing analysis to smaller Oracle and structured query language (SQL) server-based marts. The bank has deployed computing to the desktops of its end-users with graphical user interface (GUI) tools and has implemented a Web-enabled reporting strategy that will leverage its intranet.

The complexity of allowing multiple vendors and products to play a role in the company's information provision is not lost on Butcher, who acknowledges that it might have been easier to standardize on a handful of preferred vendors. "You pay a price for integrating multiple technologies," he admits. "Our business requirements are driving our technology selection. For example one of our marts is a vendor package that only runs on specific hardware and software. And our infrastructure and processes not only support this, but enable it."

And enable it they have. Royal Bank is using its vast supply of customer information, along with a spectrum of analysis techniques from standard decision support reports through segmentation and statistical modeling, to determine such diverse behaviors as customer attrition, next likely purchase, and channel usage. The bank has launched profitability analysis and is currently able to derive account-level profitability, information that will feed a variety of organizations and business processes.

Royal's credit card group has delivered extraordinary business benefits by leveraging various levels of decision support. The card group, which uses a dedicated data mart for new customer acquisition and cross-selling alike, is able to identify points of compromise: merchants who might be at a higher risk of accepting suspicious transactions that could pinpoint fraud. Moreover, Royal is able to provide value-added reports to its top merchants that profile certain customers. This ability to provide businesses with information about their customers is data warehousing's apotheosis realized.

"We thought we knew what information was," says Pete Rider, Butcher's project manager for marketing information systems. "But now that we've implemented data warehousing, we realized that we haven't even scratched the surface."

Butcher and his team have grateful business users thanking them for delivering this information. Recently, some happy end-users even bought one of Butcher's groups a celebration breakfast. While a small gesture, its implications aren't lost on Butcher. "I don't think the specific technology choice is the issue," he demurs. "It's what you do with it that matters."

Telecommunications

When the U.S. government divided Ma Bell into seven regional phone companies and AT&T back in 1982, the goal was to foster competition. No one imagined that the decision would unleash a host of new players and technologies, not to mention an eventual blurring of market boundaries.

While telecommunications companies are not traditionally known as technology early adopters, data warehousing has spurred massive change in the way they are doing business. Gone are the days of the plodding, regulated utility company where employees were guaranteed lifetime employment and customers didn't have a choice.

The Telecommunications Act of 1996 further mandated competition among local and long-distance carriers in the hopes that the regional Bell operating companies (RBOCs), cable companies, and long-distance providers would target each other's customers. Finally, telephone company customers would have a choice, and the companies would have to pay attention to what their customers wanted. As *Business Week* proclaimed in 1996:

> In the dawning era of deregulation and digital communications, it will take more [for telephone companies] to keep ahead of the competition. It will take great services and aggressive pricing—at last![8]

Data warehouses can transform telecommunications in the same way that they helped transform modern merchandising for retailers: by fundamentally

---

8. "Think Local—And Invade!", *Business Week,* April 8, 1996.

changing business processes and job roles and rendering data analysis an industry "core competency." Indeed, telephone companies are shedding their old, monopolistic cultures and processes to become retailers, wholesalers, and resellers. And this vast transformation is inciting a rush into new ways of marketing telecommunications products and services.

For all their competitive and attrition fears, telecommunications companies have the luxury, however temporary, of knowing that a full two-thirds of consumers don't shop around for telephone service. Most American consumers, for example, still use AT&T for long distance. But the rush to turn all this around and transform telephone service into a consumer product is changing the way telephone companies need and use data.

There have been some false starts. Telecommunications companies originally tried to fend off competition by forcing high-value business customers to sign long-term contracts, sweetening the deal by offering lower prices. However, in many cases the customers benefiting from these price cuts were never in danger of leaving, and the providers were left with lower revenues and profit margins as a result. Now these companies have begun taking their cue from other industries, cross-selling products to customers who fit a particular profile.

The degree to which telecommunications companies are performing advanced analysis using their data warehouses is proportional to the market segment they serve. Unlike most other industries, the individual market segments in the telecommunications industry define the type and level of decision support analysis being performed.

U.S. Local Service Carriers

The RBOCs are still feeling the sting of deregulation, which has resulted in new competitors entering markets that had hitherto been competition-free. The new competitive climate has motivated local service companies to be less concerned about their products and networks and more customer-focused. This development in turn has introduced a veritable frenzy of new customer care and customer acquisition and retention initiatives, not to mention new demands for data analysis.

Because of the new competitive pressures, RBOCs are rushing to differentiate themselves through their various products and services. One of their biggest fears is that because of their massive infrastructures and costly organizational structures, they won't be able to compete on price, typically the most significant differentiator in a commodity business. (See the next section on transportation.)

In the meantime, competitors are cherry-picking the RBOCs' best customers, and they're starting with the biggest ones.

U.S. Long-Distance Carriers

Because long-distance deregulation occurred before local service deregulation, domestic long-distance carriers have a marketing jump-start on their local service brethren, meaning more sophisticated marketing has already become entrenched. Domestic long-distance carriers have adopted churn analysis and are seasoned in the identification of high- and low-value customers. Since they normally have fewer products than the RBOCs and are selling a commodity, domestic long-distance companies must focus heavily on target marketing, market niches, and price flexibility.

Long-distance companies will grow by increasing their usage and by diversifying—going after data, Internet, and wireless services. They can also realize additional revenues by reselling services to other telephone companies (long-distance resale, operator services, and network management). Cost containment, including fraud reduction and churn reduction, continues to be a large justification for data analysis.

Customer segmentation is much more sophisticated in long-distance companies than it is in the RBOCs, the former having long ago realized that data mining is the key to establishing truly valid customer segments. MCI's legendary "Friends and Family" campaign was an example of a successful pricing plan based on advanced customer segment analysis.

International Long-Distance Carriers

There has been little difference between the marketing issues of U.S. long-distance companies and international long-distance carriers since the European Union deregulated international long-distance companies in 1999, allowing, for example, Deutsche Telekom to sell into France.

It's worth mentioning that the United Kingdom is by far the most mature market in the international long-distance industry, with over 22 different carriers. Having instituted deregulation even earlier than the United States, British carriers are further along with marketing initiatives such as cross-selling and call win-back.

Unlike the United States, privatized long-distance carriers in other parts of the world are more immediately threatened by newer, upstart companies. For example in Mexico, Telmex, the dominant long-distance carrier, has lost 25 percent of its market share to both Avantel (an MCI partner) and Alestra (an AT&T partner) within the last two years.

Wireless Carriers

Wireless is the fastest-growing sector of the telecommunications market in terms of new customer (subscriber) acquisition. Wireless companies continue to introduce new products and services, though their core offerings remain cellular phone service and pagers.

Compared with land-line companies, wireless companies have less experience analyzing data, and the newest providers have not yet considered the potential impact of data warehousing on their business strategies.

Fraud is a major issue in wireless telecommunications, since cellular phones are ubiquitous and can be stolen much more easily than conventional equipment, thus increasing the opportunity for making fraudulent calls. Theft of service, or number cloning, results in significant costs to wireless companies both domestically and internationally.

Because the vast majority of wireless service is sold via alternative sales channels, the performance of these sales channels is of utmost interest. Wireless companies are constantly seeking new ways to motivate service providers to sell their products.

Since wireless companies in the United States are not regulated, they can charge whatever they like for their products and services. Many U.S. metropolitan areas have five to seven wireless carriers competing in the market for car phones, cellular phones, and pagers. The larger carriers have more money to spend to target their best customers while proactively addressing the occasional price war introduced by any number of upstart firms intent on harvesting new customers at any cost.

Uses of Data Warehousing in Telecommunications

The telecommunications industry's move away from a utility mentality and toward a retail mentality means that the types of analysis companies undertake have evolved to resemble those of the retail and banking industries.

Churn

While they are dissimilar in terms of both the data and the algorithms used, churn prediction and fraud analysis invariably come together to form a kind of telecommunications mantra. When the topic of data analysis arises, either within the telephone company or among its various vendors, churn and fraud rise like a collective Buddhist chant—mysterious, ubiquitous, and reaching every corner of the landscape.

The rule of thumb with customer churn analysis in telecommunications is that the better established the carrier, the more likely it is that a churn solution is already in place.

As we discussed in chapter 3, customer churn refers to a customer leaving one service provider, usually for another. It's important to distinguish between the propensity to churn and actual churning. Some telephone companies endeavor to prevent churn without having any intelligence about who might be leaving. The term "churn" can therefore imply either prediction or post facto analysis.

It's also important to differentiate between customer churn and product churn. Product churn means the cancellation of a product or service, sometimes in favor of another. It's common in local service, where customers acquire enhanced services, disconnect them, and then reconnect them. Product churn is often misinterpreted as customer churn. If, for example, I change floors in my office building, I will disconnect my telephone service but immediately reconnect it elsewhere. The telephone company has not lost me as a customer; I have simply moved. Unfortunately, telecommunications companies often fail to differentiate between product disconnects and product upgrades, and many still confuse product disconnects with customer churn. The ability to analyze product churn is very important to them, since it can indicate "phantom churn" or dramatically affect product pricing.

In the best cases, churn analysis and prediction go hand in hand with customer retention. Once a carrier knows which customers are likely to leave, it can deploy methods to motivate them to stay.

Fraud Detection

Fraud means the act of subverting a normal telephone call, or registering a telephone call not attributed to the call's originator. Fraud has always been a problem for telephone companies, and new fraud techniques are introduced as fast as new communications technologies. From telephone theft to bootleg switches that can generate false dial tones, fraud perpetrators are getting smarter.

But so are telephone companies, and data warehousing has a lot to do with it. There are two types of fraud analysis: proactive, where the company is able to detect fraud before it happens, and reactive, where the company takes steps to deal with fraud that has already occurred.

New methods of online fraud detection are being heavily used by long-distance companies. But contrary to popular belief, business intelligence via data warehousing is not the ideal method of proactive fraud *detection*, since it can detect fraud only after the fact. Data-mining tools, however, can *predict* fraud by spotting patterns in consolidated customer information and call detail records (CDRs).

Product Packaging and Custom Pricing

Because of their dire need to differentiate themselves, seasoned telecommunications companies are citing product packaging as one of their most promising business opportunities.

Of particular interest to such companies across market segments is the packaging of vertical features, those voice products such as caller ID or call waiting that already exist on the switch and simply need to be enabled. These products are not only highly profitable—estimated margins can reach as high as 80 percent[9]—but sell well together when bundled.

Most regional telephone companies now sell a "call feature package" that includes add-ons such as call forwarding, call waiting, and caller ID for one price. In fact there is no additional cost to the company to provide a customer with one service versus three. Since the features themselves are already in place and just need to be turned on, the only cost incurred is the activation of the order. So the telephone company collects additional revenues and higher profits. And since the three products are actually one, the order desk has fewer items to process, thus streamlining the entire order process.[10]

Product packaging was once a guessing-game for telecommunications companies. They would combine unprofitable products with profitable ones, announce the new package, and sit back and wait for orders. Now, however, using knowledge discovery and modeling, they can tell which products will sell well together, as well as which customers or customer segments are most likely to buy them.

In addition, companies can employ price elasticity models to determine the new package's optimal price. In some cases they may choose to price a

---

9. Cullen, Lisa Reilly, "The Bells: Babies No More," *Money Magazine,* March 1999, 38. The author was quoting Dan Ernst, a consultant with Strategis Group.
10. This is a good example of how data warehouses help reengineer business processes by making them more efficient, faster, and thus ultimately less costly.

product package differently depending on the attributes of certain customer segments.

Network Feature Management

While data warehousing's biggest "bang for the buck" for telecommunications companies is in the sales and marketing area, it is frequently identified with helping to track network equipment and plan network routing. These activities in turn can enable the support of planned feature upgrades, equipment upgrades, or new equipment installation.

Moreover, it can prevent a company from having to guess where a new piece of equipment should be installed. By monitoring call patterns and traffic routing, a carrier—wireless or land-line—can install a switch or cell in a location where it is liable to route the maximum amount of calls. Historical activity analysis can help telecommunications companies actually predict equipment outages before they occur, resulting in both higher network availability and more positive customer satisfaction rates.

The optimal way to make network and asset decisions is by examining the actual call data. This requires the loading of CDRs onto a data warehouse.

Call Detail Analysis

Usage data, as CDRs are otherwise known, is gathered by storing information in the data warehouse each time someone picks up the telephone and dials a number. Nirvana for many telephone companies would be a centralized data warehouse containing months or years of online CDRs.

Contrary to popular belief, few companies actually maintain such data, not because CDRs are not useful, but because storing the amount of data is both difficult and expensive. Never mind getting the data off the switches, where it originates. While the goal is understandable, most companies cannot justify the expense and are implementing some variation of years of detailed storage.

Most telecommunications companies keep the previous 3 to 6 months of call detail on a warehouse, summarize months 7 through 13 by week or month, and then condense annual call records even further. While flexibility is compromised—I can't verify which pharmacies called which hospitals during a given period—storage problems and costs are reduced.

Put another way, analysis of specific call records is next to impossible without a centralized data warehouse. Operationally, CDRs must be extracted from switches in order to be used, and much of the record is discarded before it appears in a company's billing system. The data warehouse offers a centralized repository of CDRs, separate and discrete from the billing or other operational systems that might contain switch data, and is thus available for unlimited business use.

> *Show me the Affinity Card subscribers who have*
> *called other Affinity Card subscribers.*

This type of analysis can provide powerful information about origin and destination patterns that could spur additional sales to important customers, and even dictate new product or service programs.

Customer Satisfaction

The return on investment from data-warehousing and database-marketing programs is closely tied to their integration with improvements to customer service. Call centers and customer care facilities are no longer limited to complaints departments receiving irate diatribes from angry customers. Newer channels such as fax, e-mail, and Web sites lengthen a company's reach to new and existing customers, and vice versa.

The business activities discussed here in the telecommunications field can use either basic or advanced decision support tools. In basic cases, end-users may simply need to access data for a specific customer or product in an ad hoc fashion to see if further analysis is warranted. In more advanced analysis, specialized churn, fraud, or trouble-tracking prediction tools can be used with detailed data to detect patterns (see figure 4-5).

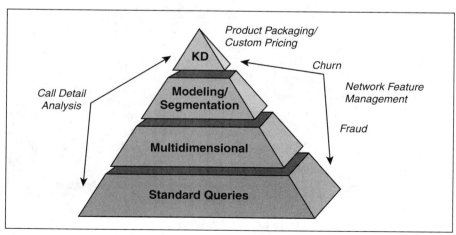

Figure 4-5: Types of Analysis in Telecommunications

The Good News and Bad News in Telecommunications

It is worth noting that the majority of telecommunications companies do not begin with enterprise data warehouses, or even with data marts. Indeed, some never intend to adopt this technology and do so only after they've experienced significant churn rates or loss of market share.

Instead, most begin with what is normally a sales and marketing system, or some sort of customer information application, intended to perform basic customer analysis on a nonoperational platform. In doing so, marketing staff, product managers, lifecycle managers, and strategic planners are no longer forced to wait the customary 60 days for monthly paper roll-up reports.

As these users become more adept at running their own marketing reports, which are normally customer- and product-based revenue reports, they begin clamoring for more data.

Figure 4-6 lays out some of the data subject areas that can ultimately populate a telecommunications data warehouse. The order in which they're implemented depends on the robustness of the corresponding legacy systems.

Some telecommunications companies, immensely relieved at receiving basic customer reports that previously took weeks to deliver, don't journey beyond analyzing basic customer billing data. The ability to access billing data online represents an exponential improvement in information availability. Others, as they increase their infrastructure to source and load other types of data from var-

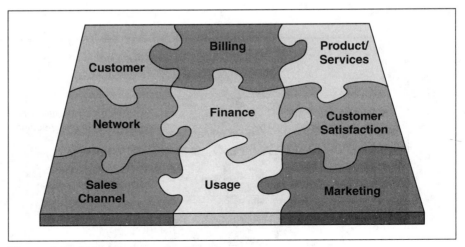

Figure 4-6: Telco Data on the Warehouse

ious operational systems, move from having a stovepipe marketing system—actually, an independent data mart—to a cross-functional database, becoming a de facto enterprise data warehouse.

The problem with many telephone companies is that—long-distance companies possibly excepted—many aren't effectively leveraging the information from their data warehouses once they obtain it. While the problem for retailers is that they are not actually measuring success, telephone companies are still having trouble incorporating data warehousing into their overall visions. The results of decision support aren't promoting business process changes, never mind new business actions.

A few years ago I worked on a data-mining prototype at a U.S. RBOC that uncovered a likely return on investment (ROI) of $9 million with the adoption of new product-packaging techniques through affinity analysis. And that was with a 1 percent response rate! The customer was thrilled. But no one would step up to fund the data mining required to formalize the process. Lots of internal budget discussions, but no game plan, left $9 million revenue dollars unrealized.

While cultural problems and resistance to change are often the culprits here, marketing in telephone companies doesn't carry the internal prestige that it deserves. Some companies are remedying this problem by hiring seasoned marketing executives from consumer packaged goods and retail companies.

Case Study: GTE

Most case studies of telecommunications companies that have been successful with their data warehousing efforts begin like this:

> Bell Company says that by using Data X to turn customer billing data into valuable analysis, the company is on the cutting edge of business intelligence. "We're using billing data like nobody's business!," exclaims Joe, director of marketing, and the results are simply staggering. . . .

Well, almost any telephone company worth its salt has managed to get customer billing data onto a data warehouse. And the resulting analysis is indeed valuable to the business. But a few visionary companies are taking this approach a few steps further.

Ask David Yamashita how GTE's data warehouse has helped the business, and you'd better have more than a few minutes to spare. Yamashita, GTE's director of enterprise data warehousing, has a broad perspective on decision support that cuts across technology and straight to the value proposition. Yamashita can portray the business benefits of his data warehouse as nimbly as he can discuss its architectural features.

Like many telecommunications companies, GTE embarked on its decision support journey with independent stovepipe systems. While these systems were independent and could not share information, they were far from ineffective. For example, GTE Wireless's original PIMS system stored years of customer billing detail that was used by marketing for a variety of reporting needs. The system was, in fact, the foundation for GTE's migration to enterprise data warehousing.

But despite its early success in data delivery, the stovepipe paradigm was tough to justify. A few years back, a large consulting firm had estimated that GTE had over a terabyte of redundant data. Independent systems were not only less and less practical in terms of their business value, they were costly.

In 1998, GTE adopted an enterprisewide initiative in which data from the company's disparate systems was integrated onto a centralized platform to produce an eclectic array of new decision support capabilities. Indeed, the classic stovepipe approach gave way not only to a new architecture but also to a new way of evaluating data warehouse requirements. Yamashita and his staff are constantly gauging new business requirements and system enhancements with two parallel questions: *Does this make sense from a cost standpoint?* and *Does this make sense from a business standpoint?*

"You'll always live with what you have unless you're constantly reapplying these metrics," he explains. GTE is applying them to some of its older applications to determine whether they should be rewritten, or done away with altogether in order to free up technologies and staff for new requirements.

The company has encouraged its end-users to perform their own data analysis. Yamashita defines GTE's data philosophy as one of "centralized processing, but decentralized data access." For instance, each GTE marketing director is empowered to create his own custom reports and encouraged to use the resulting e-data to launch marketing programs that best suit the customers and prospects in his region. Why the push toward end-user empowerment? "We want our business users to do their own reporting," Yamashita explains, adding, "It's impractical to ask end-users to submit requirements in writing each time they want to do something new. This way they can get their data directly."

GTE faces three of the classic telecommunications challenges: churn, customer retention, and channel management. The company now understands how to treat different customers in different ways. The resulting knowledge means a broader array of new products and services, which in turn triggers further growth of the warehouse.

As a result, GTE end-users—who include managers, marketing analysts, and financial staff from Florida to Hawaii—use tools such as Cognos Impromptu and MS Access to locate, interpret, and manipulate data subject areas as disparate as customer billing information and usage data. "GTE's strategy is to deliver 'anytime/anyplace' ad hoc reporting to our end-users," says Yamashita, pointing out that the company has succeeded in reaching this lofty goal. "When our end-users realized they could run their own reports, even do their own aggregations . . . well, it was very powerful."

That GTE end-users have adapted well to running their own reports has everything to do with easily accessed data. Yamashita drives the point home, stating: "People around here understand that knowledge is power. And that knowledge must be public and easily accessed in order to be leveraged."

Transportation

When I was a systems engineer for Teradata Corporation—the company that pioneered large commercial data warehouses—one of my first customers was American Airlines. This was back in 1985, before data warehousing was on people's radar screens, so to speak, but American had been dabbling with databases and understood data exploration, particularly statistical analysis. The company foresaw the potential for large quantities of detailed information about customers and flights. American not only wanted to store ticket sales information in a large database, it also wanted to compare sales to flights, particularly those made by their AAdvantage members.

Ahead of their time? You bet. The transportation industry is fiercely competitive, and as in most commodity businesses, price remains the driving factor in customer travel decisions. Thus, many airlines have made cost cutting a major priority—justification enough for a data warehouse.

In the past few years however, service quality, market share, customer loyalty, and profitability have emerged as equally critical business drivers for transportation firms. In 1995 Sir Colin Marshall, the chairman of British Airways, explained the evolution away from the commodity mindset:

We must: get passengers where they want to go, do it safely, go when they want to go, provide some nourishment, and let them accrue frequent-flier miles. But our research shows that customers now take the basics for granted and increasingly want a company to desire to help them, to treat them in a personal, caring way.[11]

Data warehousing is increasingly used by, among others, airlines, railroads, and package delivery companies to deconstruct and examine schedules, routing, traffic patterns, and customer behavior. The business activities described in the following sections and illustrated in figure 4-7 reflect some of the principal uses of data analysis among transportation firms.

Yield Management

Not only did transportation companies invent yield management, other industries have since adopted the term to describe the sales-per-capacity ratio for certain products. Perhaps the biggest payoff of the data warehouse for the transportation industry has been, in airline parlance, "getting butts in seats."

The principle behind yield management is analyzing flight data to determine the price/yield ratio for seats. Looking at the number of seats, costs per flight, and ticket prices can help an airline or railroad fill as many seats as possible on a given trip and thus determine the optimal price per ticket.

At its simplest, yield management analysis means reactively monitoring the relative capacity of various flights, rendering changes to equipment assignments or routing. By facilitating the analysis of reservation data, scheduled versus actual flight data, equipment assignments, and seasonal travel history, a data warehouse not only helps the company make reactive decisions but also enables it to plan for future flights. Yield management can dictate new target-marketing campaigns, discount programs for certain routes, booking incentives, and other types of promotions.

On the planning side, transportation companies use decision support to dictate any number of possible business actions. For example, if a flight from Dallas to Omaha is regularly only half full, the airline has several choices:

- Change equipment to a smaller aircraft.
- Promote/advertise the flight.
- Offer discounts to frequent fliers.

---

11. Prokesch, Steven E., "Competing on Customer Service: An Interview with British Airways' Sir Colin Marshall," *Harvard Business Review*, November–December 1995, 100.

- Raise the price of the flight.
- Reduce the number of other flights on that route.
- Cancel the flight altogether.

Predictive yield management analysis, known as "passenger demand forecasting," helps travel carriers to forecast loads and thereby modify fares, often right up to flight time. This type of analysis can also help a carrier gain greater operating efficiencies, giving an airline the information it needs to decide against adding a flight to Europe and opting instead to promote one of its alliance partners. Such decisions can save an airline the expense of launching unprofitable flights or opening underused hubs, both of which can soar into the hundreds of millions of dollars.

For cargo, yield management examines flight traffic, equipment capacities, number of units, and unit volumes to determine freight capacities for certain legs. Railroads regularly use their data warehouses to predict and modify the ratio of freight cars to passenger cars.

Frequent-Passenger Programs

Most carriers have some sort of incentive program for repeat passengers. This tool has become a balancing act for many airlines, which want to retain loyal customers but don't want to give too much away. Consider the following query.

List frequent fliers who have flown less frequently this
year to date than last year at the same time.

This type of question can become a valuable competitive weapon, potentially curtailing passenger attrition through new marketing and sales initiatives.

One U.S. domestic airline performs this query for frequent fliers who are also members of its airport club lounge. The company examines the customer profiles, looks at current flight behavior, determines the customers' overall value, and in many cases renews the lounge membership at no cost, stimulating loyalty while decreasing the likelihood of attrition.

Frequent-flier analysis provides a carrier with insight into specific customers' flying habits. This intelligence can in turn be used for target marketing: providing discounts to loyal customers (preferably on profitable routes); offering customized packages of flight, hotel, and car rental; and tracking the use of mileage awards. Indeed, frequent-passenger programs go hand in hand with customer loyalty.

In mature data warehouses, demographic information, which is easier to obtain from frequent fliers than from other passengers, offers a new way to understand and predict flight purchases, as well as to analyze customer characteristics relative to routes and other carriers.

Travel Packaging and Pricing

In addition to flight tickets, some airlines also sell other travel products, such as hotel reservations, car rentals, and packaged tours. A data warehouse with detailed information about these products, their costs, and their profitability can aid a transportation company in customizing profitable packages of flights, ground transportation, and lodging to attract an optimal volume or specific demographic of customers.

In addition, a data warehouse provides intelligence about "loss leader" products. A bus company may be losing money on a certain route, but by bundling a ticket on that route with a profitable hotel reservation and car rental for an optimal number of days—all for a fixed price—the company can turn a net profit. As with telecommunications product packaging, these types of marketing programs have historically been developed through trial and error. Using the detailed data from a data warehouse, companies can now base them on facts and potentially generate new revenue much more reliably.

With the right data, the data warehouse can provide answers to questions such as the following:

- What hotels are offering the steepest discounts?
- What is my flight profitability on legs to that destination?
- Which customers have flown to that destination at least twice a year in the last three years?
- Which businesses are headquartered in that destination city that might benefit from price breaks?

Answers to these questions can provide new knowledge of customer behavior, as well as material for new marketing campaigns and promotions.

Fuel Management

According to *USA Today*, an airline's operating expenses increase $19.2 million annually for every penny increase in the price of fuel per gallon, based on 1998 consumption. Indeed, fuel is one of the largest expenses transport companies incur, second only to labor. Airlines with large fleets can optimize fuel costs by using their data warehouses to proactively plan where and when to refuel their planes.

This issue is particularly powerful for international carriers who fly to countries where fuel costs may fluctuate dramatically. Fuel costs can vary within the United States too. At the time of writing, airplane fuel was 66.5 cents a gallon on the West Coast, compared with 58 cents on the Gulf Coast.

By understanding available fueling locations, their fluctuating prices, and where they are in relation to important routes, airlines can save millions of dollars a year by planning contracts that allow refueling in areas with the lowest fuel costs. This means not only optimizing refueling locations, but understanding optimal fuel volumes per type of aircraft, fuel availability, and even turnaround time for refueling.

A data warehouse can store up-to-date fuel data—including costs, location, availability, and fuel capacities for various equipment—as well as historical information about where a transport company has fueled its fleet, revealing best times and locations for refueling, expected price fluctuations, secondary refueling locations, and preferred fuel providers.

Customer Retention

While all industries are focusing on customer retention, the issue bears special mention in transportation. Because it's a commodity business, and because it's much easier for a consumer to switch a rail or airline carrier than, say, to change banks, airlines have stepped up their customer retention programs.

In order to do justice to customer retention, airlines are redefining just who their good customers are in an effort to pay special attention to their needs. The fact is, consumers have figured out the complex and ever-changing rules of airline travel. Back-to-back ticketing so that both tickets include Saturday night stays and steep fare discounts offered by consolidators have cut into airline profits. The consumer who flies often, sometimes at a moment's notice, and pays retail prices for the privilege is being targeted for a higher class of service, be it first-class upgrades or ground services at departure and destination points.

For the airlines, being able to find these high-value customers and change business practices in order to keep them ensures a higher level of customer satisfaction among the most desirable customers.

In addition to predicting customer attrition, transportation companies are implementing advanced systems to analyze actual individual customer contact experiences and use the data to generate improvements in operations and service. Constantly monitoring customer satisfaction levels can provide a "closed loop" feedback system from customers to management, allowing a transportation company to refine its services over time.

When British Airways' research showed that every pound sterling invested in customer retention efforts generated two pounds in revenue,[12] the company began to invest in strategic technologies to retain customers, as well as in new processes to garner customer feedback, measure performance, and experiment with new methods of customer communication. This data was used by BA's customer retention system to track customer case histories and to prevent problems from recurring.

Figure 4-7 illustrates the range in complexity of the transportation industry's various DSS activities.

The Good News and Bad News in Transportation

Like other industries, the transportation business is confronting increased competition, mergers and acquisitions, and regulatory issues in its efforts to maximize profits. However, transportation companies rely so much on their data warehouses that stories of failed data warehouse projects are less frequent than in

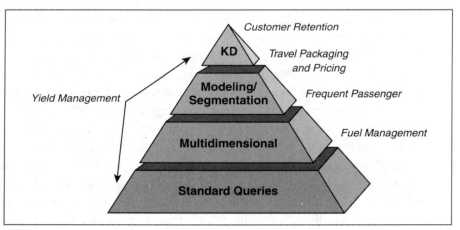

Figure 4-7: Types of Analysis in Transportation

12. Weiser, Charles R., "Championing the Customer," *Harvard Business Review,* November–December 1995, 113.

other industries. While the service glitches, strikes, and hostile takeover bids aren't going away anytime soon, transportation companies have excelled in incorporating data analysis findings not only into their marketing activities, but also into other business processes. So everybody wins.

Case Study: Qantas

Michael Vodicka's corner office features a 90-degree panorama where one can view, among other things, Boeing 747s taking off from Sydney's Kingsford Smith International Airport. Vodicka, group general manager of delivery systems for Qantas Airways, doesn't have much time to contemplate takeoffs and landings, however. He's heading up Qantas's efforts to leverage business intelligence across the enterprise.

If success breeds higher expectations, Vodicka's challenges are growing, as Qantas is already a transportation industry leader in the use of data warehousing and decision support technologies. Since 1991, the world's second oldest and eleventh largest airline has had a centralized data warehouse centered on NCR Teradata technology. "In '91, we realized that there was a better way to do yield management," notes Vodicka, explaining the company's initial foray into decision support. "But we soon discovered that yield management was just the tip of the iceberg, and it's enabled us to do a variety of other things with our data."

Those other things include a laundry list of analytics, from the tactical to the strategic. Qantas uses its data warehouse for a variety of cross-functional decision support functions, from monitoring changes in the travel patterns of frequent fliers to planning and optimizing its fleet to predicting customer attrition. The company can even take just-in-time actions based on the answers to questions such as, "Which Gold frequent fliers are traveling tomorrow?"

Notwithstanding the value of reservation, frequent-flier, scheduling, and inventory data, a critical differentiator has been tying these disparate data subject areas together. "We're not building disconnected and inconsistent islands of information," says Jay Gurjar, Qantas's senior consultant and one of the data warehouse's original advocates. Confirms Vodicka: "Our ability to look at our business in different ways and always link it back to our customer accounts for a lot of our business users' satisfaction with our systems."

And Qantas business users are happy indeed. As he demonstrates the functionality of Qantas's Worldnet application, Steve Goudie positively beams. Goudie, manager of forward analysis, uses Microsoft Excel to produce reports that not only indicate the key yields from certain routes but can also extrapolate future loads, thus aiding decisions about equipment, route planning, pricing, and marketing.

Forward booking information allows Goudie both to examine past flight activity and to compare next month's projections to bookings held at the same time last year. By analyzing who intends to fly and thereby projecting yields, Qantas can decide whether to drop prices on a sparsely filled flight, cancel it, wait for last-minute bookers, or add more services where demand is high. "I want to know what the market is doing," claims Goudie. "That's the real indicator."

The dollar savings have indeed been significant, reportedly well into eight figures. But the data warehouse has also paid off in other ways.

For instance, due to its ability to project flight activity, the airline was able to predict the Asian economic crisis and react by cutting back flights and shifting aircraft in the area before the Asian market—and regional passenger travel—plummeted. This rapid remobilization capability, widely reported in the press, was directly responsible for a surge in the airline's stock price.[13] Qantas is now using similar analysis techniques to project activity for Sydney's 2000 Olympic Games.

And the airline isn't (pardon the pun) standing still. Rather than focusing on acquiring new technologies that may simply address problems the airline is solving now, Vodicka and his team are honing in on extending current DSS capabilities to a broader user base. Despite his stellar technical credentials, Jay Gurjar understands the true value to the business at large and is circumspect about the technical nuts and bolts. "As technically exciting as it all is, the data warehouse should really be transparent to the end-users. It should just be part of people's daily business lives."

Qantas's corporate data warehouse has in fact all but eliminated the guesswork that, while part and parcel of decision making in other industries, carries an especially sensitive stigma for an airline. The company's ability to measure flight history and predict upcoming activities accurately, based on high-quality, reliable data, allows it to make business decisions with an inordinate degree of confidence.

And this confidence translates to customer service, the one key differentiator in a commodity business. Qantas's attrition rate among frequent fliers is dramatically lower than the industry average. "Our customers are obviously our top priority," confirms Michael Vodicka. "Our data warehouse not only lets us

---

13. "S&P Praises Nimble Qantas," *The Australian*, April 2, 1998.

maximize our operational efficiencies, it keeps our customers coming back." As if on cue, a jet rises into the sky behind him.

Government

"We need substantially different actions to get us substantially different results," claimed James Belasco and Ralph Stayer in their 1993 book, *Flight of the Buffalo*.[14] Government organizations, from municipal to federal, have heeded the call.

From detailed taxpayer histories to air traffic "incidents" to global weather patterns, the federal government has relied on data warehouses for some time to keep the country humming. But state and local governments too have deployed their data warehouses in some surprisingly original ways.

Reasons vary, but a few specific phenomena have driven the move toward greater efficiency and innovative knowledge gathering:

- Elected officials, many of whom run on a platform of lower taxes, are calling for cost-cutting measures.
- Local and state governments are newly empowered by the federal government.
- Funding to these same agencies is being cut.
- Crime is a greater political "hot button" than ever before, and information is an important factor in solving crimes.
- Taxpayers—the government's customers—are demanding a return on their investment, insisting on better service levels and response rates.

"Government working smarter!" the campaign posters read. And they're doing it with e-data.

Those of us involved with data warehousing in the early days worked on the same types of projects over and over again: customer profiling, billing analysis, inventory tracking, etc. So imagine my surprise when an international intelligence agency requested help to develop a criminal-tracking database. The agency wanted to gather and store all identifying characteristics of known criminals with past histories that could indicate terrorism and deploy the information to the country's police stations and border control points. When such a suspect was

---

14. Belasco, James A. and Ralph C. Stayer, *Flight of the Buffalo*, Warner Books, New York, 1993, 270.

spotted, the individual's whereabouts were entered, and the agency could monitor the offender's movements over time.

Suffice it to say that data warehousing in government isn't the staid, boring administrative stuff one would imagine. In states across the United States agencies such as those listed below use data warehouses to track down delinquent taxpayers or drivers whose licenses have lapsed.

- motor vehicle departments
- law enforcement and corrections
- tax collection
- airport administration
- Medicare and Medicaid monitoring
- budget and capital investment
- contract management for external suppliers
- public works and roadwork departments
- utilities
- fire and forestry agencies
- family services
- city and county infrastructure management—from the mail room to the city council chamber

ROI can be an alluring justification for a data warehouse in the government sector. For instance, the state of California estimates that Medi-Cal fraud costs it $1 billion a year. A fraud detection program linked to a data warehouse delivering a mere 2 percent fraud reduction rate could save the state millions of dollars annually.

In the late 1990s, in a high-profile success story the U.S. Internal Revenue Service deployed its data warehouse to analyze taxpayer compliance. Among the findings were incidences of divorced couples in which both mother and father claimed their children as dependents. The revelations resulted in additional tax revenues of $70 million.

The Good News and Bad News in Government

Government agencies are being forced into self-evaluation: What do we do well? What don't we do well? The dearth of capital and limited resources will not go away anytime soon; nevertheless the pressure to reform and improve constantly is nonstop. Given that government agencies are measured against achieving their objectives to a much higher degree than private-sector businesses, the push to succeed is overwhelming.

In fact, the good news and bad news are identical when it comes to the use of data in government: The success criteria are changing all the time. New federal programs, slashed budgets, and improved business processes are here to stay, and so is data warehousing.

Case Study: State of Michigan

From a nondescript building in downtown Lansing—one of a series of Michigan state offices—it's hard to believe that groundbreaking activities have been taking place. The hustle and bustle of public service goes on as usual, and hyperefficient government employees go about their workaday duties. But the State of Michigan's Family Independence Agency (FIA) has been chipping away at the routine. Moreover, it could be saving the state's taxpayers millions.

Like the legions of other local, state, and federal agencies, those in Michigan are responding to the needs of their constituents. The FIA, which refers to families in need as its "clients," is concentrating on cost savings and customer satisfaction as any large business would. But welfare reform has triggered some major changes to which the states must respond—and fast.

"For twenty years we knew exactly what was going on, and exactly what our processes were," says Rich Burgis, the FIA's manager of database administration. "But since reform, the rules have changed radically. The federal government has added a host of new reporting requirements. Data warehousing will give us the flexibility to respond to these requirements, as well as others that come along." These federal reporting requirements concentrate on welfare activities and include information on applicants and recipients as well as outcomes. The federal government uses these state reports to track welfare demographics, determine compliance with state work participation programs, and monitor how well the states are following federal guidelines.

The U.S. government isn't the only agency requesting information. The FIA must also respond to other governments, as county administrators and state legislators request activity profiles and custom reports. Michigan's "Project Zero" program has charged individual counties throughout the state with eventually reducing the welfare caseload of employable clients with no income to zero, and county directors need to monitor their progress. The FIA data warehouse will provide counties with status updates and also help them identify new tactics for reducing welfare. In addition, it will expand Project Zero from the current handful of counties in which it is currently implemented to every county in Michigan.

With an architecture revolving around a Teradata data warehouse connected to a Bull mainframe, the FIA data warehouse stores data on client family demographics as well as information on payments, services, foster care, adoption, and delinquency programs. The warehouse provides simple reports describing the client base—for example, which families or individuals are currently receiving aid, or where in the state clusters might exist —and more sophisticated simulations and "what if" analysis to help the FIA predict how certain policies could affect expenditures. "Our legacy systems took months to perform the scenario analysis we're able to perform on the data warehouse in days," says Burgis.

Because state governments are responsible for ensuring child support payments, the FIA's child support enforcement system is leveraging the data warehouse in order to track down "deadbeat dads."

Before the data warehouse, eight state employees relied on referrals to locate absent parents and enforce collection of support payments. Now centralized name and address data can be used by case workers and enforcement officers statewide to find the last place the individual lived. This data is also compared with federal data, improving the possibility that the absent parent will be found and payments will be collected.

In addition, the data warehouse will aid the state in reducing fraud. Recipients who changed their addresses just before payroll and then changed them back again previously went undetected until it was too late. Now the state can identify abusers quickly, resulting in significant cost savings.

But the real savings lie in the fines the state will avoid by submitting federally mandated reports on time, fines that can add up to millions of dollars each year. "By avoiding federal sanctions, we've paid for our data warehouse, and will ultimately pay for it many times over," Burgis says.

"We don't even know all the capabilities this data warehouse will be able to provide us," adds Sue Doby, the FIA's director of application software development. The data warehouse not only facilitates savings, it will bring about improvements to the state's very infrastructure. "Our users are so used to being told what they can have. Now they'll be able to tell us what they need."

Doby speculates that private industry would be surprised at the work going on in government. "The private sector believes that government is in the dark ages," she says, "but we're far from it." In fact, they can't afford to be in the dark ages: The Freedom of Information Act means that when it comes to requests for information, government agencies—unlike private companies—can't say no.

The fact that the Michigan FIA's ROI amounts to more than just the millions of dollars in cost savings isn't lost on Rich Burgis and Sue Doby. After all, it's hard to put a dollar figure on feeding a hungry family. But once the agency meets its long-term goals, it might not have to.

Health Care

For the last several years the health care industry has been faced with a tough challenge: to reduce costs and improve care. And as if this weren't enough, the national spotlight has been shining brightly on the industry, with politicians and consumers both petitioning for major reform. This fresh focus has heightened the awareness of how information technology can help health care organizations solve many of their problems.

The health care industry encompasses public, private, and nonprofit institutions. Health care is in fact the rubric for a diverse set of businesses, including the following:

- hospitals
- pharmacies and drug distribution companies
- managed care organizations (HMOs and PPOs)
- private practices and clinics
- insurance companies

The industry is in the unique and unenviable position of marketing to consumers who are unaware of the real price of the products and services they're receiving. The fact that prices are not available prior to consumption is exacerbated by the fact that the industry is dominated by third-party providers such as insurance companies and Medicare, who are in effect barriers to price gathering.

Most health care companies would not necessarily characterize themselves as being part of an information culture. Nevertheless, these days they are making significant strides in the gathering, access, and deployment of data, sometimes with life-saving consequences.

Uses of Data Warehousing in Health Care

Data warehousing in health care has been adopted, albeit warily, to support cost control efforts. While revenues and profits do matter, health care companies are being pressured to keep costs down. There are several reasons for escalating costs:

- the increase and variety of new treatments
- duplication of treatments and tests
- malpractice insurance

- legal fees
- increased life span
- new regulations that require additional expenditures
- costly new medical technologies

A 1993 study published in the *New England Journal of Medicine* found that administrative costs account for one out of every four dollars spent on hospital care. Health care organizations are using data warehouses to measure these rising costs and to examine ways to reduce them, while increasing patient satisfaction at the same time.

Besides cost control, health management companies now rely on data warehouses to perform basic business functions such as revenue analysis and, increasingly, to perform more strategic work such as fraud prediction. Yet even day-to-day functionality in the form of basic reporting capabilities is in growing demand. In a 1998 study, the Healthcare Information and Management Systems Society asked health care organizations for their information priorities over the next two years. "Improved decision support" was cited as the top priority by 61 percent of respondents, second only to improvements in managed care.[15]

Health care companies are using data on their warehouses for a variety of purposes:

- patient records storage and analysis
- case management
- risk management
- provider monitoring and profiling
- complaints tracking
- contract tracking and processing
- actuarial and underwriting functions
- rate analysis
- monitoring of trends in quality of care
- quality/outcomes analysis
- profit-and-loss analysis
- claims analysis
- patient relations

---

15. Carlos, Lawrence G. and Kay M. Comaford, *Future Trends in Health Care Enterprise-Wide Knowledge Distribution,* The Healthcare Information and Management Systems Society, 1998 (see *http://warehouse.chime-net.org/software/eisdss/98s112.pdf*).

While these business drivers may seem diverse, they are ultimately all linked to patient care. One of the overriding value propositions of data warehousing in health care is the potential for a "single version of the truth" about a patient, accessible and sharable across the continuum of care, as illustrated in figure 4-8.

This centralization of data and resulting one-stop shopping for information has allowed health care companies easier access to historical information to develop profiles for both care providers and patients, providing new knowledge of both their staff and their patients.

For example, an outcomes analysis query might be expressed like this:

> *Of the bypass surgeries performed by Provider x*
> *in 1999, show the percentage of patients who*
> *experienced postoperative complications.*

The response to such an ad hoc query can have far-reaching effects, from singling out specific providers for further analysis to targeting individual patients for follow-up or home care to confirming payment rates with insurance carriers. As simple as the query is, few health care organizations are currently capable of providing this level of on-demand access by clinicians and hospital staff. But the changes are coming.

The goal for many health care companies is to move beyond simply processing paperwork and reporting on events after the fact to managing in-process care

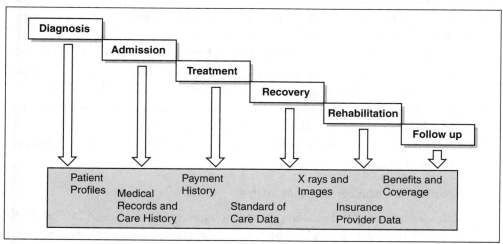

Figure 4-8: A Health Care Data Warehouse

and predicting financial outcomes. While health care has followed other industries in terms of acquiring advanced business intelligence, care providers and payers alike are highly motivated to incorporate that intelligence into their core business once it's understood.

Claims Management

Hospitals and insurance companies are leveraging claims history to track individual customer activities, modify prices for certain customers or providers, and determine new contract renewal rates. One HMO is using its claims data to model price tolerance for certain services, as well as to find and recover excessive procedure charges. This same data is also used across the HMO's accounting, patient relations, and utilization review departments.

Care providers can also use claims data to calculate expected reimbursements and compare them to actual payments to discover cases of underpayment. Payment detail, such as underpayments, variances, or denied charges, can aid health care organizations in traditionally paper-based loss recovery processes.

Risk Management and Fraud Analysis

Risk management allows health care organizations to follow the claims management process by tracking incident reports with the aim of preventing patient fraud. For example, a patient with a history of wrist injuries and resulting workers' compensation claims might warrant either preventive treatment or further investigation. The data warehouse can provide a record of patient visits and follow-up contacts in a simple canned report, which clinicians may then use to develop care plans for specific patients or ailments.

Fraud, waste, and abuse are rampant in health care, notably in Medicare programs. Both government and health care organizations are using data warehouses to pinpoint inappropriate activities, reduce waste, and look for trends in abuse by both patients and providers. Compliance is the name of the game here, and health care organizations are using their data warehouses to define and implement appropriate compliance measures—avoiding the cost and negative publicity of lawsuits.

Patient Case Management and Analysis

New advances in decision support technologies specific to health care allow the use of patient data to track a case across the continuum of care. This process has traditionally been paper-based and bureaucracy-laden. Patient responses to acute episodes—from surgery and recovery to home care—provide hospital administrators and treatment teams with invaluable trend data about patient responses to care. This data can also motivate hospitals to implement additional services, such as enhanced rehabilitation facilities.

The centralization and resulting sharability of data in the data warehouse means that the patient information is standardized and accessible across the many touch points of a patient's care, from the admissions representative to the treatment team to the pharmacist. Indeed, the advantage of the "single version of the truth" provided by the data warehouse is nowhere more vital than in health care.

Health care companies are also using data warehouses to store discrete patient contact information, from checkup visits to satisfaction survey responses. Often, patient demographics can be compared with patient visit or complaint rates, as well as with care denials and appeals, enabling care facilities to profile patients or segment patient groups. This information dictates how best to respond to patient input and ensures a higher degree of follow-up and resolution.

The Good News and Bad News in Health Care

The holy grail for the data warehouse in health care is to link the patient to the cost of care and subsequently modify prices, improve the quality of care, and increase patient satisfaction. The Balanced Budget Act of 1996, which promised to reduce Medicare outlays by billions of dollars, provided yet another incentive for cost containment, and rumors of Medicare's impending bankruptcy have kept these efforts in the public eye.

The bad news is that health care has been slow to automate some of its more complex processes and is experiencing some of its worst market pressures just as it begins to implement strategic technologies. These pressures put a burden on each point in the health care supply chain to define, find, and gather data that will be needed for later analysis. Indeed, companies such as Pacific Health Network are outsourcing their decision support processes to third parties in order to leverage online claims data for provider profiling and utilization management, among other business initiatives.[16]

Other good news is that health care organizations have mandated rapid change and that vendors are responding with decision support technologies

16. Greengard, Samuel, "Assembling a Hybrid Data Warehouse," *Beyond Computing,* March 1999, 22.

specifically geared to the diverse analysis demands of the industry. Health care and insurance providers are entitled to be vigilant in their efforts to contain costs and are right to use advanced technologies to help them do so. And in cases like the one below, they are succeeding in their use of e-data to improve the standard of care.

Case Study: Aetna U.S. Healthcare, U.S. Quality Algorithms

For someone with an "M.D." after her name, Dr. Carol Diamond certainly knows a lot about data warehousing. Dr. Diamond is the president of Aetna U.S. Healthcare's U.S. Quality Algorithms (USQA) division, Aetna's information delivery subsidiary. As adept as she is at discussing data warehousing and data analysis, Diamond's true goal is to leverage technology to improve the quality of care for Aetna's 13 million members nationwide.

Since the mid-1990s, USQA has evolved from a small team of researchers running ad hoc reports into an organization that has garnered worldwide recognition for its analysis of health care performance. The company's award-winning data warehouse is an IBM RS/6000 that runs the DB2 universal database and houses over three terabytes of data (and growing).

USQA performs an array of analysis techniques, using data as diverse as provider profiles, member information, benefit plan information, outcomes data, and disease statistics. The company is charged with providing a range of information-based services, from analyzing the effectiveness of managed care programs to ensuring regulatory adherence to risk modeling for chronically ill patients.

One of its key initiatives is monitoring physician performance. This means not only tracking Aetna U.S. Healthcare's nationwide network of care providers and the accompanying point-of-care data but also determining patient satisfaction levels in an effort to make ongoing improvements. Besides generating the cost savings associated with early detection of disease and tracking quality of care, USQA has used physician performance measurement to increase patient satisfaction.

With the data on the warehouse, USQA analyzes member activity nationwide in order to, for instance, assess the percentage of members with diabetes who have not had an eye exam within the last year. Findings result in a range of business actions, from triggering a member education campaign about diabetes and eye disease to sending care providers a list of patients who are candidates for eye exams. With OLAP technology that uses products from Seagate Software,

USQA can also observe trends in patient office visits and monitor year over year uplift in vaccine rates.

In health care business, acting on suspicions alone can literally be a life-or-death decision, so hard data plays a critical role. "Once we began formalizing our process for gathering performance metrics," says Dr. Diamond, "we had the data to really demonstrate measurable improvements." Performance reports measure quality across several domains, including members' satisfaction with their primary care physician. This data can, among other things, result in physician bonus payments, offering continual incentives for optimal patient care.

A victim of its own success, USQA regularly receives requests from physicians who have received new reports and want more. So it's no surprise that USQA's data-warehousing strategy prominently features the Internet. Diamond's staff is currently considering mechanisms to ensure secure Web-based delivery of information to members and physicians.

"Member satisfaction is a theme in everything we do," Dr. Diamond affirms. "We're constantly communicating with members and providers, and the common denominator of that communication is information." No doubt millions of members and providers will be logging on.

Insurance

Many insurance chief executives are suspicious of data warehousing because they don't understand how it works. While this phenomenon isn't unique to their industry, entrenched processes seem to maintain a stranglehold in insurance more than in other industries. Many insurance companies have kicked and screamed toward customer knowledge, in many cases outsourcing their IT departments and their data warehouses altogether.

Of course, as in other industries, some pioneers continue to make great strides in maintaining competitive edge. Companies such as Transamerica and Liberty Mutual in the United States and Royal Insurance in the United Kingdom, both of which acquired and began using their data warehouses in the 1980s, remain ahead of their competitors now. Good news for them, since customer defections are mounting, and deregulation threatens to spread insurance sales out to a larger provider community.

Insurance companies may deal in all types of insurance or may specialize in health insurance, property and casualty, life insurance, or other areas.

Uses of Data Warehousing in Insurance

As with health care, claims data make up the bulk of most insurance companies' information, and claims analysis continues to take priority as a business driver. However, with customer retention and fraud demanding increased attention, other areas of analysis also beckon the data warehouse:

- risk management
- product cost and pricing analysis
- target marketing
- attrition[17]
- cross-selling
- product packaging
- campaign management
- provider profiling
- fraud detection

While all of these areas parallel the analysis efforts undertaken in the other industries described here, the insurance industry is unique in that both its growth and its profitability have actually been eroding. This slippage is mostly due to the combined forces of tighter regulatory controls and tax laws with increased competition. At the same time, health care costs have skyrocketed. The challenge for insurance companies is threefold: (1) to control their costs, (2) to maintain market share, and (3) to improve customer service and perception.

Many insurance companies are also struggling to overcome their outdated legacy systems, and their focus on rewriting these systems has put data warehousing on the back burner. As proprietary claims-processing systems age and expertise wanes, some insurers have given into temptation and outsourced IT operations, rendering in-house data expertise difficult to find. Thus, data modeling and sourcing have become the insurance data warehouse's ball and chain.

Data warehouses have both an operational and a strategic advantage for insurance carriers. Tactically, data allows insurance companies to calculate price changes and track possible fraud quickly and accurately, resulting in loss prevention and cost savings.

---

17. We're referring to "attrition" instead of churn here because customers who leave one insurance company for another are unlikely to return to the original company. Thus, churning in the insurance industry is less of a problem than losing customers for good.

Strategically, though, insurance companies can leverage their data warehouses not only to reduce expenses but also to increase profitability and customer satisfaction, as well as nimbly quelling competitive threats via the timely introduction of new campaigns and promotions. Their challenge is moving beyond the reactive analysis, which has resulted in limited business benefits, toward more proactive activities with higher payoffs, such as establishing high-value customer segments using claim and profitability data and predicting fraud using modeling techniques.

Claims Reporting

Insurance companies continue to use their data warehouses primarily for storing and reporting claims data. This reporting can take many forms:

- executive claims reporting, including summaries of the number and type of claims and payments for a given time period, often for use by executives
- claims comparisons (by claim type, number of claims, etc.) against industry averages
- claims tracking for certain service providers, comparing payment and volume history with that of other providers or sales channels
- subrogation services, whereby insurance companies research and pay third-party claims
- customer satisfaction measurement, obtained by using claims data as a springboard for customer surveys, and feeding customer input back to the data warehouse for comparison against future claims

Cost analysis is a superset of claims data analysis. Since insurance companies don't actually know the true cost of a policy until claims are made, claims evaluation must occur regularly. Cost analysis also involves evaluating treatment or repair costs against similar cost data, which is often linked to state or federal averages. A simple query comparing podiatrist charges in a certain geographical area with the regional averages for the same treatment types could save an insurance carrier tens of thousands of dollars.

Distribution Channel Analysis

Insurance companies today are selling their services in a variety of ways. The neighborhood agent has made room for the Internet, and insurance companies, like banks, are calculating their most productive and profitable channels.

Channel analysis can result in significant cost savings. Monitoring claims and policies per agency or agent can result in increased efficiency in a variety of areas, such as weeding out problem agents or motivating the most productive agencies to sell a specific product. Here's an example of a simple query:

> *Of the policies sold by Agency X in the past year,*
> *how many have resulted in claims, and what*
> *percentage of those claims are "open"?*

Such a query can result in a variety of business actions, from dropping an agency to expediting claims processing for high-value policyholders. Finding the claims-to-policy ratio for a given agent, agency, or regional office is often the initial requirement for an insurance company's first data warehouse application.

When combined with claims data, channel data can indicate trends in claims severity, premium payment rates, and overall sales trends. It can also aid in the target marketing of specific insurance products to specific sales channels.

The optimal decision support opportunities for the insurance industry arise through the use of existing detailed data to help determine differentiating products and services, spurring more sales as well as enhancing customer perception. This differentiation at the policy or channel levels, combined with the opportunity to target new markets or identify market niches, helps insurance companies reach more consumers, and in fact may keep many in business.

The Good News and Bad News in the Insurance Industry

A friend of mine, a director for a property and casualty insurer, recently oversaw the development of a DSS reporting tool designed to distribute internal information and updates to third-party sales agents. Senior managers were invited to attend a demo of the new reporting tool, which would make it easier for the company to gather and monitor claims as well as improve customer service.

As soon as he saw that the tool included the ability to access the company's research materials—summarized studies that would provide sales agents with historical claims and sales data to facilitate regional marketing efforts—one executive jumped up and cried, "I don't want agents seeing market research! They don't understand this stuff! How much is this costing us?" The executives then proceeded to debate the benefits of distributing more limited, paper-based reports to agents. So much for improving customer service! Insurance companies have a long way to go in transforming their culture to support and adopt new knowledge, not to mention share it.

The good news is that forward-thinking insurance companies who realize the value of customer knowledge and the different ways to analyze, manipulate, and act on it will end up acquiring and keeping new customers—probably those who have left the insurance company run by the executive described in the previous paragraph.

Case Study: California State Automobile Association

Nearly one hundred years ago, Auto Club charter member Hermann Oerlichs told a reporter that "the proliferation of motor cars is a sign to awaken every serious-minded horse to an uneasy consideration of its future." Almost four million members later, the California State Automobile Association (CSAA) is readying itself for the new millennium.

That the insurance industry is late to the business intelligence game doesn't seem to faze Alexandra Morehouse McReynolds, CSAA's vice president of customer relationship marketing. A veteran of financial services firms, Morehouse McReynolds has spent much of her career putting in place state-of-the-art database marketing systems. So what's she doing at CSAA?

As it turns out, plenty. Morehouse McReynolds has landed smack dab in the middle of a company—and an industry—undergoing significant change. This change ranges from the en masse replacement of outdated operational systems to the onslaught of new competition. Morehouse McReynolds's marketing strategies are poised at various levels to leverage this transformation while bolstering the company's ability to respond to newfound market pressures.

As one of the insurance industry's *grandes dames*, CSAA offers a range of services beyond automobile insurance. The company's travel, financial, and emergency roadside services have generated word-of-mouth repeat business for years. The historical processes that have maintained the company's reputation as a solid service provider—particularly to a growing traveling public—are the same processes that are now changing to drive a more proactive market presence. In the face of emerging competitors and an aging customer demographic, CSAA has begun to embrace the transition.

"We have no more excuses," states Morehouse McReynolds. "The technology is finally available to do what we need to do." And her to-do list is a long one. Instead of selling the advantages of online claims data, Morehouse McReynolds and her team are proselytizing the value proposition of data warehousing.

The holy grail for CSAA is to have accessible customer information online for a wide variety of marketing uses. Morehouse McReynolds can illustrate the promise of ad hoc reporting as deftly as she can articulate the tactics behind lifetime value scoring. Data subject areas such as membership status, policy cancellation, product purchases, and customer demographics figure heavily into programs for customer acquisition, retention, and cross-selling.

CSAA's initial end-user community for decision support comprises both actuarial and marketing staff. While the former benefit from consolidated data, leveraging it into their own set of computations and processes, the marketing organization can already analyze different data in ways unimaginable before data warehousing. CSAA has deployed end-user desktop reporting via E.piphany querying Oracle data that originates from the company's mainframe IBM DB2 system. While the reports provide straightforward point-and-click claims analysis, the fact that end-users can get information on demand constitutes a significant breakthrough.

Eventually, scores from attrition and cross-selling models will make their way onto CSAA's data warehouse to supplement desktop reporting. So, too, will data about marketing campaigns, denoting which customers have responded to a given campaign and furnishing comprehensive profiles. The Oracle system will also store contact history, recording each customer touch point. This closed-loop strategy will not only aid CSAA in refining its marketing offerings but also provide a single, integrated view of the customer over time.

The ideal is direct access to both claims data, and a host of customer and product information in order to help the company nimbly navigate new marketing territories. "Just the ability to write a mailing plan and track it through fruition will be very powerful for us," says Morehouse McReynolds.

"Our entire corporate heritage has been taking care of people," she concludes. "If we can get the data we need into the hands of the people who need it, we can do an even better job."

Entertainment

The entertainment industry is a special case. Entertainment companies could be considered consumer packaged goods firms or retailers, but in other ways they warrant their own category. Truth be told, though, a sophisticated server is more likely to generate whiz-bang special effects for a studio than to provide it with business information.

The most pervasive use of data warehousing in the entertainment business is in monitoring product distribution and sales. A product can be anything from a home video to a T-shirt featuring the logo of a television show. Web merchandising is emerging as a hot area in entertainment, and understanding sales and revenues from these products can go a long way to help an entertainment company earn add-on revenues.

The world of theatrical screenings also holds promise for decision support. The ability to predict ticket sales down to a certain theater, model syndicated television ratings, or distribute weekend box office results over the company intranet can help a studio optimize release schedules as well as save millions in marketing costs.

Case Study: Twentieth Century Fox

In an industry that still relies on gut feel for many of its business decisions and on focus groups for market research, Justin Yaros might well sit on his laurels after throwing together some Web sites and deploying corporate e-mail. But Yaros, senior vice president and chief information officer for Twentieth Century Fox, has other things in mind. And decision support is one of them.

"There are a number of areas where DSS is beginning to take root," says Yaros. "Principally, it's in sales and marketing analysis. While we're not yet as advanced as other consumer packaged goods companies, we're learning a lot from our data."

Log on to Fox.com and you'll see why business intelligence is critical. The company markets merchandise ranging from *X-Files* mouse pads to videos of *Dr. Doolittle* to *The Simpsons* refrigerator magnets. Who buys this stuff, anyway? Plenty of people, it turns out. And Fox's ability to track these purchases can help the company better understand its supply chain, as well as construct profitable licensing and merchandising agreements.

But don't assume that an entertainment organization is nothing more than a high-gloss consumer packaged goods firm focused on product movement. In this business, the money's in the theatrical area, and so is the data warehouse.

Fox uses an Oracle data mart with DSS Agent to analyze box office results together with marketing expenditures relative to specific films. "On a Monday morning," says Yaros, "we can look at a movie's box office performance that weekend. We can examine our marketing expenditures, not just for the film as a whole, but for specific DMAs [demographic marketing areas] and even for individual theaters." Although in its early stages, this type of analysis can help Fox evaluate its marketing expenses for a given film as well as assist the company in determining its distribution strategies, potentially dictating which regions or theaters can sell the most tickets.

This analysis strategy will help Fox establish optimal distribution channels and enable it to develop relationships with high-volume theaters, perhaps inducing them to hold over a film that's doing well. Moreover, using its data warehouse, Fox can present the theater owner with the data to back up its claims. It's a new spin on CRM, and one that promises improved revenues.

Yaros and his team are also considering data-mining technology, especially predictive models. Yaros hints at the ability to predict the performance of certain films or genres prior to their release, potentially saving the company millions. "There are people here who have been in the business for so long that they can feel how a film will perform," he says. "Our data warehouse has to be as or more reliable than their intuition."

Data warehousing and the accompanying analytics will ultimately allow Fox to invest its marketing dollars more wisely, as well as schedule release dates and test out distribution scenarios well before the fact. And there's little doubt that the technology will also help the company forecast just how many Homer Simpson fridge magnets to have on hand.

Some Lingering Questions

So, now that I understand what each industry is doing, how do they compare in their decision support adoption rates? Are some industries generally further ahead?

As a rule, industries that are experiencing the most competitive threat are data warehousing's front-runners. This is why the financial services and telecommunications industries in particular have been so fierce in deploying decision support.

In its 1999 report, *Business Intelligence and Data Warehousing: Crossing the Millennium,* the Palo Alto Management Group released a chart indicating DSS application adoption levels currently and within three years (see figure 4-9).

The report indicates that sectors with the most data also have—and are acquiring—the highest number of applications. The report goes on to point out that the highest percentage of growth will be achieved by industries that currently have lower adoption levels—namely, education, manufacturing, and government.

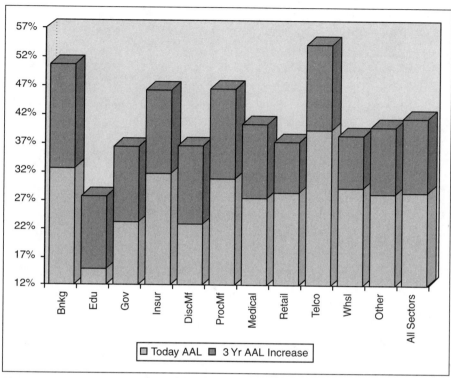

Figure 4-9: Data Warehouse Application Adoption Levels by Sector (Source: Palo Alto Management Group)

PART II

Getting the Technology

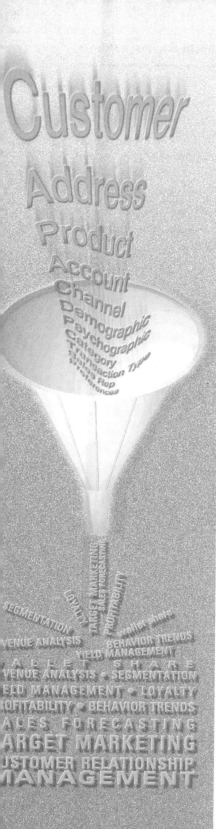

CHAPTER FIVE

The Underlying Technologies: A Primer

While this isn't a technology book, it might be helpful if we do a brief review of some of the fundamental technologies that are comprised in a data warehouse. Understanding the basics can help you sound intelligent with your colleagues and vendors and prevent some of the inevitable double-talk that occurs when technology staff and business-people meet to discuss business intelligence solutions.

If you feel comfortable with database terminology and basic client/server concepts, feel free to skip to the next chapter.

Data Warehouse Architecture

Many people, particularly end-users, view their data warehouse as a software tool rather than as a principal component in their company's technology infrastructure. While this might sound like definitional nitpicking, a holistic understanding of the data warehouse can affect everything from its budget to its staffing to its usage.

As explained in chapter 1, the data warehouse comprises hardware, software, networking, and data. There are two basic types of data warehouses: (1) the enterprise data warehouse, which is used by multiple organizations across a company for multiple purposes; and (2) the data mart, which is typically a single-function data warehouse used by one organization.

The architecture of an enterprise data warehouse is characterized by the size of the hardware platform, the number of source systems that feed it, and the number of users. An enterprise data warehouse architecture looks something like the one in figure 5-1, which is fed by three separate operational systems; each of its users might belong to a different organization.

Conversely, a data mart's architecture can vary with its specific usage. In the case of a dependent data mart, the data mart is connected to an enterprise data warehouse and performs a discrete business function using a subset of the data from the enterprise data warehouse. The enterprise data warehouse is, in effect, the source system for the dependent data mart, as shown in figure 5-2.

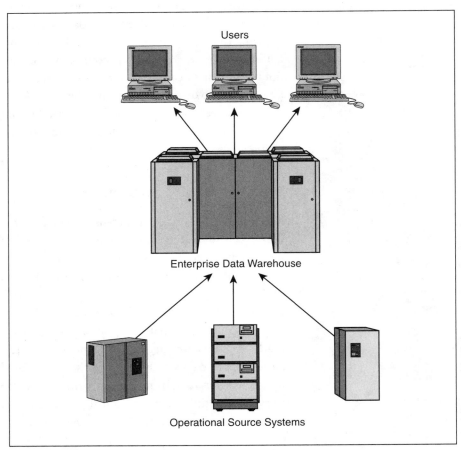

Figure 5-1: Enterprise Data Warehouse Architecture

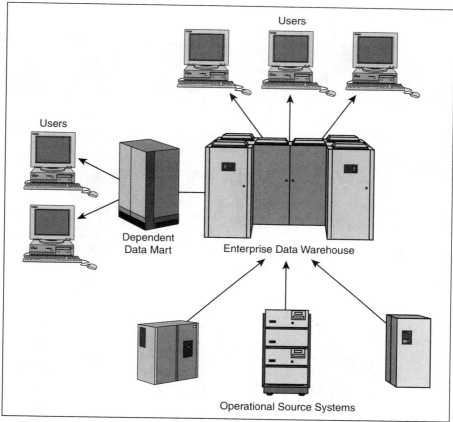

Figure 5-2: Dependent Data Mart Architecture

The dependent data mart might house campaign information to be used specifically by marketing staff looking into new advertising ideas. At the same time, the enterprise data warehouse could also offer marketing data to the company at large, along with other data on areas such as sales, finance, or product development.

The independent data mart is a stand-alone system. Its data can originate from operational systems, as with an enterprise data warehouse, but it may also be generated or in some cases even manually fed. Figure 5-3 illustrates the independent data mart.

The independent data marts shown in figure 5-3 are each used for separate business purposes. For example, one might contain drug research results while

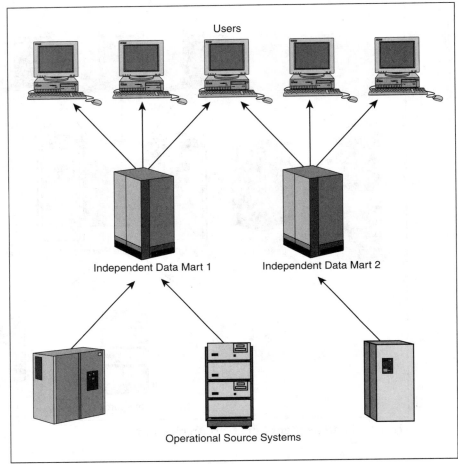

Figure 5-3: Independent Data Mart Architecture

the other contains actual sales data. Note that although each mart is focused on a specific business function, users can access a company's various marts for different purposes. In this case, the user logging on to both marts might be a pharmaceutical employee relating clinical research trial findings to drug dispensing figures.

Data aside, data marts and enterprise data warehouses are extremely different in terms of their value to an organization. While the former do an excellent job of offering tactical solutions to business problems, the latter are widely regarded as a strategic tool that provides a cross-functional view of the business.

The Operational Data Store

It's worth mentioning the operational data store (ODS). The ODS is an operational construct used to prepare detailed data between the various operational systems. Its function is to help gather and integrate nonaggregated data from the various source systems before the data is loaded into the warehouse.

For example, a middle-market bank uses its ODS to synchronize account and record information from individual customers. One customer might own a gas station with its own bank account but might also have a personal checking account and a home equity line of credit with the same bank. Rather than trying to match all of this data to the same individual, the bank uses the ODS to correlate each customer's records, as shown in figure 5-4.

Furthermore, the bank updates the ODS each time the customer performs another transaction, keeping a current and rolling history of activity. When the results of this correlation are loaded onto the data warehouse, it stores a single and integrated view of that customer.

Depending on their data warehouse technology architecture, some companies elect to perform this type of work on the same hardware platform as their data warehouse. ODS processing involves a lot of detailed data and simultaneous updates, making computing horsepower essential. Conversely, the amount of history stored on the ODS is normally less than that kept on the data warehouse.

Whether the data is correlated via an ODS, directly from the various source systems during extraction, or only after it has been loaded onto the data warehouse, it is crucial for the business to wind up with a single version of the truth.

Two-Tier Versus *n*-Tier

If you browse the Web from time to time, you know that entering "www.whatever.com" gets you access to your requested Web site. What you may not know is that you're logging on to a server, which dispatches the request to an application. A Web server for a data warehouse does the same thing; it's like a research librarian who knows where to hunt down specific information.

In a two-tier architecture, business logic, data management, and data presentation functions reside on the "client," traditionally the user's workstation. In an architecture with three or more tiers, any or all of these functions could rest on an intermediate server.[1]

---

1. Three-tier architecture is the normal term for what might really be called an "*n*-tier" architecture, with multiple servers having different functions within the same architecture.

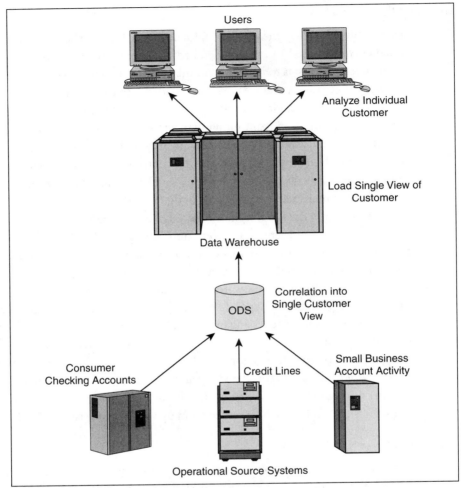

Figure 5-4: Operational Data Store

Figure 5-5 depicts a three-tier architecture on the right, in which an application server represents the "second tier." Note that the second tier can be a Web server, an application server, or even a data mart.

The architecture to the left represents a simple two-tier architecture in which the desktop PC accesses the data warehouse directly.

The two-tier architecture refers to the traditional "client/server" relationship between a workstation on the desktop and a separate server. In this case, your

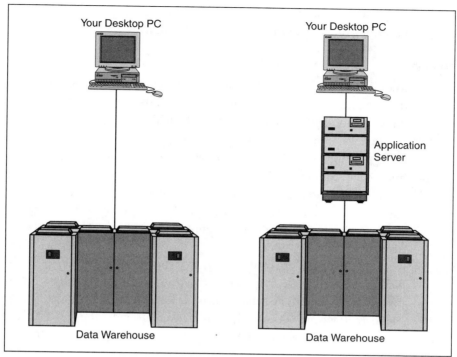

Figure 5-5: Two-Tier versus Three-Tier

desktop PC would be the client and the data warehouse would be the server. The processing is divided: The application runs on the PC, and the data processing occurs on the data warehouse.

The three-tier architecture includes a second tier that is usually reserved for application-specific functionality. While more complex to implement, the three-tier architecture removes the burden from the client workstation, which simply runs the application. The second tier serves to run the application logic and can be accessed by numerous clients, eliminating redundant processing.

"The biggest advantage of the three-tier architecture is business flexibility," says Barbara Britton of BEA Systems, a leader in middleware technology. "With three-tier architectures, you separate your business logic from the more mundane technology tasks of data management, security, etc. This allows you to change business rules or even your business approach and still leverage your technology architecture to deliver scaleable, reliable application results."

In more complex environments, the three-tier architecture simplifies navigation when one tier houses software called "middleware."

Middleware

Middleware is software that enables systems to talk to one another while hiding the complexities of network connectivity. Middleware is an important data warehouse component, since it's the means by which applications communicate with the data warehouse. Middleware technology allows clients to talk to servers, but more critically, it shields the application programmer from the complexity of finding and combining data.

Middleware exists for transactional systems, communications systems, and data warehouses. Database middleware, the type used for data warehouses, connects the data warehouse to client applications as part of either a two- or three-tier architecture.

When you call a friend in England, you dial the country code (44) before dialing the actual telephone number. You really don't care how the number is routed and accessed, just that the call will result in a telephone ringing at your friend's cottage in the Cotswolds. Middleware provides the best available route to the data, in effect freeing you from having to know how to navigate to the data in the data warehouse.

When most people think of middleware, they think of ODBC, which stands for Open Database Connectivity, the name of Microsoft's database middleware product. ODBC is a standard for the Windows environment and provides a uniform interface that lets application tools—from spreadsheets to custom programs—connect to any database system.

From a data warehouse perspective, the benefit of database middleware is that a programmer need not write the same application multiple times for multiple different database products. The middleware allows the application to know things like specific data types, network protocols, or the type of network in use—without that information being specified in each program. It can also be used to connect data marts to one another, to direct certain processes to the optimal platform in order to minimize work and data volumes, and to provide Web access and throughput management.

Though it can be very complex and offers a range of functionality, middleware's principal function in data warehousing is to create a uniform way of accessing databases.

Databases and What They're Good For

Database products were flourishing before anyone ever thought of data warehouses. This is because databases, in particular relational databases, offered hope for the storage of meaningful information in understandable ways.[2]

Relational databases are by far the most common means of storing data in data warehouses and data marts. They represent a means of storing data in tables, much like the spreadsheets you're probably used to filling out for budgets and expense reporting. Relational tables comprise horizontal rows and vertical columns, the rows representing discrete objects and the columns representing their classifications.

Table 5-1 is the "Product" table for a cheese shop that helps the store track its different types of cheeses. The table could contain even more information, such as a flavor rating for each cheese, brand names, or the number of wedges on hand. The database could contain other tables, such as a table of cheeses on order, or a table of different suppliers. A collection of related tables is, in fact, a database.

Table 5-1: Cheese Product Table

Cheese Code	Cheese Name	Country of Origin	Milk Type	Texture
10001	Stilton	England	cow	SH
10002	Vacherin	France	cow	S
10003	Cairnsmore	Scotland	ewe	SS
10004	Sbrinz	Switzerland	cow	H
10005	Halloumy	Australia	cow	H
10006	Prince-Jean	France	cow	S
10007	Buffalo	United States	buffalo	H
10008	Juustoleipa	Finland	cow/reindeer	SH
10009	Ackawi	Middle East	ewe	H

---

2. The tenets of relational databases were laid out by C. J. Date in his watershed book *An Introduction to Database Systems,* Reading, MA: Addison-Wesley, 1983.

The important thing to know about relational databases is that the tables within them can become very large and complex. The complexity of these tables depends on a number of factors, for example, the number of rows in the table, the number of columns in the table, and the relationship tables have to one another.

The intersection between a row and a column is an individual data element, much like a single cell in a spreadsheet, and is called an "attribute." The SH attribute indicates that Stilton cheese is "semi-hard."

Indeed, it's the multiple tables, ranging from under ten to hundreds at a time, that make up the data in the data warehouse. Each of the boxes in figure 5-6 represents a table in the database.

This diagram could be called a high-level data model. The data model graphically illustrates relationships between various components of the business. When translated into actual tables on the data warehouse, complete with attributes, these data structures can answer a range of questions about when certain cheeses were sold, and to whom, for example:

Who bought Stilton in the Winter Park
store last week?

Suppose we've solved the data-modeling problem and now have a set of interrelated tables. Just as a database can comprise one or more tables, a data warehouse can comprise one or more databases (see figure 5-7).

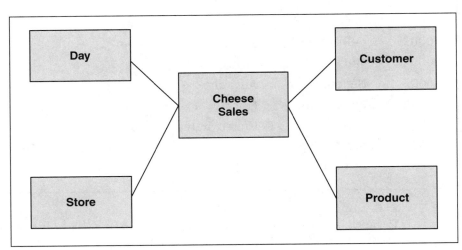

Figure 5-6: The Tables in a Database

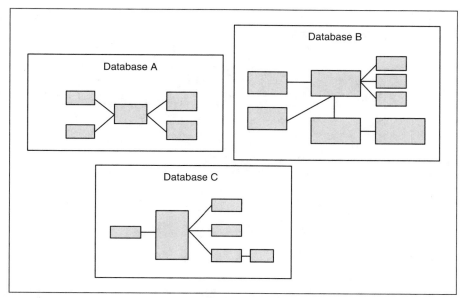

Figure 5-7: Three Databases That Together Make Up a Data Warehouse

A data warehouse's data structure can be as simple as a database containing a few tables (this would probably be a data mart) or as complex as tens of databases with hundreds of tables in each.

When people talk about a "large data warehouse," they're usually talking about a data warehouse consisting of many tables, with each containing a large number of rows representing detailed information.

How large can a data warehouse become? Figure 5-8 shows the scale to which data in a warehouse can grow. Most companies have gigabytes, meaning one billion bytes of data on their warehouses, and many data warehouses have hit the terabyte level, meaning they hold a trillion bytes of information. In a 1999 research report, META Group concluded that 30 percent of companies with data warehouses would exceed one terabyte of data, the equivalent of 700,000 floppy disks.

Note that the following illustration is not to scale. (If it were, we'd need several thousand pages for the terabytes and petabytes!)

The largest of today's commercial data warehouses, including some featured in this book, are in the terabyte range. Why so much data? Think of every credit card transaction each of a bank's 400,000 customers has ever made in a lifetime,

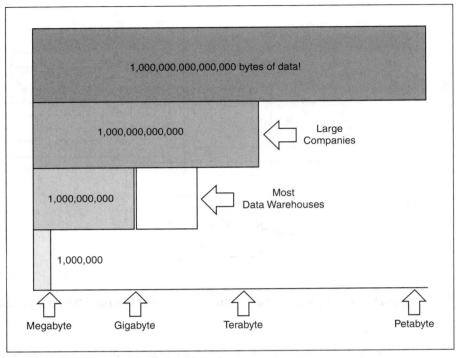

Figure 5-8: Relative Data Volumes

combined. Or the number of times a product is scanned at a supermarket. These are examples of discrete business events—someone getting cash from an ATM or buying corned beef hash at a supermarket—that are recorded by an operational system and subsequently stored onto a data warehouse with millions of similar events. Of course the longer the data stays on the warehouse, the more of it there is. The greater the amount of detail, that is, nonsummarized information, the larger the databases—and thus, the data warehouse—become.

Only a handful of commercial companies have experimented with petabyte-class data volumes, which remain the domain of research laboratories and universities. But by the time you read this, your bank or telephone company might just be there.

Multidimensional Databases

Multidimensional databases (MDDs) have advanced over the data-warehousing landscape like a stormy weather front, hard to ignore and threatening the status quo. While they often fall under the relational heading, sharing the structure of tables populated with rows and columns, they are constructed differently from traditional relational databases.

Instead of each table having a long list of attributes, MDDs contain "dimensions" that are normally separate descriptive structures. These dimensions dictate the queries that can and cannot be asked. For example:

> *Show me the average number of weekly*
> *shipments to general merchandisers in the*
> *southeast region.*

This is a valid query. However, if the shipment data available is summarized by month instead of by week, the above query will return an error message, not an answer.

You could easily compare multidimensional databases with three-dimensional spreadsheets. Multidimensional databases are generally intended for frequently submitted queries and those that deal with summarized information, much like the OLAP examples presented in chapter 2. MDDs are designed with rapid access in mind, enabling data searches through specialized indexing and intertable relationships. This prevents the RDBMS from having to pass over large amounts of tabular data to find the data elements it needs. They are ill suited for voluminous detail, so the concise, aggregated data in most MDDs can be loaded into memory, giving end-users speedy data access.

Most OLAP tools use MDD-type structures to perform the drill-down they were designed for. Beyond OLAP, there is significant debate about when MDDs are preferable to relational databases, if at all. Current theories posit that end-users have embraced MDDs more for data marts because of their ease of use. However, the greater the amount of data required, the more preferable large relational data warehouses, since MDDs become more difficult to manage and lose their performance edge with greater data volumes.[3]

It's increasingly common for MDDs to coexist with their larger relational brethren, with the MDDs serving as OLAP query engines—often on data marts—and the relational databases acting as enterprisewide data servers.

---

3. Paller, Alan, "A Roadmap to Data Warehousing," in *Planning and Designing the Data Warehouse,* Upper Saddle River, NJ: Prentice Hall, 1996, 25.

Metadata

Even businesspeople should understand what metadata is: data about data. Metadata supplies definitions about the data in a database and is stored in tables, much like the data it annotates.

Data definitions through metadata solve a variety of problems. In order for users to get value from names, postal codes, addresses, risk scores, or other data elements, these elements should be presented in a standardized and understandable way. Data that means the same thing but is stored in various ways can confound a well-intentioned end-user.

By having standard data definitions, a company protects its data warehouse, and vice versa. For example, database administrators can come and go, but the data definitions will remain meaningful and consistent. Comprehensive metadata definitions mean never having to explain what a given data element really signifies. Metadata also buffers the system from endless user searches by allowing users to query metadata in order to ensure that what they're looking for indeed exists, and where it is. The metadata can tell the user which database or table to query.

Metadata is a topic of endless discussion in data warehousing. The concept of metadata came along only after many data warehouses were already in use. By providing data definitions and navigational information, metadata thus renders data warehouses easier to use. However, the claim that data warehouses can't exist without metadata, though often made, is a bit of a stretch.

A large part of the metadata controversy is that there has been no widely accepted standard for how data definitions should be stored. Without a standard, various definitions might exist for the same logical data element. For example, is a "customer" someone with an active account, or someone with a billing address? The lack of a metadata standard makes it difficult for different software tools to share data. A group called the Metadata Coalition, comprising various data warehousing vendors, has recently defined a metadata storage model, and since Microsoft belongs to the coalition, it's likely that this standard will stick.

There are three basic types of metadata:

1. *Business Metadata.* Also known as end-user metadata, business metadata provides business definitions for specific data attributes. Business metadata is used most often by users searching for interpretations before or after submitting queries, and it usually describes specific data elements. An example of business metadata might be the following:

SIC: SIC stands for Special Industry Code, designating the customer's industry type. SIC codes represent a standard and are supplied by the customer and confirmed internally before data is loaded.

Business metadata can also include descriptions of data source systems, data synonyms, data access restrictions, valid values, and business rules to annotate derived data, among other annotations.

2. *Database Metadata.* Database metadata defines the terms used in the database, particularly names of database objects: databases, tables, and columns. For example, while the definition of a "product" might be given in business metadata, annotating the product table would be the job of database metadata:

The product table contains the attribute of a single product, including its identifying characteristics and descriptions. Product table data originates from the product information in the customer billing system and is updated monthly with each new billing system refresh. Each product has a primary name, but may also have a secondary name (see the Product Names table).

Database metadata also includes administrative information, such as source system mapping information. This metadata might include anything from the name of the source system from which the data originated to the date and time when the data was most recently loaded to the contact name and telephone number of the staff member supporting the source system.

3. *Application Metadata.* Application metadata explains certain terms and functions within an end-user's application tool and should be confined to application-level terminology to avoid confusion. For example:

Monthly Sales Report: The monthly sales report icon runs the roll-up report of monthly product sales by territory. It can be accessed by sales vice presidents, sales managers, and those with specified access rights. The monthly sales report is available three days after the last day of the previous month.

Metadata not only defines terms, it helps users and technical personnel find data without having to browse tables in the warehouse. In addition, metadata is sometimes used by the application tools to navigate through data in the data warehouse.

Metadata is usually stored in a specially designated area on the warehouse called a metadata repository. This raises another controversial issue: metadata storage. Given the range of possible information about a data element, metadata can consume almost as many resources as the data it seeks to explain, including the tools needed to define and catalogue the metadata and the additional disk space required to store it. And let's not forget the biggest cost factor of all: the staff time needed to implement and maintain it.

Disseminating the Information: Application Software

As we saw in chapter 2, various kinds of analysis can be carried out using data in a data warehouse, and each type of analysis has its own set of tools.

Application front-end tools enable a user to perform three tasks: (1) request the data (a data request is called a query); (2) inspect the data; and (3) format the data in different ways.

Even companies that have carefully choreographed their technology acquisition processes often end up spending either too much time evaluating front-end tools (usually at the expense of the underlying database) or not enough (usually focusing on tactics particular to data sourcing and loading).

The delicate dance of technology selection should be planned well in advance. Compared to the selection of the data warehouse hardware and DBMS, choosing an application tool seems simple. However, it can often be the most important decision made.

The fact is, users want a tool that's easy to use and gives them the data they need. They don't care about which database software is on the data warehouse, whether the queries are compatible with industry standards, or whether the hardware is single-platform or distributed. The fact that the user's view into the data warehouse is through the application software interface means that choosing the right application tool is one of the most important decisions of all.

Since the front-end tool is the only technology component of the data warehouse the user ever sees, it is often the best indicator of user satisfaction.

What are some of these tools deployed in data warehouses? The following sections list the various types of application tools.

Graphical User Interfaces

By far the most popular type of tool, GUIs prove the maxim that a picture is worth a thousand words. GUI tools let nontechnical businesspeople examine data via buttons, arrows, and icons rather than text. Thus, instead of typing out queries using a programming language like SQL, the user can simply click on a desktop icon that represents a query.

Depending on your company's environment, GUI tools normally work under the Windows operating system, but they may also work in Macintosh and Sun environments. Figure 5-9 shows an example of a GUI application screen.

Of course, some behind-the-scenes work takes place before the user can log on and retrieve data. An application programmer must customize the user interface to present the functions the user requires. The user can perform further customization by saving her own canned queries and arranging the desktop so that certain icons represent certain functions.

GUI tools have proved a boon to business users by moving data reporting from the programmer's desktop to the hands of the everyday businessperson in need of more data, and faster.

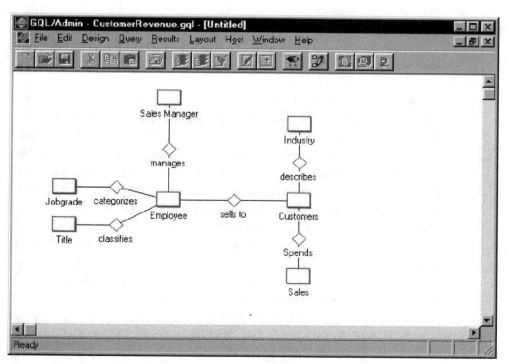

Figure 5-9: A GUI Screen

A Word About the Web

Web-based tools are quickly catching on in data warehousing because companies can quickly deploy these applications to a large number of people using existing Internet technologies.

Even the easiest-to-use GUI tools present a deployment nightmare. Many companies have experienced the short-lived euphoria of completing their first data warehouse application: The data is on the warehouse. Users have signed off on its quality. The GUI front end has been developed and tested. And one hundred impatient users are waiting to get the application tool onto their PC workstations in order to start submitting queries.

So how does the GUI tool get on everyone's PC? Most companies use communication software to distribute the tool electronically. Users receive the tool via e-mail or some other mechanism, along with documentation on how to install it on their PC.

Companies are using the Internet more and more to obtain information from a variety of sources. Since the Internet is external and global, it offers an ever-increasing panoply of data. Conversely, a company's intranet—its internal, proprietary network—allows information to be distributed across company organizations and staff, and enables even greater access to both internal and external data.

Companies lacking a robust communications infrastructure are forced to install data warehouse applications manually on each end-user's desktop. I once worked with a pharmaceutical company whose employees were first-rate database experts. As we readied the front-end tool for distribution, one poor guy was elected to load the tool on a floppy disk and go around logging on to the PCs of all 46 new users to install the application. Of course, the users weren't about to give up their passwords, so the hapless installer was forced to wait for every user to be physically present and logged on before he could load the new tool.

This, of course, took weeks. And don't even ask about maintenance versions (user-requested updates and fixes to the application). Until the company marshaled its own intranet, all new data warehouse tools were installed manually.

What's the difference between Web-based applications and standard GUI tools? The major distinction is the ease with which Web applications are configured and deployed. For one thing, they don't require significant system resources such as memory and hard disk space, because the processing occurs on a Web server (remember the second tier?). This setup is drastically different from that of a desktop PC, which requires a specific hardware and software configuration in order to support and run a GUI tool.

The Web server enables the processing to take place outside the user's desktop environment, which makes it easier to ensure that adequate technology exists for the Web application. Also, since GUI tools require significant memory and disk space, a data warehouse user's PC is often configured with decision support analysis as the worst-case scenario. "GUI tools are pigs," as a techie might put it, in that they consume significant workstation resources.

Since Web-based decision support applications are run on a separate server, they are more efficient at preserving computing resources and could save significant money on PC upgrades over time.

Development Definitions and Differentiators

Most of the tools used to implement and access a data warehouse can be categorized as "development tools." Here are a few additional classifications you should be aware of before we move on to implementation.

OLAP Subcategories

New product categories pop up all the time. In the race to come up with the latest technology marvel, vendors constantly reinvent or, worse, redefine technologies and their classifications.

Consider OLAP (*online analytical processing*), as we did in chapter 2. Once OLAP functionality arrived on the scene, people were captivated by its functional capabilities. Enter ROLAP (*relational online analytical processing*). ROLAP allowed OLAP to access relational tables directly with SQL. To differentiate themselves from ROLAP tools, non-ROLAP products began referring to themselves as MOLAP (*multidimensional online analytical processing*). These tools load data into an intermediate structure—usually a three-dimensional "cube"—in order to speed up response time. Figure 5-10 illustrates MOLAP versus ROLAP tools.

Believe it or not, there's also DOLAP—database OLAP—a variation of ROLAP that migrates OLAP functionality directly into the relational DBMS, not to mention HOLAP, which stands for hybrid OLAP—if the data is already stored in the MDD structure, it will be used; if not, it will be accessed from the underlying relational database.

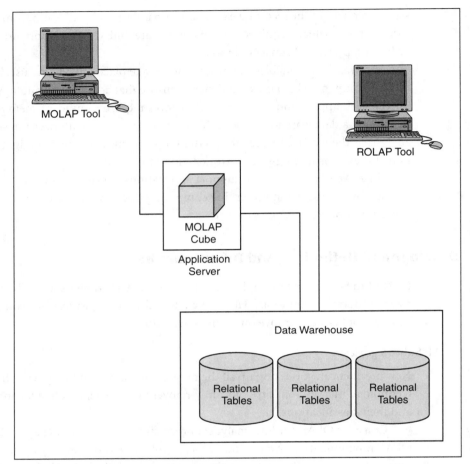

Figure 5-10: MOLAP versus ROLAP

Try to understand the difference between the many products that adopt these acronyms and you'll be frustrated. Try instead to define the specific functionality that you and your company need and then find the tool that best meets those needs; the importance of the acronyms will quickly recede amidst the value of the resulting application.

Data Modeling and Design Tools

Another important term in data warehouse implementation is data modeling. We'll talk about data modeling a little more later in the book, but for now let's define it as the means for identifying the data elements in the data warehouse, the relationships among them, and the overall structure of that data.

The practice of data modeling—that is, developing a logical view of the business entities that will serve as the basis for the eventual tables on the data warehouse—occupies a significant share of the data warehouse practitioner's mindset. A myriad of books and magazine articles have expounded on the subjects of logical data modeling (developing a conceptual view of the business components that mandate data) and database design (translating those business components into actual table definitions). Data modelers like arguing about the best methods with which to develop data models and design databases. This takes lots of time.

Data-modeling tools help data warehouse developers—principally database administrators—delimit what the tables in the database will look like, how they are defined, and their relationships to one another. They also define metadata and help generate certain programming code that defines table layouts to the DBMS.

In instances where the tool transcends the simple illustration of data objects and validates relationships, sometimes translating a data model from its logical form to a more physical and thus implementable structure, data-modeling tools are called CASE (computer-aided software engineering) tools. Similar to the system an architect might use to design a house, CASE tools automate database design. They replace work that might previously have been performed manually and are characterized by their ability to display various database objects—tables, databases, and indexes—graphically and generate code to create these objects.

There are many CASE tools on the market from vendors ranging from those that specialize in development tools (Popkin, Rational Software) to those that manufacture key components of the warehouse (Oracle, Hewlett-Packard). However, off-the-shelf data models are increasingly available from various software companies. These data models are usually industry-specific and can be customized to suit a company's specific data inventory. This customization drastically reduces the time it would otherwise take to develop a data model from scratch.

We'll talk about data modeling and its significance to implementation in the next chapter. Suffice it to say here that data modeling and database design, while small parts of the overall data warehouse development lifecycle, are critical to the successful development of a useful data warehouse. As a result, they receive the lion's share of attention when it comes to debates about methods and conventions.

For now, it's important to understand that data modeling and CASE tools are assumed to be part of your collection of data warehouse development tools.

They help delineate the structure of the data warehouse tables and can prepare the data warehouse for what the source data—the data from the operational systems—will look like.

The selection of modeling tools and conventions is one of the few areas where end-user input is not required. Indeed, arguments among the database administrators (DBAs) for your company's databases should keep modeling tools in the foreground without a lot of involvement from the business side.

Data Extraction and Loading Tools

Savvy technology vendors saw the potential for data extraction tools as soon as the first data warehouses emerged, mainly because extracting data from source systems and loading it onto the data warehouse was more complicated than anyone had imagined.

It wasn't so much the extraction itself that was the problem, nor was it the data loading. In fact, it was all the work that needed to be done in between to "transform" the data from its often cryptic transactional formats into meaningful information that could be queried by business users.

The cottage industry in extract-conditioning tools, known either as data migration tools or ETL (*extraction, transformation,* and *loading*), soon became a booming business for database, hardware, and specialty vendors alike. These tools do not merely gather data from one place and put it someplace else; they are also capable of the following:

- gathering data from disparate operational systems
- converting the data from one format to another
- changing the data to be more meaningful or complete
- loading the modified data onto the target data warehouse

ETL technologies (see figure 5-11) have evolved over the years and have become increasingly easy to use. Most of them are GUI-based and provide the data transformation process with additional rigor through procedures and rules for data transformation. They can also generate metadata, yielding definitions for both the source data coming in and the resulting data being loaded onto the warehouse. Often, ETL tools are coupled with modeling tools to provide a comprehensive, end-to-end data definition environment that tracks and annotates data from its system of origin through to its destination on the warehouse.

If you are an IT manager or staff member, you probably already know that different data extraction tools have different features, and you should do your

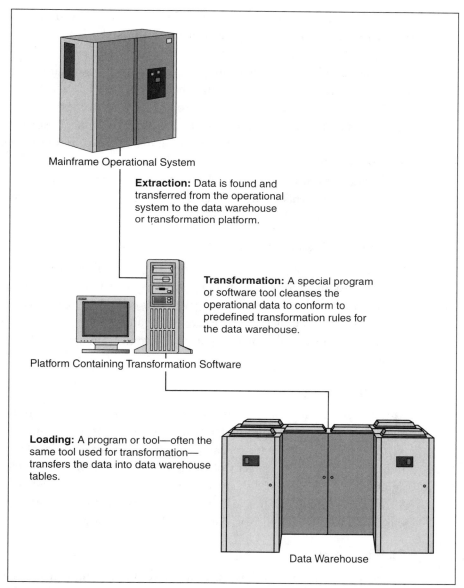

Mainframe Operational System

Extraction: Data is found and transferred from the operational system to the data warehouse or transformation platform.

Transformation: A special program or software tool cleanses the operational data to conform to predefined transformation rules for the data warehouse.

Platform Containing Transformation Software

Loading: A program or tool—often the same tool used for transformation—transfers the data into data warehouse tables.

Data Warehouse

Figure 5-11: Extraction, Transformation, and Loading

research before choosing one. Keep the skill sets of your data administrators and DBAs in mind when selecting such a tool. Although "report extractors" are emerging that shift database population responsibilities away from IT to end-users, be careful what you wish for. The end-user who can transform her own source data isn't far from implementing her own personal data mart.

If you are an executive or manager from the line of business, you should have the end result in mind: clear, consistent, meaningful data that business users can interpret once they access it. If data must be manipulated or reformatted by an end-user before it is understandable, the ETL technology or process has failed. Don't forget that it's the responsibility of the end-user community—not the IT group—to clarify what "understandable" ultimately means and to define how the target data should look once it's loaded.

Management and Administration Tools

There is an array of additional tools to manage and fine-tune the data warehouse environment, particularly on the database side. Once a data warehouse is up and running, IT staff are constantly working behind the scenes with a diverse set of technologies to perform a variety of ongoing activities. The following list describes the principal management and administration tasks that regularly occur.

Capacity Planning

As the data warehouse grows and more data is added, its ability to handle the ongoing load must be monitored. Capacity planning means continuously gauging the capability of the hardware and software to support additional data and/or additional users. Often, capacity planning results in a hardware upgrade, usually signifying the addition of disk space or processing power to the data warehouse. A software upgrade involves loading the vendor's most recent software release, which usually results in increased functionality or performance.

Backup/Restore

The more a data warehouse is used, the more precious the e-data becomes. To ensure the data's ongoing availability, a system or database administrator will regularly back up the data warehouse, copying some or all of the critical data to tape. This safeguard ensures that if something goes wrong and data is corrupted, data from the last backup can be restored onto the data warehouse. The more frequently backups are made, the more current the restored data will be.

Security Administration

Data warehouses store valuable cargo in the form of information about your customers, your proprietary products, your cost allocations, or your revenues. Not everyone should be looking at all this data, which is why security is so important in data warehousing. Security can be implemented at three different levels:

- The database level—only certain users can access certain databases or tables in the data warehouse.
- The application level—certain users can access certain applications (each of which in turn has its own data access rights).
- A combination of database security and application level security—this can be customized for each user.

There are several automated ways to enforce data warehouse security, most notably by using middleware to perform certain gatekeeper functions before allowing an end-user to submit a query.

Access Tracking and Usage Logging

Access tracking means monitoring what data users are looking at on the warehouse. Access tracking lets database administrators keep track of which data is most in demand, plan regular data refreshes, and know how often certain data should be backed up.

Usage logging means actually keeping an online record of who logs on to the data warehouse, either directly or through a specific application. This step allows database administrators to know exactly which users access and use the data warehouse, and how often.

Knowing who uses the data warehouse most can help a company determine anything from hardware upgrades to budget allocations. I once saw a group of several financial analysts lobby for months to gain access to revenue data on the warehouse. However, once the application was ready and the logon IDs had been allocated, not one person from the angry mob had actually logged on to the data warehouse! You can be sure that this fact was considered the next time this group clamored for data.

Performance Tuning and Monitoring

There's an old data warehouse adage about reports taking longer to run than queries, making the point that users' expectations about performance can be very subjective. Performance monitoring involves watching the data warehouse's utilization of resources—disk space, memory, etc.—for individual queries. Tracking query response time on a regular basis can show a system administrator if database resources are becoming saturated, thus providing information to aid in upgrades or capacity planning.

At a lower level, performance monitoring can result in special access privileges or additional resources for specific users or user groups, who either use the data warehouse more often or require faster turnaround time for specific queries. In addition, the DBA can make certain adjustments to the tables in the database to speed up data access, tuning the database according to the ongoing and changing dynamics of its usage.

Performance tuning also means recalibrating end-users' response time expectations at certain times, for example, when more data is loaded or during certain maintenance activities.

Putting It All Together

The process of combining the range of disparate technologies described in this chapter is called "integration." Entire consulting firms have sprung up overnight to answer the call of harried companies trying to tackle the integration of their systems or applications. While the process is not confined to data warehousing, integrating hardware and software products and making them work with as little customization as possible now constitute an IT holy grail for many companies.

The integration issue is often avoided altogether by customers seeking the path of least resistance, who instead choose a single large company to provide all the pieces and parts of a data warehouse, from the hardware platform to the DBMS to the middleware to the application tools.

However, this isn't always the best approach. Your users could adore their new application tool, but the DBMS could be tediously slow, making businesspeople yearn for the paper reports of yore. Conversely, the e-data in the data warehouse could be pristine and the responses to queries lightning fast, but if users were to find their tools arduous to handle, the data warehouse would become nothing more than a very large and expensive paperweight.

The great technology dilemma—not limited to data warehousing, but encompassing a range of business systems—continues: Should a company rely on one vendor to supply all of its data-warehousing needs, or should it pick and choose from a variety of "best of breed" products?

Companies such as Oracle, NCR, and IBM have come up with packaged solutions, many not limited to data warehousing, explicitly designed for single industries. These companies and others offer tool "suites," which are integrated with the vendors' metadata and database management tools. The advantage of this approach is that information can flow easily between the products' different modules, and users and technicians alike can have a seamless view of the use and management of the data warehouse. A single vendor's varied tool sets can talk to and understand one another, and terminology and data definitions are consistent across the different technology layers.

But what about functionality? Imagine the very likely scenario that at some point your company's end-users see a demonstration at a conference or read a magazine article about a software tool that does exactly what they need. The only problem is that the tool is not currently in use anywhere in the company. Furthermore, it is not subsidized by the IT department, and the vice president of business systems has never heard of it. Do you want to be the one to explain that the new product that will address their needs does not show up on your company's approved vendor list?[4]

If your data warehouse is going to meet the disparate and ever-changing business requirements that necessitated it in the first place, it will become a microcosm of technology, leveraging products with a diverse set of functions from a variety of hardware and software vendors. Figure 5-12 typifies a data warehouse platform architecture that incorporates a variety of hardware and software products.

The more mature your data warehouse becomes, the more likely it is that different components of its architecture will come from different vendors. The company looking to one vendor to solve all of its problems is asking to be held hostage, straitjacketing its business users as they become more data-savvy. The vendor willing to do it is asking for a delivery nightmare.

---

4. Most companies have an approved vendor list, but few people actually know about it until they want to purchase a product or service from a vendor that's not on the list. Then, suddenly, the approved vendor list assumes the authority of the Ten Commandments. In their effort to control prices and prevent overkill, approved vendor lists usually hurt companies by limiting vendor competition and thus driving prices upward. So be a rule breaker. Go with the vendor offering the best service for the best price.

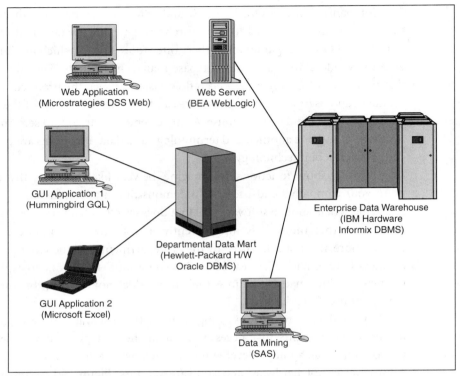

Figure 5-12: A Multivendor Data Warehouse Scenario

Some Lingering Questions

As detailed as it was, this chapter was by no means an exhaustive review of every possible data-warehousing technology category or product. Hopefully, it answered some of your basic questions and illuminated some of those nagging definitional doubts you had in the back of your mind.

Reading this chapter made me nervous: I'm a financial analyst, not a technician. Do I really need to be on intimate terms with the architecture of my data warehouse and the administrative work that takes place?

Not if everything's working fine. The problem comes when the data warehouse is too slow, or your application can't access certain data, or the data you want doesn't exist. Often the answers to these problems involve technology, and the more you know, the greater the degree with which you can become part of the solution—or at least sound extremely well informed!

My department is developing its own data mart. We're being realistic and know we'll end up using products from different vendors. So which ones do we call first?

Keep two things in mind:

1. The RDBMS is really the heart of the data warehouse. It's a lot easier to change your hardware platform or add another application software tool after a false start than it is to transfer everything over to a brand-new database product. Include your IT department in discussions of specific database functional requirements and performance expectations.

2. Having said that, get your users to start thinking now about what they need from an application. Develop two lists of features: an "A list" of required features, and a "B list" of nice-to-haves. Start researching tools that meet the needs on both lists, making sure that at a minimum they are ODBC-compliant. That way it's more than likely that when the time comes, your selected tool(s) will work with your selected database.

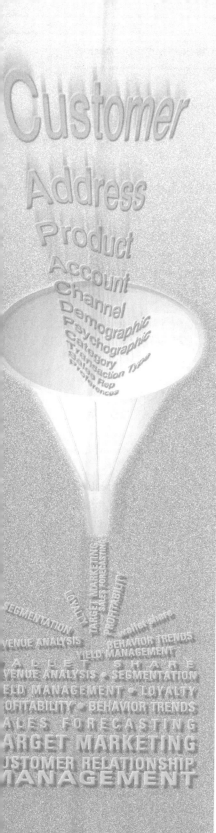

CHAPTER SIX

What Managers Should Know About Implementation

If Sophocles was right and nothing vast ever entered human life without a curse, then the curse of data warehouses must surely be the suffering that companies go through to implement them.

There's a data warehouse project plan on the desk of almost every chief information officer (CIO). Sometimes it's been developed with the help of a good consultant. Sometimes it's homegrown. Either way, most companies have a data warehouse methodology or standard project plan, and most feature the old standby tasks:

- Develop the business case.
- Create the project plan.
- Hire staff.
- Design the database.
- Identify data sources.
- Load data.
- Test.

Of course, the above list is incomplete. There are other things involved in data warehouse implementation. This chapter serves to fill in the blanks, guiding you through the subterranean alleyways of data warehouse development in order to reveal some of its secrets.

We're not discussing "how to implement your data warehouse" here. There are plenty of books that already do a fine job of that. Instead, we'll introduce implementation steps and discuss the areas that will be helpful for you to understand in case you're preparing your next project, recruiting staff, evaluating a new consulting firm, or considering adopting a development methodology of your own.

What You Should Know About Data Warehouse Methodologies

Up till recently, data warehouse conferences focused more on the intricacies of the evaluation, architecture, design, installation, loading, development, integration, and deployment of data warehouses than they did on discussing how they were being used. Seminars on everything from data cleanup to workload management to implementing process controls drew awed attendees hoping to glean a few as yet unlearned tidbits that they could put into practice.

In the late 1980s and early 1990s, the showpiece presentation at these conferences was alternately named either "A Methodology for Implementing Your Data Warehouse" or "A Rapid Approach to Data Warehouse Development." These presentations were always particularly well attended, and one's peripheral vision always revealed participants scribbling away on their handouts. I too succumbed to the surefire methodology mania. My presentation was called "A Data Warehouse Implementation Roadmap."

This roadmap, shown in figure 6-1, is one of several examples of a methodology that works.

This roadmap represents only a high-level view. Each step shown is really a process in its own right. The extraction step involves several activities, for example:

- choosing extraction and loading tools
- performing migration planning
- identifying source systems
- identifying discrete source data elements
- developing extract routines or code

As important as these steps are the three major phases of the roadmap: (1) business analysis, (2) database development, and (3) application development. These phases ensure that consideration is given to each area, that the phases— not the steps—are linear, and that the output of one phase serves as input to another. Let's look at each phase in turn:

1. *Business Analysis.* This phase ensures that the organization obtains a thorough understanding of the business problem(s) the data warehouse is intended

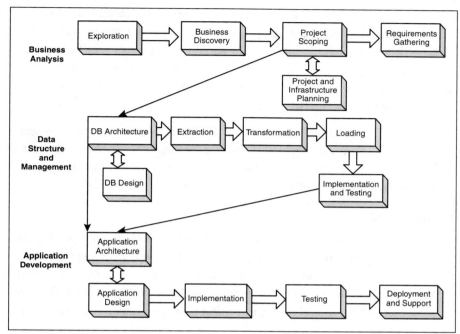

Figure 6-1: The Baseline Data Warehouse Implementation Roadmap

to solve. War stories of failed data warehouses that didn't conform to stated requirements abound in the industry. Business analysis ensures that requirements are gathered, understood, documented, and authorized before formal implementation begins. Furthermore, this phase ensures that the pieces are in place before development begins.

The business analysis process should reveal answers to the following three questions:

    a. What is the fundamental problem or problem set?
    b. Does someone "own" the problem?
    c. Is the problem data-related? Can data help solve it?

2. *Database Development.* Since the database is the foundation of the data warehouse, the objective of this phase is to enforce the necessary rigor on selecting, designing, extracting, transforming, and loading the data. It also ensures that the database is designed separately from the application, resulting in the best approach, rather than just the easiest.

3. *Application Development.* This phase guarantees that the tools used to access the data are developed to coexist and conform seamlessly to the overall data warehouse architecture. In addition, it enforces specific tasks related to the programming and deployment of the data warehouse application to end-users. (Application testing, deployment, and training are often ignored even by seasoned practitioners.)

Ever hear the one about the difference between a methodologist and a terrorist? (You can negotiate with the terrorist.) So it goes with data warehouse implementation methods. Every consultant has one—and only one—and will lay down his life in order to justify its superiority over all others.

Evaluating a Methodology

Regardless of whether you already have a methodology, are looking into acquiring one, or are thinking about building your own, here are a few questions to which you should have the answers before your friendly consultant slaps a fat binder in front of you introducing his sacrosanct data-warehousing methodology, or before your project manager wants your signature on his project plan.

- Does the methodology combine phases or activities that should be separate? If there is a large step called "Development," be careful! Certain activities in data warehousing, including requirements gathering, project scoping, project planning, application testing, and data validation should be distinct from one another so as to avoid overlap and ensure execution.
- Is the methodology or project plan incomplete? Many do not go beyond the point when the data is loaded onto the data warehouse. Stopping here omits some of the most important development work of all: application development, testing, and deployment. The best methodologies actually consider end-user training and ongoing support as part of the deployment process. Make sure that your candidate methodology or project plan considers post–database development tasks.
- Has the methodology been reengineered? Look closely and you might find that the methodology is a reworked version of an older client/server development procedure, or that the project plan mirrors that of your most recent operational system. While data warehouse development has a lot in common with other technology implementation undertakings, the implementation plan should support the following capabilities:

—separate data-sourcing and data-loading activities

—distinct user-interviewing and requirements-gathering activities

—testing for data quality, application acceptance, and integration[1]

—discrete application development steps

—data validation and data-testing activities

—dedicated time for tuning once deployment occurs

- Does the methodology require external consultants to fill key positions? It should, in fact, enable your full-time staff to lead the project, with consultants acting as guides or subject matter experts. Ideally, the project manager should come from your organization. Look askance at any methodology that requires external consultants to assume the helm for all principal activities. Unless you're considering outsourcing development or have found it impossible to obtain the adequate skill sets, your staff should fill lead development positions.

- Does the methodology consist only of a big document full of lists? It should, at a minimum, contain both instructions and sample deliverables for key tasks. Better yet, the methodology can combine documentation with software to help enforce the tactics along the way.

Should your company spend time developing a customized methodology for data warehousing? Probably not. You're better off purchasing a sound development guide that is clear, tactical, and contains repeatable tasks. After the first few implementation iterations, your staff will have turned into the experts you've spent years looking for. Moreover, they will have learned enough to use what works and toss what doesn't, resulting in a development method that is de facto tailored to your organization.

The Data Warehouse Implementation Process

In this section we'll take a more detailed look at some of the principal steps illustrated in figure 6-1. First let's briefly examine each of the steps.

---

1. "Integration testing" means ensuring that newly developed technology works with existing technology that it may need to communicate with. For example, the new application works with the company's standard workstation environment, or the new data warehouse can send and receive data over the network. Since data warehouses can often be orders of magnitude larger than other corporate technologies, and since they often rely upon mission-critical systems such as corporate networks and mainframes, integration testing is critical.

The Steps in Business Analysis

The following five steps make up the business analysis phase of the roadmap:

1. *Exploration.* This step ensures that data warehousing is truly the right answer to the company's questions. During exploration, a company may choose to perform a number of different activities that may not be directly related to data warehousing but can nevertheless provide clues to whether data warehousing is a solution whose time has come. These activities may include best-practice benchmarking,[2] strategic technology alignment work, corporate process redesign, or the establishment of a balanced scorecard.

2. *Business Discovery.* Business discovery is the high-level examination of the relative need, pain, or problem, documenting business drivers and high-level requirements that can justify a data warehouse. This process confirms that the problem the company aims to address with its data warehouse can actually be solved by e-data (instead of, for example, instigating process improvements). While in most cases business discovery is done for enterprise-level data warehouses, data marts can also benefit from the activity. Business discovery identifies a hierarchy of need and defines the boundaries of the initial implementation project.

3. *Project Scoping.* Scoping a data warehouse project should be a discrete step carried out before project planning occurs. While many organizations are tempted to treat scoping as a mere formality, it in fact helps narrow down specific time and resources for the project and defines initial deliverables. Most of all, scoping ensures that staff members can be lined up before actual development begins. Scoping also helps cement budget estimations. In short, scoping your data warehouse project is an insurance policy against failure.[3]

4. *Project and Infrastructure Planning.* This step readies your organization for the development of a data warehouse by ensuring that your chosen methodology is reflected in a tactical project plan and that the requisite infrastructure is put in place to support it. This means everything from making sure that develop-

---

2. Best-practice benchmarking is the process of examining other companies that are acknowledged industry or technology leaders. In the case of data warehousing, it's sometimes used to evaluate if and how new ways of e-data distribution have indeed resulted in benefits. See chapter 9 for more on best-practice benchmarking.

3. See: Dyché, Jill, "Scoping Your Data Mart Implementation," *DBMS*, August 1998.

ment workstations have compatible software products and versions to securing adequate seating space and meeting rooms. It also establishes a communications planning strategy to be followed throughout the initial and successive projects.

5. *Requirements Gathering.* This stage comprises consensus building, interviewing, and often complaint sessions. Requirements gathering lays out the functional objectives for each decision support application, large or small, and is considered by many to be the linchpin of implementation. Requirements gathering can define objectives, for example, loading three years of customer sales history in the data warehouse, or displaying results via pie charts. It identifies initial subject area data and should include the documentation of objectives and success metrics.

The Steps in Data Structure and Management

Given our prior assertion that the database is the hub in the wheel of data warehousing, the database itself must be well understood and implemented prior to application construction. The database structure development and management phase comprises the following steps:

1. *Architecture.* Architecture involves not only evaluating and selecting specific database and database-related technologies but also planning how those technologies work with one another, and with the company's in-place systems. This step ensures that the data warehouse is both functional and compatible with the existing technology infrastructure.

2. *Database Design.* Database design can begin in tandem with architecture development, since the initial design will focus on business requirements and evolve to incorporate actual available data. The database design task encompasses both the development of a data model and a physical design that defines the actual table constructs and involves tuning for performance. Design activities also establish the level of detail.

3. *Extraction, Transformation, and Loading.* The purpose of these steps is to examine the physical database design in order to source specific data elements, as well as actually create the transformation and loading routines. In the best cases, data extraction and loading can often be performed using a database vendor's utilities, warranting little or no programming. However, many companies still spend time coding custom programs to extract cryptic data from their various source systems. In either case, this step is never quite as easy as it first appears.

4. *Implementation and Testing.* Your DBA will probably load the database(s) onto the warehouse several times before the final load. The database is tested to ensure that it accurately reflects the business's information needs and can support its processes. End-users are often involved in the data validation part of database testing. Once testing has been completed, the final load can occur, and the application development can begin.

The Steps in Application Development

Once the physical design of the database has been confirmed, application development can begin. This phase encompasses the following steps:

1. *Architecture.* Just as database development involves selecting and integrating the relevant technologies, application architecture involves identifying development and support technologies. These technologies aren't limited to the application software to be used for end-user queries; they are also tools to synchronize different versions of software, aid developers in integrating their programs, and enable remote access, among other tasks. Application architecture also entails tying back the proposed technologies to the already chosen database technologies to ensure seamless integration.

2. *Design.* Amidst all their development responsibilities, programmers often forget about application design. This task leverages the requirements that have been gathered, as well as additional end-user input, to evaluate how users expect to see and use the information on their desktops. This step helps programmers define data presentation techniques and ensure an acceptable "look and feel" for the application.

3. *Implementation.* Application implementation represents the actual programming of the application software and may include design reviews, prototyping, and query development.

4. *Testing.* Thorough application development requires several different testing steps:

- test design and development
- functional testing
- integration testing
- user acceptance testing

Testing, which involves developers and end-users, employs various methods of validation and authorization.

5. *Deployment and Support.* The distribution of application code and database access to users is known as application deployment. Deployment doesn't mean making an application available to a set of users just one time; it represents an iterative approach to constantly tuning and fixing applications to make them more functional and usable over time. Supporting these applications can mean anything from designating a subject matter expert to help end-users adopt and learn an application to setting up a help desk for ongoing assistance. This stage also takes user training and application documentation into consideration.

Who Should Be Doing What?

The nature of staff involvement in a data warehouse project depends heavily on several factors, including the type of company, the internal organizational structure, the existence of a formal IT department and its influence, and the executive who's sponsoring development of the warehouse.

Figure 6-2 illustrates a sample data warehouse development organization. The picture represents a real-life organization chart for an ongoing enterprise data warehouse development project. (Data mart development doesn't involve as many separate roles.) Note that each development team is organized a little differently. When it comes to organizing yours, although the actual reporting structure and titles will probably vary, make sure that each of these functions is covered in some way.

Your development team may not need every role, or you may well be able to combine several roles into one (the DBA might also load the data, for example).

The main functions shown in figure 6-2 are described in the set of tables discussed in the next section.

Development Job Roles and Responsibilities

While your particular data warehouse development organization may not require every function described here, you can use the following tables to evaluate whether and how you will fill the described roles. Each table covers the key roles and responsibilities involved in each function illustrated in figure 6-2. You might want to use the descriptions as a checklist for your existing development team, or as a recruiting guide once you do launch your development project.

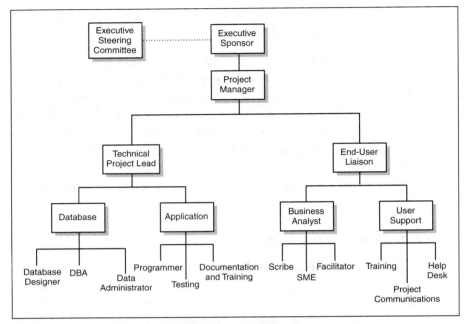

Figure 6-2: Data Warehouse Development Roles

Note that this section assumes that your company has some level of IT staff and processes in place. The job descriptions in tables 6-1 to 6-4 are specific to data warehouse development and thus don't include more general roles such as "chief architect" or "quality assurance manager." These functions may be involved in the development of your data warehouse, but they aren't exclusive to it.

Job titles marked with an asterisk (*) in the tables denote roles that may be filled by external consultants. All other jobs should originate—and stay—within the company, meaning that they should be performed by full-time permanent staff members.

"Wait a minute!" you cry. "Our data administrator is testing the data, our programmers are maintaining our business metadata, and I don't *know* how our data is getting into the warehouse, since we don't have a data loader!"

It's OK. These tables aren't meant to define a rigid structure for you to follow as much as they are intended to describe the individual job functions necessary. The larger the company, the more likely it is that each role will be filled by a specific person, or in many cases a team of people. (Ever seen a herd of DBAs? Scary.)

Table 6-1: Management Roles

Job Title	Description	Representative Responsibilities
Executive sponsor	The executive sponsor is normally a management staff member from the company's executive management or line of business (as opposed to IT). Ideally, the executive sponsor manages one or more departments in which the data warehouse's target end-users work. She is the focal point for high-level decision making and usually contributes some or all of the development funding.	Represent the data warehouse and its development status to upper management. Establish the data warehouse vision. Assist in authoring the data warehouse project mission statement. Participate in high-level project planning activities. Participate in hiring key contributors. Act as a tie-breaker in cases of conflict.
Technical project lead	The technical project lead works with the database and application development groups to define project activities and establish completion measures. He usually takes the lead in planning the overall solution architecture. He is also involved in the establishment of skill sets for each role and in the interviewing	Align project plan with chosen development methodology. Verify technical components of project plan. Interview and recruit staff. Participate in technical briefings and design reviews.

continued

Table 6-1 (*continued*)

Job Title	Description	Representative Responsibilities
	and recruitment of development staff.	
Administrative project manager*	The administrative project manager coordinates and manages the development project overall, oversees the project's day-to-day activities, and maintains the project plan. She works with the executive sponsor and technical project manager to define time frames and monitors progress and slippage.	Create/ maintain project plan. Hold periodic status meetings. Communicate project progress to executive sponsor. Organize facilities. Track ongoing issues and their resolution.

Table 6-2: Requirements Development Roles

Job Title	Description	Representative Responsibilities
User liaison/ project communications	This role serves as a buffer between end-users and development staff, as well as a central resource to which end-users can communicate problems and concerns. The role may be filled by one person performing multiple	Conduct periodic status updates with end-users and key stakeholders. Participate in user-requirements-gathering meetings and interviews. Perform consensus building as necessary.

continued

Table 6-2 (*continued*)

Job Title	Description	Representative Responsibilities
	functions, from business analysis to support, or by a team of people established specifically for this purpose.	Communicate development schedules and release dates to end-users.
Subject matter expert (SME)	Always an internal resource, and as comfortable with his vision for decision support as he is with the business requirements, the subject matter expert varies with the application being built. For example, he could be a financial analyst, a product manager, or a distribution specialist, as well as an expert on an internal system or other technology. The SME is usually an end-user who participates in requirements gathering.	Participate in acceptance testing of data once loaded. Provide feedback once construction is complete. Validate data and test query results. Serve as a resource for questions on requirements and "look and feel" issues. Provide ongoing expertise about a finished application.
Facilitator*	This person is the leader of all business discovery, scoping, and requirements-gathering meetings that involve multiple participants. While in most cases the	Schedule and conduct requirements-gathering meetings. Establish clear goals for requirements-gathering sessions.

continued

Table 6-2 (*continued*)

Job Title	Description	Representative Responsibilities
	business analyst also serves as the facilitator, in more complex projects the facilitator will run the meeting while the business analyst asks questions or notes responses.	Work with user liaison in consensus building. Document meeting results and open issues.
Business analyst*	Principal contact for requirements-gathering activities. Depending on the scope of the data warehouse, the business analyst may actually lead a team of analysts who specialize in facilitation, scribing, and consensus building. The analyst should have business experience as well as the ability to translate business information into technical solutions and good written and verbal communication skills. The business analyst may also be required to construct requirements documentation.	Schedule and conduct user-requirements-gathering workshops. Communicate changes in scope or requirements to project manager. Translate business requirements to database designer to ensure conformity to requirements. Propose test scenarios. Participate in application prototypes for end-users to ensure continuity.

Table 6-3: Database Development Roles

Job Title	Description	Representative Responsibilities
Data modeler/ designer*	The database modeler/ designer can perform more than one role in the development of the database, often leading a design team comprising people with different skills: logical data modeling, modeling software expertise, or DBMS expertise. The designer must be experienced in designing relational databases for decision support, including direct interaction with both businesspeople and DBA staff, and must understand the agreed-upon modeling convention.	Construct logical model with input from business analyst and end-users. Work with DBA to build physical database design based on access needs. Participate in select requirements-gathering activities to understand business issues. Select and use a database design tool to document the model. Work with DBA to make periodic changes to design for performance and tuning improvements.
Data administrator (A.K.A. data steward)	The data administrator focuses on issues of data, its relevance to requirements, its location both before and after loading, and its definition. She is responsible for addressing data issues such as establishing	Gather data requirements as business requirements are defined. Ensure data quality and integrity. Participate in data transformation decisions with database designer.

continued

Table 6-3 (*continued*)

Job Title	Description	Representative Responsibilities
	enterprisewide definitions and business rules, defining and maintaining metadata, and offering additional data requirements as business needs evolve. Depending on the size of the organization and the scope of the project, the data administrator can also create and maintain the data models in the absence of a full-time database designer.	Create and maintain metadata definitions. Identify and define source systems. Monitor data usage and act as point person for all data-related questions from users.
Database administrator (DBA)	While the DBA may be an external consultant, ideally he is a long-term resource, as he is responsible for data warehouse administration and ongoing maintenance. While the DBA is normally responsible for the physical tables in the data warehouse (those designed after the logical model), he should also be familiar with the	Work with data administrator to validate physical data. Work with database designer to perform physical design, including performance tuning. Administer various design and CASE tools. Generate and maintain database objects, including tables and indexes.

continued

Table 6-3 (*continued*)

Job Title	Description	Representative Responsibilities
	operational maintenance tasks associated with the data warehouse and should be intimate with the RDBMS product. He should also understand performance and tuning issues and the use of various production support and administration tools.	Implement ongoing production practices such as backup/recovery, data security, etc. Perform ongoing capacity planning and usage tracking.
Data loader*	Depending on the complexity of the data and the number of source systems involved, the data loading may be performed either by the DBA or by a separate data loader. The data loader is responsible for implementing the necessary tools or code to access, cleanse, and transfer data to the data warehouse.	Perform ongoing extraction, transformation, and loading. Evaluate data from source systems. Work with data administrator to define transformation rules and data quality standards.

Table 6-4: Application Development Roles

Job Title	Description	Representative Responsibilities
Application programmer*	The programmer should be experienced in the	Develop the necessary front-end application using the

continued

Table 6-4 (*continued*)

Job Title	Description	Representative Responsibilities
	development of GUI front-end tools and have knowledge of specific application software environment. She should also be familiar with at least one programming language. Experience in establishing test procedures, prototyping, and rapid application development projects is also desirable.	chosen tool(s). Administer the application tool to accept new users. Participate in user acceptance testing or interim demos.
Application tester*	The tester should also be experienced in the development of GUI front-end tools, as well as in functional and integration testing procedures.	Review end-user requirements document to confirm application objectives. Define test plans/procedures. Perform user acceptance testing and conduct interim demos.

Consultants versus Full-Time Staff

We'll talk about the pros and cons of certain types of external consulting firms in chapter 7. For now, here are a few points to be aware of when considering how—and whom—to hire externally.

The obvious metric is to hire consultants for onetime only activities that won't be repeated and for which a permanent skill set is unimportant, for example,

Table 6-5: Consultant versus Full-Time Staff Evaluation Grid

Question	Yes or No?
Does the skill set for the open position currently exist in-house?	
Is continuity across implementation projects mandatory? (For instance, will the DBA for the next project need to understand the exact same data?)	
Has the internal candidate ever performed the role on a non–data warehouse project? (For example, he developed a Windows-based client/server application for the finance department.)	
Has the internal candidate ever performed the role on another data warehouse project?	

inventorying all available source systems, guiding architecture development, or setting up security and access controls. In such cases obtaining an "injection of expertise" is cost-effective when compared with the expense of training internal staff. In many instances, hiring external consultants can be far less expensive than retaining and training permanent employees for activities that only occur once.

Differentiate your start-up costs and your ongoing development costs, and remember that your start-up costs will go away. Hiring outside consultants for start-up work definitely makes good sense. In ongoing development activities, your company's culture will have as much to do with determining how external resources are used as your requirements and budget will.

With most data-warehousing projects, time to delivery is everything. Your measure of success shouldn't simply be to develop everything in house, but to deploy the application quickly to end-users. While it's commendable that your application programmer wants to try her hand at business analysis and your DBA wants to develop training, decide what the trade-off is of using inexperienced staff and how that will impact your delivery schedule.

You can use the asterisks in the preceding tables as a general guideline for whether to look externally. Alternatively, answer the questions in table 6-5 to determine whether to recruit from within or start calling your favorite consulting firm.

If you answered no to at least three questions in table 6-5, either start soliciting resumes from consulting firms or prepare to hire and train additional full-time staff. If the experienced consultants you bring on board are any good at all, they will train your full-time staff and render themselves dispensable over time.

When staffing your data warehouse development project you should focus on skill sets. If your decision to retain a consulting firm or hire external contractors to help develop your data warehouse is based on any of the following reasons, you might want to reconsider:

- It's easier just to let my database vendor develop the entire system for me.
- I'll just hire a bunch of consultants for a few months. As they work, my people will be learning from them; then we can go it alone.
- Now that business requirements have been gathered and we've begun modeling the data, I'm starting to realize my budget's too low. I'll just send out an RFP, and whoever comes within my price range can implement my warehouse.
- I like the vendor's implementation approach, but I'll never use its technology, so they shouldn't be helping us.
- The consulting firm isn't on our approved vendor list.
- I've always wanted to work with a big management consulting firm.
- The consulting firm did a good job on our Y2K (process reengineering, strategic alignment, portfolio analysis, corporate activity-based costing) project, so it should implement our data warehouse too.
- The consulting firm did a bad job on our last data warehouse project, but now they know the data (our modeling tool, their logon IDs, our floorplan . . .).

The Lost Fine Art of Skill Set Delineation

Everyone has a funny story about a consultant who didn't do the work expected. A few have stories about consultants who did work that was unexpected. I once worked for a large company that hired lots of consultants and left it completely up to them to figure out the work that needed to be done.

Most companies today hire consultants because of the company they work for, not because of how they themselves can help. The reality is that a consulting company is only as good as the individuals who work for it, and the individual is only as good as his skill set. Read resumes, and if you have the time, consider preparing a skills matrix for each job opening you have.

A skills matrix can be simple or complex, but it basically outlines the actual skills necessary for the job. These can be high-level skills that everyone agrees upon ("The project manager should have experience with at least one project management software tool, preferably MS Project."). Or they can be specific to your company or to your project ("The business analyst must have worked in the transportation industry and must be familiar with the specifics of yield management for freight.").

A skills matrix doesn't guarantee that you'll be able to find the perfect resource for each open job role. But it does help in two specific respects: (1) by creating a rigorous way of evaluating different candidates (internal and external) and (2) by offering a unit of consensus. Current team members can work together to define the specific skills required for each job. This not only prevents discord over job responsibilities, it allows each team member a level of ownership in the composition of the team.

Data Administration for Marketing Data Mart				
	Local Development Team	Corporate IT	Tech Support Department	External Consultant
Understanding of customer data from the billing system	○	●	○	○
Knowledge of customer billing data model	○	●	◉	○
Experience in documenting data transformation rules	◉	●	○	●
Acquaintance with internal billing systems terms and SMEs	◉	◉	○	○
Logical data-modeling expertise	●	●	◉	●
Knowledge of standard metadata tool	◉	◉	○	◉

● = Known resource   ◉ = Available resources   ○ = Unknown/ must locate

Figure 6-3: A Simple Skills Matrix

At its simplest, a skills matrix simply defines the skills that are mandatory for each job role.

The skills matrix shown in figure 6-3 was created by a technical project manager for her new project's data administration function, and it provides significant information in a visual way (translation: it's easy for management to understand). The filled-in circles denote a resource that's already been found for the described skill; the partially filled circles denote a possible resource; the empty circles signify that a particular skill set is missing.

At a high level, this skills matrix tells us that knowledge of customer data from the company's current billing system, the primary source system for its marketing data mart, will be more difficult to find than logical data-modeling skills. We can also discern that the development organization will need to lean heavily on the corporate IT organization for expertise here.

Also, by eyeballing the skills matrix we can recognize that the external consulting firms—at least those currently being considered—offer no supplementary skills that aren't already available elsewhere in the company. For data administration, retaining someone from an external firm will most likely be unnecessary.

In more complex projects, skills matrices can be controversial as well as involved. The skills matrix in table 6-6 is a portion of a very complex skills matrix that took several weeks to develop. The skills listed are those that management felt did not yield obvious staff choices, and they include specific kinds of experience to determine the best of all possible candidates.

Since this skills matrix was part of a scoping activity for an enterprise data warehouse, staff candidates for the various development roles would be committing to at least a year in their respective positions. Since the project's company profile and budget were equally high, management understandably wanted to avoid any false starts once the project got under way.

The scoring scheme was as follows:

4: considered an expert in this area
3: experienced in this area
2: some experience or knowledge
1: cursory knowledge
0: never worked in this area

This skills matrix ended up being a highly guarded secret because it could have been misinterpreted as a staff "rating system." But it was invaluable in helping management understand whom to consider as candidates for specific activities, and it

Table 6-6: An Advanced Skills Matrix

Skill/Experience Level	Annette	Marja	Helene	Karl	Klair	Betti	Doug	Vanessa
Project management software	2	0	3	0	4	0	4	2
Experience managing staff of over 10	0	0	3	2	4	0	0	4
Experience managing staff of under 10	2	0	4	0	4	0	0	4
Project management experience	2	0	3	1	4	0	4	4
Experience using Baseline roadmap	3	0	4	2	3	0	3	4
End-user interviewing	1	4	2	1	2	0	0	1
Requirements-gathering techniques	1	4	2	1	2	0	0	1
JAD facilitation skills	2	4	0	1	3	0	0	2
Project scoping/readiness assessment	1	4	2	0	3	0	0	2

continued

Table 6-6 (*continued*)

Skill/ Experience Level	Annette	Marja	Helene	Karl	Klair	Betti	Doug	Vanessa
Prior database development project	1	2	2	1	1	0	0	4
Prior client/ server development project	2	0	3	2	2	3	0	4
Logical data modeling or conceptual design	2	0	2	2	1	1	0	1
Physical database design for Oracle 8i	0	0	0	0	0	4	0	0
Application develpoment skills (GUI tools)	0	0	0	0	0	1	0	0
Application development skills (Oracle Express)	0	0	0	0	0	4	0	0
Application testing (funcational/ integration)	1	0	0	1	1	0	0	0

continued

Table 6-6 (*continued*)

Skill/Experience Level	Annette	Marja	Helene	Karl	Klair	Betti	Doug	Vanessa
Knowledge of switch data	0	0	0	1	0	0	0	0
Knowledge of billing system data	0	0	4	4	0	0	0	0
Knowledge of profit/revenue data	0	0	0	4	0	0	0	0
Knowledge of network data	0	0	0	1	0	0	0	0
Knowledge of provisioning data	0	0	4	4	0	0	0	0

was also useful in identifying potential project problem areas. For example, in examining the skills matrix, the project managers and executive sponsor were able to glean the following:

- Finding appropriate Oracle skills internally could pose a problem. It seems that Betti is the only staff member with any Oracle skills at all, and her overall application development skills are also the most robust.
- Likewise, no one on the list could be considered a subject matter expert for switch data. Other people in the company might need to be found to supplement the current staff members.
- Klair, Doug, and Vanessa have stellar project management credentials, although it's clear that Vanessa has a greater degree of database project experience. This might lead us to choose Vanessa as the technical project manager and Klair or Doug as the administrative project manager, if one is needed.

- Marja seems like the clear choice for lead business analyst, and Helene has some good supplementary skill sets that would make her a good facilitator. Perhaps Marja could coach Helene on business analysis techniques during the requirements-gathering activities.
- Karl seems to be a clear choice for data subject area expertise.
- There are clear skills gaps in logical data modeling, GUI development, application testing, and data subject areas. Management might need to go outside the organization to find some of these skills and should definitely plan on conducting training.

You may choose to have a team of people evaluate or score existing skills, as was done in both of the sample cases. Alternatively, distribute a questionnaire that guides staff members through self-evaluation. The advantage of self-evaluation is that the staff members can participate in determining their involvement with the project. The disadvantage is inversely proportional to the degree of the staff's objectivity.

In extreme cases, skills are assigned weights and individuals are scored based on their overall skill sets. I don't recommend this approach, however, because the assignment of the weightings itself is usually performed by a manager who is divorced from the complexity of certain tasks and the difficulty of obtaining specific skills over others. Don't consider this level of skill set delineation unless your company has mandated staff cutbacks and you need to make some hard decisions.

Whether you create a set of simple skills matrices or one all-encompassing matrix, a skills matrix is useful not just during project scoping and planning, but as a reference throughout the project. In addition to helping you determine the extent to which you need to go outside your organization for necessary resources, it will give you the proper justification for doing so.

Good and Evil Square Off: A Tale of Two Project Plans

As with all projects, there are good data warehouse project plans and bad ones. A good project plan is characterized by a number of typical features:

- It follows comprehensive information-gathering activities, such as the creation of a business case and a project-scoping or readiness assessment.
- It identifies actual individuals, as opposed to department names or groups.
- It provides detail on discrete tasks, as opposed to just listing them.

ID	Task Name	Duration	Start	Finish	Predecessors	Resource Names	Sep 26, '99 S M T W T F S	Oct 3, '99 S M T W T F S S M
1	Project Scoping Exercise	60d	8/2/99	10/22/99		Sharon H.		
2	**Project Initiation**	14d	10/1/99	10/20/99		Klair O.		
3	Meeting with client sponsors	3d	10/1/99	10/5/99		Doug M.		Doug M.
4	Confirm budget approval	1d	10/6/99	10/6/99	3	Doug M.		Doug M
5	Develop detailed project plan	1d	10/7/99	10/7/99	4	Klair O.		Klair O.
6	Write task/responsibility	3d	10/8/99	10/12/99	5			
7	Retain outside staff (ref. skills matrix)	5d	10/13/99	10/19/99	6	Klair O.		
8	Hold project kickoff-meeting	1d	10/20/99	10/20/99	7	Marja R.		
9	**Identify High-Lefel DW Architecture**	26d	10/1/99	11/5/99		Christin		
10	**Identify technical architecture**	10d	10/1/99	10/14/99		Christin		
11	Plan and prepare for IT interviews	5d	10/1/99	10/7/99		Marja R.		Marja. R.
12	Conduct interviews	3d	10/8/99	10/12/99	11	Marja R.		
13	Create technology infrastructure	1d	10/13/99	10/13/99	12	Brian S.		
14	Map diagram to candidate	1d	10/14/99	10/14/99	13	Betti B.		
15	**Create Technology Short List**	16d	10/15/99	11/5/99	10	Vanessa A.		
16	Create selection criteria for DW	4d	1-/15/99	10/20/99		Vanessa A.		
17	Create selection criteria for RDBMS	4d	10/21/99	10/26/99	16	Betti B.		
18	Create selection criteria for application	3d	10/27/99	10/29/99	17	Helene R.		
19	Interview vendors	5d	11/1/99	11/5/99	18	Vanessa A. Betti		
20	**Select technologies**	0d	11/5/99	11/5/99	9	Vanessa A.		
21	**Gather Requirements**	15d	11/8/99	11/26/99	9	Marja R.		
22	Create interview lists	1d	11/8/99	11/8/99		Andy N.		
23	Plan and schedule interviews:	2d	11/9/99	11/10/99	22	Helene R.		
24	Prepare interview questions	2d	11/1/99	11/12/99	23	Helene R.		
25	Conduct interviews	5d	11/17/99	11/23/99	25	Marja R.		
26	Plan and schedule JAD	2d	11/24/99	11/25/99	26	Helene R.		

Figure 6-4: A Good Project Plan

- It lays out realistic schedules.
- It has a "start date" and an "end date."
- It has an "owner."
- It is a living document, meaning that its contents may change.
- Everyone connected with it understands the goal of the project that is represented in the plan.

While some of these criteria sound obvious enough, it's easy to let one or more of them slip through the cracks. Figure 6-4 represents the first page of a good project plan.

Looks simple enough, doesn't it? But this project plan was drafted only after the project was thoroughly scoped. It includes the staff members listed in the skills matrix in table 6-6, assigned to work activities in which they are experienced.

Notice also that the activity is described in detail under each task and that each task is owned by one person. This doesn't mean that others might not be

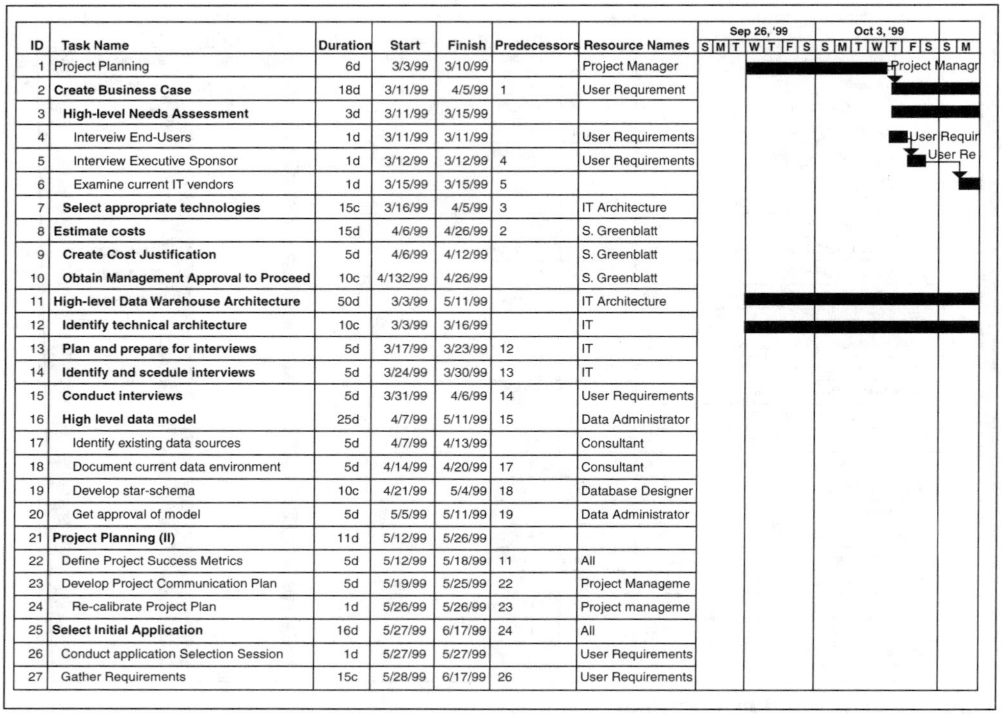

ID	Task Name	Duration	Start	Finish	Predecessors	Resource Names
1	Project Planning	6d	3/3/99	3/10/99		Project Manager
2	**Create Business Case**	18d	3/11/99	4/5/99	1	User Requrement
3	**High-level Needs Assessment**	3d	3/11/99	3/15/99		
4	Interveiw End-Users	1d	3/11/99	3/11/99		User Requirements
5	Interview Executive Sponsor	1d	3/12/99	3/12/99	4	User Requirements
6	Examine current IT vendors	1d	3/15/99	3/15/99	5	
7	**Select appropriate technologies**	15c	3/16/99	4/5/99	3	IT Architecture
8	**Estimate costs**	15d	4/6/99	4/26/99	2	S. Greenblatt
9	**Create Cost Justification**	5d	4/6/99	4/12/99		S. Greenblatt
10	**Obtain Management Approval to Proceed**	10c	4/132/99	4/26/99		S. Greenblatt
11	**High-level Data Warehouse Architecture**	50d	3/3/99	5/11/99		IT Architecture
12	**Identify technical architecture**	10c	3/3/99	3/16/99		IT
13	**Plan and prepare for interviews**	5d	3/17/99	3/23/99	12	IT
14	**Identify and scedule interviews**	5d	3/24/99	3/30/99	13	IT
15	**Conduct interviews**	5d	3/31/99	4/6/99	14	User Requirements
16	**High level data model**	25d	4/7/99	5/11/99	15	Data Administrator
17	Identify existing data sources	5d	4/7/99	4/13/99		Consultant
18	Document current data environment	5d	4/14/99	4/20/99	17	Consultant
19	Develop star-schema	10c	4/21/99	5/4/99	18	Database Designer
20	Get approval of model	5d	5/5/99	5/11/99	19	Data Administrator
21	**Project Planning (II)**	11d	5/12/99	5/26/99		
22	Define Project Success Metrics	5d	5/12/99	5/18/99	11	All
23	Develop Project Communication Plan	5d	5/19/99	5/25/99	22	Project Manageme
24	Re-calibrate Project Plan	1d	5/26/99	5/26/99	23	Project manageme
25	**Select Initial Application**	16d	5/27/99	6/17/99	24	All
26	Conduct application Selection Session	1d	5/27/99	5/27/99		User Requirements
27	Gather Requirements	15c	5/28/99	6/17/99	26	User Requirements

Figure 6-5: A Bad Project Plan

involved in the task, but rather that the person assigned is responsible for its complete and timely delivery.

Sadly, the "bad" project plan, shown in figure 6-5, is all too common and illustrates some frequent mistakes in data warehouse project planning.

Besides being disjointed and arbitrarily ordered, the tasks in this project plan intermingle individuals, departments, and the ever-convenient "All." This common mistake not only fails to assign consistent ownership, it presumes that everyone will come together and agree (often in one day). Lack of delivery accountability is a big problem on data warehouse projects, and this diffusion of responsibilities only reinforces the problem.

This project plan includes several sharp turns, as well as steps—such as "Obtain management approval to proceed"—that may thwart the effort entirely. A detailed project plan for data warehouse implementation should not be created until a data warehouse has been approved and a budget set aside. Otherwise, the time you've dedicated to planning your project may amount to nothing.

Reading between the lines of the bad project plan indicates that there is probably a significant amount of politics in the organization. This plan also suggests that the project manager who created it doesn't really have a say in either the work or the people involved in the project.

Executive Involvement on the Project

Every data warehouse project should have an executive sponsor associated with it. The broader the magnitude of the data warehouse, the larger the number of executives who should be involved.

At least two executives should be involved in the data warehouse project:

1. *Executive sponsor.* As mentioned before, she represents the major line of business that will be using the data warehouse. Ideally, the executive sponsor has business and/or revenue goals that the data warehouse can help realize.

2. *IT executive.* Be it an enterprise data warehouse or a departmental data mart, a CIO, vice president of information systems, or other technology executive of rank should be kept apprised of the project. Ideally, this executive is involved in the creation of a business case or the business discovery activity before the implementation project is launched. During the project, the IT executive attends high-level status updates and may even be involved in high-level architecture and technology selection activities.

Often, an executive "steering committee" oversees the data warehouse at the company's highest level. The steering committee may be involved in anything from budget approval to the definition of new requirements.

The data warehouse executive steering committee at a large pharmaceutical firm involves the following positions in its monthly meeting:

- vice president of strategic planning
- vice president of marketing (also the DW executive sponsor)
- director of data warehousing (IT)
- administrative project manager
- technical project manager
- selected end-users and subject matter experts

The group usually follows an agenda similar to the one illustrated in figure 6-6. While your agenda might include additional items, those featured in figure 6-6 should form the core of any executive-level data warehouse meeting. While the job titles and terms may be different, here's what goes on behind the closed doors of that executive meeting room while the data warehouse steering committee is in session:

1. The status update is a regular agenda item that basically gives the administrative project manager time to explain the development team's progress since the last steering committee meeting, as well as to highlight problems the committee

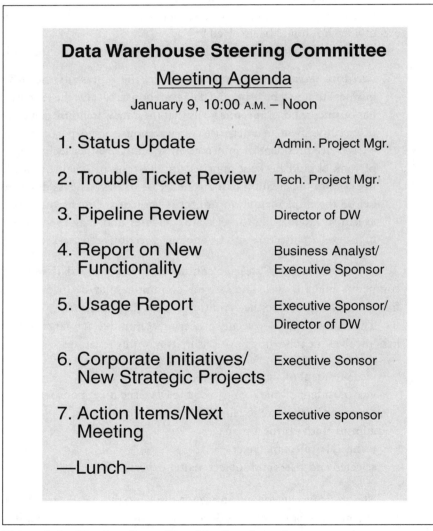

Data Warehouse Steering Committee

Meeting Agenda

January 9, 10:00 A.M. – Noon

1. Status Update	Admin. Project Mgr.
2. Trouble Ticket Review	Tech. Project Mgr.
3. Pipeline Review	Director of DW
4. Report on New Functionality	Business Analyst/ Executive Sponsor
5. Usage Report	Executive Sponsor/ Director of DW
6. Corporate Initiatives/ New Strategic Projects	Executive Sonsor
7. Action Items/Next Meeting	Executive sponsor

—Lunch—

Figure 6-6: Steering Committee Meeting Agenda

members might help resolve. Over time, the status update provides the steering committee with information about the "hot spots" in development, enables it to approve additional resources or budget, and can even pinpoint whether the company's existing business processes and technologies might be hindering development progress.

2. The "trouble ticket" review looks at problems that have been called into development or, more likely, to the help desk. The technical project manager might focus on certain high-profile problems that could divert development resources.

3. The executive sponsor reports on new applications that are already in the pipeline, meaning those that have been planned, scoped, and approved. The purpose of this report is to update steering committee members on whether new applications or systems that will access the data warehouse are on track in terms of start date, duration, and resources. Members often elect to defer some applications in favor of others.[4]

4. Discussing new data warehouse or application functionality gives the development team a chance to explain enhanced features that have already been deployed to users. The new features can be arcane ("We finally upgraded to row-level locking, so now more users can access parts data.") to the generally understood ("Field salespeople now have a report that includes compensation data with sales to date.").

5. The usage report obliges the technical project manager to cite statistics about the number of users, and which specific users from which departments, have logged on to the data warehouse. Depending on the technology being used, some usage reports provide individuals' names, the length of time they were logged on to the data warehouse, and listings of the queries they submitted. Others simply provide a list of logon IDs and dates. Either way, this report is an account of the data warehouse's usage over time, and it is an effective indicator of the company's overall receptiveness to it.[5]

---

4. See the discussion of data warehouse operations planning in chapter 8 for a way to formalize the prioritization of new business opportunities for decision support.

5. Indeed, the degree to which the data warehouse is used is the single biggest factor in its success. If more users are using the data warehouse in the last two months than ever before, the executive sponsor deserves to crow about her success. If usage decreases over time, something's very wrong.

6. The mere fact that a data warehouse is being developed doesn't mean that the rest of the business is standing still. Company management should always perform periodic reviews of strategic or far-reaching company projects, especially those that have been recently launched. It is often difficult for companies to interrelate projects with seemingly nothing in common. Steering Committee members share their knowledge of new and upcoming corporate projects or organizational changes that may affect the data warehouse. For example, a new corporatewide activity-based costing program might affect the existing cost allocation data in the data warehouse and could enable new profitability reporting. This information can help the executive team approve additional resources, as well as prepare the data warehouse development team for upcoming work.

7. Whether it be agreeing to bring new funding figures to the next meeting or researching a recent rumor that may affect head count, at least someone from the steering committee will have a to-do item for the next meeting.

Profile: Hank Steermann of Sears, Roebuck and Co.

Consumers who have in recent years seen "the softer side of Sears"—and are now leading "The Good Life at a Great Price. Guaranteed"—probably don't care about the effort that goes into supporting the company's advanced technologies. While its shoppers know that Sears offers an incredibly diverse range of products, from automotive tires and batteries to lingerie to swimming pool accessories, they're blissfully unaware of the sophisticated decision support infrastructure behind the merchandising.

Hank Steermann, on the other hand, is intimately familiar with this infrastructure. Having worked for Sears for over 26 years at the store and district levels as well as at headquarters, Steermann has a bird's-eye view of retailing and its evolution. His role as business support manager for the Strategic Performance Reporting System (SPRS) involves interfacing with an assortment of end-users who often work in jobs that he himself has performed at one time in his career.

Working for a $41 billion retailer definitely has its advantages. Steermann supports technologies especially well suited to sizable data volumes, including the company's NCR Teradata data warehouse, which supports the SPRS data. "Our data warehouse environment has simply allowed us to change the way we do business," he declares. But unlike other retailers, who have solved various business problems with smaller, disconnected systems, Sears has consistently thought bigger. "The changes we're experiencing because of decision support are at the enterprise level. People all over the company use this data."

Who are they, these worldwide users of decision support? Steermann's team supports executives, who rely on user-friendly screens to perform high-level sales and revenue reporting; headquarters merchandisers, who need data to make informed purchasing decisions; divisional merchandisers and buyers, who analyze product sales; district merchandise managers, who monitor sales trends and maximize sales potentials in their markets; and store managers, who review weekly sales summaries by product line or class. And there are many users in between, from general merchandising managers to clerical staff. All told, Sears has over four thousand decision support end-users.

The SPRS application helps these users analyze data at different levels, aiding business processes as diverse as inventory management, sales forecasting, product purchasing, and promotions. It can tell a product manager the top one hundred stores for her product during the back-to-school period, as well as calculate monthly revenues for socket wrenches for a particular store or district. The data warehouse has helped Sears's marketing department evaluate product placements in advertising circulars, enabling more effective promotional campaigns.

"The business we've been in for the last several years has been ensuring a 'single version of the truth,'" Steermann explains. To get to that truth, Sears shrewdly formed the SPRS team. Effectively a data warehouse steering committee, the SPRS team is a cross-functional crew comprising both business and IT subgroups. Steermann heads up the former team, the SPRS business support team, whose members bring to it experience in buying, marketing, and inventory management, among other retail disciplines.

The SPRS team's main purpose is to bridge data warehouse development with the end-user community, ensuring that new data warehouse projects meet objectives while old ones continue to provide value. In regular weekly meetings the team comes together to discuss a panoply of topics relating to the data warehouse, from production schedules to future application enhancements to new user requirements.

One topic of discussion has been the retirement of legacy systems, some of which duplicated data stored in the data warehouse. (Sears has over 23 legacy systems sourcing the data warehouse with POS, inventory, replenishment, vendor, and product data.) But change can be good. Sears's vigilance about data quality and accuracy has paid off in end-user confidence. "Once end-users know you're delivering quality data," Steermann says, "they're willing to trust your decisions about source systems, data cleansing, and new functionality."

The business support team enforces end-user education. Users aren't allowed access to SPRS without first attending a two-and-a-half-hour training session. Indeed, SPRS training is deemed a key success factor, is held in various remote locations as well as at headquarters, and boasts different modules for different types of users. This comprehensive approach to end-user education socializes decision support as an enterprise initiative and ultimately saves back-end support time.

Each new data warehouse initiative undergoes a structured requirements-gathering activity supported by Steerman's team, which also backs up the help desk, ensures data accuracy, plans new features, and develops and conducts end-user training. And in the end, the entire SPRS team reports not to IT, but to the vice president of the merchandise planning organization, who is responsible for the data and how it can benefit individual business units as well as the entire enterprise. This guarantees that business goals, not technology decisions, continue to drive decision support at Sears.

"Ultimately," concludes Steermann, "our job is to give our users a window into the data warehouse so that they can view their world." And with five terabytes of raw data—updated daily—it's a pretty big world indeed.

Some Lingering Questions

You talk a lot about consultants in this chapter. It's clear from the job functions listed here that my company needs to retain some external people. How do we know whether to set a fixed price for their deliverables or pay as we go?

It depends on the proportion of consultants you need and what they'll be doing. If the work is finite and straightforward, establishing a fixed price for the project—even for one consultant—is a good safety net for both parties. But don't be surprised if negotiation takes a bit longer and the contract is more complex as a result.

Having said this, one of the best indicators of a company's understanding of its own weaknesses is its willingness to entertain time and materials (T&M) development projects. T&M means "pay as you go," and the term is often synonymous with cost overruns and mercenary consultants who milk clients while doing marginal work.

However, T&M projects also allow practitioners to "fix as they go," focusing on quality work and deliverables over the project's lifecycle. Inevitable problems and changes can be worked into the project plan with minimal impact.

Conversely, fixed-price projects don't adapt well to change, and change is a staple in data warehouse development. Larger fixed-price projects require forms to be filled out in order to accommodate scope changes and sometimes even warrant contract renegotiation, both of which can significantly bog down development. They often pit client and consultant against each other, with the customer intent on squeezing the maximum number of staff resources from the vendor and the vendor trying to pass off its least experienced consultants in order to reduce costs while providing on-the-job training.

To be sure, this is a worst-case scenario. The problem is that many clients prefer paying a fixed price for projects for the obvious reason of financial security: They know how much the effort will cost and have a general feel for the resulting deliverable. But fixed-price development efforts for decision support projects are always vastly more complicated, because deliverables often evolve due to requirements changes and prototyping. Unfortunately, many companies are accustomed to fixed-price development because of its success with previous operational systems projects for which the end-result was—unlike many DSS requirements—crisply defined at the beginning.

If your budget constraints or policies require you to request fixed-price development, be certain that you've spent time exposing your weak areas—be they skills shortcomings, staff availability, outdated technology, unavailable work space, or other limitations. If not, working with a fixed price could end up costing you more in the end. In either case, knowing the skills of the practitioners about to do the work is the best insurance policy of all.

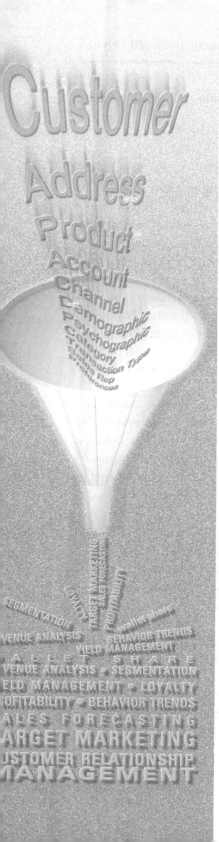

CHAPTER SEVEN

Value or Vapor?
Finding the Right Vendors

If you happen to be in Transylvania and are blighted by an irksome vampire, you have one of two choices. You can go for the garlic, which reputedly can be hit or miss. Or, if you have money and connections, you can invest in a silver bullet. The silver bullet is a surefire way, so to speak, of getting rid of that pesky vampire once and for all.

Unfortunately, many of us seek out the silver bullet to solve other problems, namely, how to address challenges in data warehouse development, or whether to add new decision support functionality. We'll call a company that specializes in one technology and ask it to deliver another or, worse, call a single vendor and expect it to solve all our problems.

It's worth noting that these days, being a "major player" in data warehousing has little to do with company size. Some small emerging companies promise great things when it comes to packaged applications and data mining. This chapter will help you interact with them as well as providing some questions to ask the "big guys."

You might think that the evaluation metrics in this chapter are only for readers who don't yet have a data warehouse. Jacques Nasser, Ford Motor Company's president and CEO, has been known to say: "Five years from now, we will be a different company, and five years from then, we'll be *another* different company."

Even if you have a production data warehouse, the constant of change is ever present. So it's a good thing to constantly reevaluate your technologies. That way, when it comes time to reengineer, redesign, rearchitect, or revamp your data warehouse infrastructure, you'll know where to turn for help.

The Hardware Vendors

Just as with the database vendors, it's a little misleading to lump all the data-warehousing hardware vendors into one bucket. The range of servers on the market that can deliver decision support is astonishingly broad, between vendors as well as within them. IBM, for example, can deliver servers from single micro-processor-based PCs to large multiprocessor parallel computers all the way to enormous mainframes running complex database software.

Choosing data warehouse hardware is more complex than it seems—at least, it should be. Fortunately, your IT department has probably already standardized on a data warehouse hardware platform. Unfortunately, most companies do one of two things: (1) use existing hardware that might be available or underutilized or (2) run performance benchmarks on a few select vendors to see which hard-ware platform is fastest.

What most companies don't do is evaluate hardware based on features and functionality as well as processing power. Take the *symmetric multi-processing* (SMP) versus *massively parallel processing* (MPP) issue. MPP hardware links fast processors and leverages software to balance the workloads, performing the major-ity of the work in parallel with significant performance and concurrency benefits. Conversely, SMP products distribute differentiated tasks between processors.

While more detailed definitions aren't important here, your company's IT department should be able to profile data warehouse workload, concurrency, and usage requirements to identify whether MPP or SMP is the better choice.

Unfortunately, most companies embarking on data warehousing haven't mapped out their usage requirements thoroughly enough to understand which type of architecture makes the most sense for their specific environment. Sometimes this lack of planning results in companies overspending on too much processing power. More often it means costly and unforeseen hardware upgrades, frequently at critical junctures in the data warehouse's usage, in order to support unexpected processing or data volumes.

I can't tell you which hardware is right for your data warehouse, but you should be sure to have some specific information before selecting which hard-ware vendors to talk to. In fact, a good vendor will request the following data from you.

1. The average and maximum number of users you foresee using the data warehouse once it's up and running. Since, as we've said before, a data warehouse is a process and not just a technology, you probably won't have the "final" answer to this question. But you should at least understand which departments or groups within your company will be needing to query the data warehouse and how many people from each department will be logging on. Try to identify specifics, such as "5 percent of the marketing staff will need to use the data warehouse twice a week." Focus on an 18-month time frame, longer if you can project that far. Use worst-case estimates.

2. A classification for the type of work that will be done on the warehouse. Again, you won't be able to anticipate everything that occurs on the data warehouse, but you should at least have an idea whether users will be doing simple canned queries, more complex and unpredictable ad hoc work, or data mining. Using the pyramid we've discussed throughout the book can help you classify the types of work that will be done on the warehouse (see figure 7-1).

3. Finally, you'll need to anticipate the amount of data that will ultimately reside on the warehouse. Again, you won't know the long-term answer. But understanding what your data requirements are will pinpoint the operational systems from which it originates and give you an idea of the relative

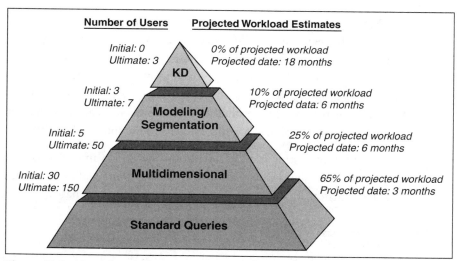

Figure 7-1: Anticipating Data Warehouse Workload

amount of data coming from each source system.[1] A database sizing estimate can be made before the hardware is purchased.

Armed with this information, you'll be able to evaluate hardware vendors on your terms, not theirs, and thus compare apples with apples.

Five Questions to Ask Your Hardware Vendor

As unlikely as it is that you'll even need to ask the questions listed below—your IT folks have probably taken care of it, and that's great—it's helpful to understand the role of the hardware platform in the overall data warehouse architecture, as well as the role of the vendor in ongoing development and maintenance.

1. Are you selling us a hardware platform for our data warehouse, or are you playing solutions integrator?

The answer to this question speaks to the role the vendor wants and is willing to play in your development. Some vendors want to play systems integrator, bringing together disparate hardware and software products, while others are content to do a "box drop." Be sure to differentiate between a vendor looking for commission on multiple products and services and one that plays the development and support role of a true systems integrator.

2. Why should I buy the RDBMS from you rather than directly from the vendor?

Most hardware vendors package software into their hardware offerings. For example, HP regularly bundles Oracle's database product, selling the complete solution. A worthwhile hardware vendor will offer end-to-end support—and centralized accountability. This approach provides the vendor's customers with one-stop shopping, as well as a centralized address for handling problems, upgrades, or new product evaluations. It also cuts down on intervendor finger pointing: "It's the hardware's fault!" versus "It's the software's fault!"

Another interesting response might involve the optimization of the RDBMS to the particular hardware platform, meaning that a database product would have been customized to work with specific features of the hardware product.

---

1. This is the main reason hardware selection should ideally occur only after requirements have been gathered: it's much easier to delineate what data will be needed on the warehouse once business analysis has been done. The Baseline Roadmap in chapter 6 allows for database and application architecture to be done only after the business analysis phase of implementation.

3. If something breaks, whom do we call? What type of service assurance do we have? How long does it take before problems are resolved, and what contingencies are in place if you are unable to resolve the problem within a reasonable time?

The answer to this set of questions establishes the vendor's commitment to support, as well as the boundaries of its accountability. Understand the escalation procedures, that is, how a problem or system outage climbs up the vendor's support hierarchy, and make sure the vendor understands the impact such an outage could have on your business.

4. Do you offer application development assistance, or do you simply use third-party expertise that we can retain ourselves? What phases of development do they specialize in? (Database design? Application construction? Data extraction and conditioning?)

Some vendors have only recently transformed themselves from order takers into complete systems integrators. As they catch up, they often use third-party providers. While increasing reliance on your in-house expertise is a good idea and certainly cost-effective, make sure you understand the abilities of the vendor's own staff relative to its outsourced help.

5. How are you going to protect my company's intellectual property and investment?

Every vendor employee working on your site will be exposed to specific information about your business. While it is unrealistic to expect the vendor to leave key learnings behind, you do want assurances that your business's intellectual capital remains secure.

Differentiate between implementation expertise and intellectual capital, and make sure the vendor knows you're concerned about the latter. Don't focus on noncompete contracts—vendors have a right to sell their products to a range of businesses—but rather on nondisclosure agreements.

The Database Vendors

The risk of writing about database vendors is that their technology features are changing so quickly. Notwithstanding a customer's ability to take "an interesting little database product" and make it into a mission-critical solution, a few common players in the market today are the acknowledged leaders.

The analysis firm Dataquest Inc., a division of Gartner Group, predicts that the database market will reach $10 billion by 2003. Is it any wonder that the leading database companies are in a neck-and-neck race to win customers and claim market share?

But in order to win customers, these vendors often make lofty claims about a product that sometimes doesn't work or, worse, doesn't even exist. This is where the term "vaporware" comes from. As account teams become more aggressive, customers must become more savvy, in regard to both who offers the best technology and which company's technology best meets the given set of business requirements. An RDBMS can be Web-enabled until the cows come home, but if it can't support a company's requirement for 500 gigabytes of data and 237 concurrent users, the Web capabilities won't do much good.

Five Questions to Ask Your Database Vendor

As a manager, consultant, or practitioner-to-be, it's more likely that you'll have a say in the acquisition of a database product than of a hardware platform. This is particularly true in relation to dependent data marts, which are popping up as adjuncts to enterprise data warehouses and have their own specific set of business requirements.

Regardless of what the data warehouse or data mart will be used for, asking your RDBMS vendor the following questions will give you an idea of the role it would be likely to play, as well as the ongoing resources it might provide.

1. What if we have to add a lot more data? Can the product you're selling us now handle our data needs in the future?

This question is one of those disingenuous ones that vendors don't like much, but should be able to answer. It raises the possibility that data requirements might change, the implication being that you don't want to have to change database products or releases in midstream in order to support new requirements. The vendor that has a clear and ready answer—which should involve its product's ability to grow (scale) with more data—is in a good position to be a partner.

2. Is it more cost-effective for us to have a site license? (for services? for the number of seats? for the number of end users?)

If you expect to have more and more users over time, the database vendor should be able to offer a site license for which you pay one flat fee. This way you won't be writing a check each time a business user asks for a logon ID to the data warehouse.

3. Do you have data model templates or functionally specific tools already developed for particular industries?

Many database vendors have industry-specific application tools that are tightly integrated with their RDBMS products. If yours does, it will save you time as well as the headache of having to research tool vendors. The initial design of the databases and selection of the appropriate tool can take months. Also, the database vendor might have experts in both products available to help you with implementation.

4. Could you describe the consulting expertise you offer and explain why I should staff my consulting positions through you?

These days, all of the database vendors offer consulting services, many transcending the particular product set and delving into industry specialization or management consulting. The vendor should be able both to explain why its consultants are preferable to those at the body shop around the corner and to justify its prices. While few vendors will give you a uniform hourly rate, they should be able to offer a price range that takes into account the seniority and staff levels of the consultants in their professional services organizations.

5. Can I call a reference or two?

This issue is discussed below in the consulting section, but it applies equally to technology vendors. Don't settle for marketing collateral, white papers, or data sheet testimonials. Get the names and addresses of clients who are implementing systems similar to yours, and call them. Ask them if they're happy with the product, if they're satisfied with their ongoing support, and whether they consider the vendor a technology provider or a partner. If you're uncomfortable with any of the referee's comments, whatever answers you get to the other questions in this list don't matter a whit.

TPC Benchmarks

When evaluating an RDBMS vendor, prospective clients often inquire about that vendor's "TPC-D numbers." The Transaction Processing Performance Council (TPC) has established a set of performance tests, or benchmarks, that enable comparisons within the eclectic range of database products. Other TPC benchmarks have measured transaction-processing performance, but TPC-D—the council's decision support benchmark—has been the benchmark of record for most DSS processing until recently.

"TPC-D's original intent was to give an apples-to-apples comparison of different vendors' ability to perform ad hoc decision support type workloads," explains NCR's Carrie Ballinger, one of the original TPC-D architects and current industry benchmark analyst. But, Ballinger cautions, "Over time, TPC-D has evolved into a showcase for preplanned query speed-up techniques, such as preaggregation and sophisticated indexing. Many of the more recent TPC-D techniques involved extensive setup and planning, thereby eroding TPC-D from its ad hoc roots." Ballinger explains further:

> While TPC-D results are no longer useful for assessing ad hoc performance, they can demonstrate some interesting approaches to query tuning. Producing industry benchmark results acts as a qualifier for a platform's data warehouse readiness, affirming a platform's ability to support certain data volumes or a particular level of concurrent queries. But in comparing the primary metrics of current TPC-D benchmarks, as with all industry benchmarks, it is important to do so with an understanding of the techniques being used, and to consider the setup and maintenance efforts involved.

The TPC Council has recently replaced TPC-D with two similar but contrasting benchmarks: TPC-H to simulate ad hoc performance and TPC-R to continue showcasing preplanned query speed-up techniques in order to represent business-reporting capabilities. Regardless of the changing dynamic of the benchmarks, Ballinger urges those interested in TPC benchmarking to get the full picture. "To get the most value from a TPC benchmark, read the benchmark documentation," she recommends, "and understand the tactics behind the metrics."

The Application Vendors

The selection of an application software tool is arguably the most important decision in data warehouse technology acquisition, since it's the application software that is seen by end-users. This decision can, in fact, be a "make or break" one for a data warehouse, since end-users will measure the value of the entire data warehouse by the questions they can—and cannot—ask through their application tool.

Companies evaluating application tool vendors normally do so according to how the information is presented to the end-users. While this metric—known as "look and feel"—is critical, not as much attention is paid to how end-users interact with the system and how they specify what they want. In other words, input isn't given as much weight as output, although the input is where the user spends the most time, telling the tool what to bring back and display.

Some of the tools currently on the market are geared toward average businesspeople who submit standard queries in the course of their everyday jobs. Other tools are meant for experienced data analysts only. While there are exceptions, the bottom of the pyramid usually means the greatest ease of use, and thus the highest number of data warehouse users. As users move up the pyramid, as shown in figure 7-2, they become fewer, more specialized, and usually more knowledgeable about the data and data structures.

It's not the terms that are important here: One person's data analyst is another person's knowledge worker. The point is that skill sets change with the type of tool being used. Thus, an everyday business user isn't likely to use a statistical-modeling tool, any more than a statistician would use a query tool to do sophisticated data mining.

Indeed, if we spin the pyramid again (see figure 7-3), we can match the analysis type and user category to the type of tool being used.

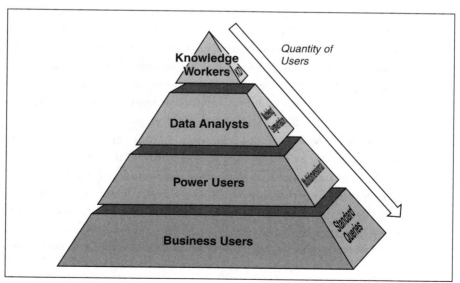

Figure 7-2: End-User Classifications

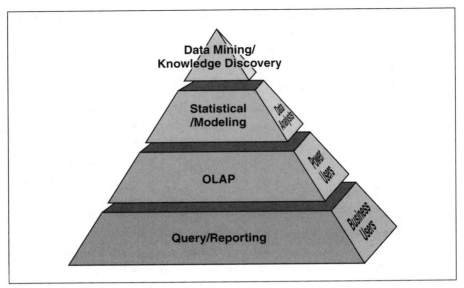

Figure 7-3: Tool Classifications

"Developing great business intelligence applications is a bit like creative research," claims Bob Doss, senior consultant at Spirit Lake Consulting. "Great business intelligence applications deliver functionality that alters the business landscape." Doss cautions companies against rote development and hard-and-fast technical specifications, advocating instead "lateral thinking, tenacious experimentation, and innovation." He insists that creativity during development is key: "Give the right people ordinary tools and they might do something special. But give the wrong people any sort of tool and you'll get no value at all."

Some of the tool vendors currently marketing business intelligence software offer a variety of different decision support products. For example, Business Objects offers both query and data-mining tools, and SAS Institute offers both statistical-modeling and true knowledge discovery products.

Notwithstanding the myriad development tools such as Visual Basic or C++ that allow developers to build custom applications from scratch, most companies have standardized database application tools.[2] Products from companies such as

---

2. Sometimes specific functionality or data access requirements make custom-developed applications a better choice. Certain business questions can't easily be translated into straight-forward queries, and there may be a discrete set of business or display functions that a packaged tool doesn't provide.

Microstrategies, Brio, and Business Objects specialize in the data access and volume characteristics of data warehouses (as opposed to, for example, PC databases). While such off-the-shelf "third-party" products have taken hold, there are also vendor tools such as Oracle's Express and IBM's Intelligent Miner that are sold by their respective database vendors and are quite good. These guys have the advantage of being able to snag business along with the sale of their database products.

Also, while the functionality may be similar between certain tools, the prices may vary significantly. Check with a tool's vendor for the cost per seat as you rate and compare its features.

Five Questions to Ask Your Application Tool Vendor

When evaluating a business intelligence software tool, you should focus first and foremost on who will be using it and how. To this end, try classifying your end-user community in a way similar to the pyramid in figure 7-2. This includes gauging how intuitive the tool is—more important for queries than for knowledge discovery—and how much training it will require.

You should also understand how flexible the tool is and its ability to function within your company's existing technology infrastructure. In addition to the support and maintenance questions we've covered in other sections, you should be prepared with the following questions for your software vendor.

1. Do you require your tool to be installed on every PC, or is it server- or Web-enabled?

The answer to this question will dictate the work involved in deploying the application. Does the tool need to be installed on every discrete client workstation, or can it be deployed over your company's intranet? The answer will help you determine whether things like the client workstation configuration are an issue, whether an application server should be purchased, or whether you can simply leverage your company's existing network infrastructure.

2. Will the tool work with our existing database design, or does it require a special database layout?

While all application software tools claim to have ODBC interfaces and standard SQL language generators, the real issue is how well the tool works with your database. Some databases will require summary tables or "application support" tables in order to support a given tool.

3. Does the software allow GUI application construction?

Does the tool allow your programmers to customize the "look and feel" for end-users who may be already accustomed to certain screen layouts or icon names? Can they copy data to tools like spreadsheets or word processors? Tools that allow for customization can also simplify end-user training by allowing the developer to incorporate familiar formats or terminology.

4. Does the tool require the end-user to understand how the underlying database is constructed?

Some tools shield end-users from having to navigate the databases in the data warehouse by giving end-users a list of data fields from which to choose. In reality, these data fields may actually represent combinations and joins of underlying data elements in the database, rendering querying and reporting much simpler. Tools that don't shield end-users from underlying database structures require a level of database knowledge that many end-users don't have—and don't want.

5. Is the tool technology-focused or industry-centric?

For example, there are tools that specifically calculate banking customer profitability or predict credit card fraud. There are several data-mining tools that were built around specific industry uses and retrofitted to other industries later on. Conversely, some tools enable multidimensional reporting against Oracle or Informix regardless of the business use.

Data-Mining Tools: A Breed Apart

While the questions listed above apply very well to all vendors no matter where they fit on the pyramid, there is a specific set of questions that apply only to data-mining vendors. Why? Because there's a broader range of potential functional differences between these products. Also, it's more difficult to determine if a given data-mining tool can truly solve your business problem. And nowadays, everyone's claiming to be a data-mining company.

If you are evaluating data-mining tools or numerical analysis tools, add the following set of questions to your list. Rather than reinvent the wheel, I've extracted these questions from Evan Levy's "The Lowdown on Data Mining," which appeared in *Teradata Review*.

Ten Questions to Ask Your Data-Mining Vendor[3]

1. Does your data-mining tool support continuous or range value analysis? (Can the system identify relative groupings for a continuous set of values, or is the user required to identify those values? For example, does the tool subdivide age ranges, or must the user define the ranges?)
2. Does your tool scale? (Can it break problems into multiple concurrent steps? If so, how?)
3. How many algorithms does your tool support?
4. What do the results look like?
5. What data formatting does it require?
6. How does the tool acquire data?
7. How does the user or business analyst interact with the tool? Is it a GUI interface? Is it command-line?
8. What level of data or statistical analysis experience is necessary to use the tool?
9. Is your data-mining tool business or functionally focused? A "business-focused" data-mining tool focuses on a specific function such as "churn." A functionally focused tool is more aligned with the type of algorithm (i.e., cluster), and can usually apply to more than one business problem.
10. Is it a learning or static model–based tool? (A static-based tool requires the user to identify the specific attributes and their relative weightings. A learning model tool analyzes all available data attributes and determines the appropriate weightings and values itself.)

The Consultants

Having worked with and for several consulting firms both large and small, I can confidently state that if you've seen one consulting company, you haven't seen 'em all. Indeed the cultures, hiring practices, work ethics, training, delivery methods, annual revenues, and management styles of these companies can vary in the extreme, and with the current rash of acquisitions, they're changing all the time.

---

3. Levy, Evan, "The Lowdown on Data Mining," *Teradata Review,* Summer 1999. Reprinted with permission from Miller Freeman, Inc.

This section could be an entire book on its own. While it's tempting to list every consulting company out there—each having its particular strengths and weaknesses—I've divided the diatribe into two: the "big guys" and the "little guys," which by the way is how most clients categorize them. The questions at the end apply to any consulting firm you might retain, regardless of size.

The Big Guys

The mythical squad of young MBAs descending on a strategic project and going to war is still a fact of modern business. So is the quiet consulting company that relies on word-of-mouth recommendations and has no direct sales force. And there are dozens of descriptions in between.

In a recent article, Mort Meyerson, ex-president of EDS and CEO of Perot Systems, described the "big consulting company" mentality he witnessed at EDS, and its fallout:

> Of course we delivered what we promised. But there were two problems: we made sure we won virtually every negotiation that decided what would be delivered; and our tone was often paternalistic, almost condescending. Customers felt like they were outgunned at every turn. Too often we made them feel incompetent or just plain stupid—after all, they had called us to bail them out of trouble.[4]

When talking to clients of the big consulting firms, battle imagery looms large. Being "outgunned" by a bunch of "young guns" just out of "boot camp" can be disconcerting, and the war stories abound. Nevertheless, the big consulting firms offer advantages to clients that smaller firms simply can't match.

In Europe in the early 1990s, my company subcontracted to Peat Marwick, better known in the United States as KPMG, and I can vouch for its consultants. Peat was hiring some of the best minds in the business, consultants who not only had the academic credentials so prized in Europe but had hands-on experience as well. Not only did Peat consultants understand data warehousing and database design, they usually did so in three different languages. Clients loved them.

Larger consulting firms have a clear advantage in the critical mass department. Need someone to start on your project on Monday—and today's Thursday? No problem for Andersen Consulting, KPMG, Deloitte and Touche,

---

4. Meyerson, Mort, "Everything I Thought I Knew About Leadership Was Wrong," *Fast Company New Rules of Business,* volume 1 (supplement to *Fast Company* magazine), 4.

or Ernst and Young. In fact, they're used to it. Never mind that this kind of last-minute staffing request should be a big warning that the project may be poorly planned.

These companies also have a leg up in the infrastructure department. Several of them have sophisticated knowledge management setups that include centralized methodology and proposal documentation available over a secure Internet Web site for consultants to access and use. These companies excel in providing their necessarily disparate employees with a range of tools they can apply to client projects.

Training is also usually superior and more structured at the larger firms, many offering the aforementioned boot camps to all new consultants. PricewaterhouseCoopers recently opened a training facility in Tampa, Florida, to accommodate 750 new recruits for 12 weeks of training.[5]

But what may be attractive for recent college graduates could spell trouble for clients, and there's the rub for some of the larger consulting firms. While the image of a 12-year-old Stepford consultant emerging from two months of initiation chanting, "Billable hours! Billable hours!" is a bit of a stretch, the effort to "engineer" good consultants from scratch can backfire. With data warehousing becoming more pervasive than ever, it's hard enough for seasoned consultants to keep up with their clients' knowledge base. What exactly does a boot camp graduate with no real experience offer a client who's had a data warehouse since the consultant was in grade school? A running gag in the HR department of one large consulting firm goes like this: "Does he have three of the five vital signs? Hire him!"

The larger consulting firms have also been known to "reengineer" consultants from their industry, accounting, or strategic planning areas into data-warehousing experts. While knowledge of these areas is helpful, it's no substitute for experience with data-warehousing technology, implementation processes, data, and business value.

"The business models of the 'Big 6' require that they develop efficiencies in scale across common technology and business issues," says Barbara Britton, president of BEA Systems e-Commerce Integration business unit. "In other words, they do the same things over and over for different customers. This works well when you have predictable, labor-intensive technology challenges like SAP implementation. The problem is, it doesn't give customers unique added value, nor is there motivation on the supplier's end to complete the task in an accelerated fashion.

---

5. According to *Information Week*, April 12, 1999, 150.

"Remember to round each billable hour off to the nearest week."

Figure 7-4: The Dark Side of Consulting

This affects competitiveness and time-to-market planning—both critical issues in the age of the Internet, e-commerce, and data warehousing."

Many clients choose larger consulting firms out of comfort, the logic being, "They're a big company. If something goes wrong, they'll be around to fix it." Another rationale is, "We're already using them on Project X." These aren't the best selection criteria when engaging a firm to deliver an expensive, high-profile data warehouse.

Some companies have paid the price. According to the *Wall Street Journal,* Ernst and Young recently agreed to pay $185 million to settle claims that it provided "incompetent advice,"[6] and the press has carried similar stories of consulting firms that were retained to run enormous projects subsequently being kicked out.

---

6. Elizabeth MacDonald, "Ernst & Young to Settle Merry-Go-Round Claims," *Wall Street Journal,* April 27, 1999.

In chapter 6 we discussed skill set delineation. It would be an interesting exercise to poll the clients whose projects managed by the large firms they retained failed and ask them how closely they had read resumes.

The Little Guys

A band of upstarts is snapping at the heels of the big guys with legitimate bragging rights over lower rates and more specialized products and services. These companies are bidding against the big firms, and in many cases they're winning. "Would you rather have a platoon of blue suits build your e-business—or one goateed artist?" crowed *Forbes* magazine recently, trailing a piece about the looming challenges for large consulting firms.[7]

Why are some of the world's largest commercial companies turning their collective heads toward the "niche players"? Some have failed with the big guys. Others understand the value of specialized expertise at the outset of their projects. The wisest customers understand that the smaller consulting firms are often staffed by the larger firms' ex-employees, many of whom were disaffected or simply craved more autonomy.

Baseline Consulting Group, the firm I work for, is a good example. The company works only on data-warehousing projects (with some industry expertise thrown in). Its employees come from vendor companies like Andersen, IBM, and NCR, as well as large data warehouse users like BellSouth and J. C. Penney. All are senior, all have hands-on expertise, and all have interesting reasons for joining a smaller company. And clients in the *Fortune* 50 have retained the firm for some of their most mission-critical projects.

Other smaller firms such as Cambridge Technology Partners, Reliant Ventures, and DB Assist have not only delivered high-quality work but have literally transformed standard implementation tasks such as application development or database design into tightly defined and highly successful deliverables. These companies often find themselves "cleaning up" after the big guys, and their satisfied customers call them back again and again. Indeed, word-of-mouth references are critical for smaller consulting firms, many of whom do not have direct sales staffs.

Lest you think I'm biased, there's plenty wrong with the smaller firms, critical mass being the main problem. It's simply harder for a small firm of 40 or 50 consultants to mobilize what may amount to half the company's employees in

---

7. Joanne Gordon, "Webster Boutiques," *Forbes*, May 31, 1999, 182.

order to launch a large project. Such firms often seek out project work that employs a team of consultants for a period of time. Thus short-term or piece-meal work is more difficult to staff.

Moreover, the smaller firms have a harder time attracting talent. Many data-warehousing practitioners who decide to become consultants are attracted to the name value of the Big Five firms. Recruiting is thus a challenge for smaller consulting organizations, for whom "I've never heard of you guys" is a constant refrain. The problem is compounded as, with a few exceptions, smaller firms don't offer the extensive training programs or published methodologies from which these practitioners can learn new skills. Some smaller firms are able to hire staff only after they are actually awarded new business.

The main problem for smaller firms is that there are so many of them, and well-meaning clients intent on giving these firms a fair shake are forced to sift through numerous Web sites and brochures to determine which ones can do the job. Those in doubt should let the references speak for themselves.

A Word About the Analysts

Gartner Group, META Group, Forrester Research, et al. There are dozens of analyst companies out there, but just a handful focus on data warehousing and business intelligence as a core practice area. They're not exactly consultants, and they're not exactly think tanks. What are they, and why do you need them?

In providing a broad view across vendors, technologies, and customers, the analysts perform a very valuable function. In the best case, their research provides a handle on the acceptance of an emerging technology, for example data mining, and puts it in context with other activities in that area.

Analyst companies originally came into being as clearinghouses for vendor product Ts and Cs (terms and conditions) and pricing. They are among the best resources for determining the credibility of vendor references as well as pricing information. They act as an advocate for the customer looking for the best deal. They are especially helpful to companies that may be starting out and need a subjective opinion about a given vendor or experience with a well-known product. The analysts are also adept at predicting which products will be widely adopted, which will be niche-based, and which have precarious prospects.

But their clients pay for the privilege. One client of mine pays upwards of $120,000 annually for a firm's research papers, the majority of which, according to him, offer no new insights. "Until these guys have as much data warehouse implementation experience as I do, I won't take anything they say to be gospel," he says. Indeed, as recently as a few years ago, it was the data warehouse analysts who were making the brash and completely unjustifiable claim that "If you build it, they will come."

Thus, the same issue with consulting firms exists with the analysts: They are only as good as the individuals who deliver the end product. Some analyst firms release breakthrough research that can end up defining a certain class of technology. Others publish reports that merely echo what industry trade magazines and actual practitioners have been saying all along.

A Word About the Vendors

Some hardware and database vendors also have large consulting organizations that not only deliver high-quality consulting on the company's products but also include expertise on other technologies, development methods, and industries. IBM's Global Services division alone is larger than many of the large consulting firms, and Oracle, NCR, Siemens, and Informix have consulting organizations that support their technology delivery projects.

While it's often better to have a consulting firm that is not product-oriented during the data warehouse business discovery or technology acquisition phase, the vendor companies can provide a range of skills during the "post-sales" phases that go beyond technology expertise. If you are looking for delivery help, consider the consulting arm of your technology vendor of choice.

Five Questions Your Consultant Should Ask You

Notice that we've turned around who asks the questions on this one? That's because you can learn as much about a consultant from the questions she asks you as from how she explains her credentials or wistfully recalls past projects.

The most important thing to remember when retaining a consulting firm is that the whole is *less than* the sum of its parts. After the corporate sales pitch, the client reference list, the visions and values presentation, the two-martini lunch, and the four-course dinner, a consulting firm should be ready to discuss the talents and credentials of its individual staff members, and it is these qualities that should drive your decision whether to retain the firm or not (no matter how good the dinner). Big or small, your discussion with any prospective consulting firm should eventually hinge on the individuals slated to perform the work.

The best way to determine whether a consultant can do the job you want done is to read her resume, mapping her experience to the skills you've already delineated. Then listen to the questions. Here are five that are good indicators of a solid, delivery-focused approach:

1. What was the original business problem that led you to undertake this project?

This question indicates that the consultant is interested in the big picture—regardless of whether he is being hired to gather requirements or to customize an OLAP application. He'll keep the answer in mind as he does his work, which is a measure of quality assurance.

2. Where are you in your current implementation process?

A consultant who asks this question knows not to make any assumptions about how much progress you've made. She probably also understands that you might be wrong. There are plenty of clients who have begun application development without first having gathered requirements. Understanding where the client thinks he is is just as important as understanding where he wants to be. It also helps the consultant suggest improvements or recommend additional skills or technologies.

3. How long do you see this position being filled by an external resource?

While the question may at first seem self-serving, a good consultant is ever mindful of his responsibility to render himself dispensable over time. Your answer will give him a good idea of how much time he has to perform the work, as well as to cross-train permanent staff within your organization. A variation on this question is, "Is there a dedicated person or group targeted for knowledge transfer in this area?"

4. What deliverables do you expect from this engagement?

The consultant who doesn't ask about deliverables is the consultant who expects to sit around giving advice. Beware the ivory tower consultants, those who are too light for heavy work, too heavy for light work. Every consultant you talk to should expect to produce some sort of deliverable, be it a requirements document, a data model, HTML, a project plan, test procedures, or a mission statement.

5. Would you like to talk to a past client or two?

The fact that a consultant would offer this is testimony enough that he knows his stuff. Many do not. Those consultants who hide behind nondisclosures as a way of not giving references should be avoided. While it's often valid to deny prospective clients work samples because of confidentiality agreements, there's no good reason not to offer the name and telephone number of someone who will sing the consultant's praises. And don't be satisfied with a reference for the entire firm. Many good firms can nevertheless employ below-average consultants. Ask to talk to someone who's worked with the person or team you're considering. Once you've hired that consultant and are happy with his work, offer to be a reference. It comes around.

One last tip: When interviewing consultants, watch out for convention or methodology bigots. Regardless of what you hire them to do, they'll try to commandeer a certain activity, sometimes doing more harm than good. In fact, a consultant's experience and references should carry a lot more weight than his favored data modeling approach or preferred programming language.

A client once put me in the unenviable position of having to interview consultants for several open positions on a data warehouse development team. One interview went like this:

JILL: Thanks for coming. So, you've read our application brief and understand a little about what we want to do with the data warehouse. Any initial questions?

CANDIDATE: Yeah. I noticed the data model looked weird.

JILL: (eyeballing candidate's resume) OK. But you know the position we're talking to you about is for project manager.

CANDIDATE: Oh yeah, I know, but . . . is that data model dimensional or isn't it?

JILL: Well no, actually, the client uses an entity-relationship model for its enterprise warehouse, but let me ask you . . .

CANDIDATE: You know, star schema can really handle a range of processing requirements.

JILL: We're actually pretty well staffed in that area, but would you like to talk to someone in data administration about a data-modeling job?

CANDIDATE: Are you guys programming in JAVA yet?

How do you know for sure that your consulting firm will do the job? Unfortunately, apart from past experience, there's no true predictor that a single firm will do the job any better than another. As the project moves forward and the real work begins, you'll realize quickly enough whether you've made the right staffing choices. Put another way, you never really know who's swimming naked until the tide goes out.

The RFP Process

If you don't yet have a data warehouse, you're probably considering drafting an RFP (Request for Proposal) to obtain an idea of the prices and features of various hardware and software products. If you already have a data warehouse, you've probably deployed at least a few RFPs already, and you may well continue to do so as you supplement your business capabilities.

Regardless of where you are, understanding how to submit an RFP will not only guide your vendors in delivering optimal responses, it will save you a lot of work in evaluating the resulting proposals. An RFP is often the only written communication a candidate vendor will receive from your company. If done right, it will make you look good. If done badly, well . . .

The Components of a Good RFP

Many companies in search of technology solutions have tried the "throw it at the wall and see what sticks" method of generating RFPs. This means vaguely outlining what the company is thinking of doing, distributing the RFP to a hundred or so vendors, and wading through all the responses to see which one's cheapest.

If price is your only evaluation metric, then fine, choose a vendor based on the lowest price. This makes the RFP creation a lot easier. But, since you'll be drafting a second RFP for the next vendor to clean up the resulting mess, I'd recommend drafting a structured and well-thought-out RFP the first time around, and evaluating responses based on a number of different metrics, including price.

The list below details nine essential components of an effective RFP.

Company Overview

This section should briefly describe your company and its industry and then review its history, revenues, and market share. Historical information and important company milestones such as recent mergers and acquisitions and changes in executive staff should also be included.

Problem Description

The RFP should explain the company's original business drivers and provide all necessary background information, including details about failed projects or false starts. The problem overview should give respondents a general idea of the "need, pain, or problem" that the proposal should address.

Solution Guidelines and Objectives

This part of the RFP should outline a set of questions or issues for the vendor to address. If the proposal is for technology, it is appropriate to list detailed questions about functions and features here. If you are requesting a consulting proposal, ask for details about job roles, methodologies adopted, and software tools used.

The RFP should present a pro forma implementation solution description to help respondents craft the right approach or propose the optimal technology products. For example, if the proposal involves building a new front-end application for an existing data warehouse, you might see your project occurring in three stages:

Phase I: Business Analysis
Phase II: Prototyping and User Acceptance
Phase III: Implementation

Ask the vendor to describe a concise solution for each of the phases, including product, consulting, and approach. Be sure to specify the objectives of each phase, as well as the ideal outcome, for example:

At the end of phase II, the Bank expects to have a functional prototype for financial reporting, including at least 13 canned reports and a range of ad hoc capabilities that match the requirements outlined in phase I of the project.

If the proposal involves technology products, be sure to specify the exact type of technology on which you would like the vendor to bid. Asking the vendor to describe and price a solution from scratch without describing the existing technology infrastructure or intended product purchases can foment misunderstandings and confusion, resulting in disparate responses. Better to specify the components you're interested in (hardware platform, operating system, database software, industry data model and Web-enabled tools) and how you expect them to fit together with what you've already got.

To maintain objectivity and ensure completeness, many companies retain a third-party vendor—who is not involved in the bidding—to help produce this section of the RFP, as well as to help judge the resulting responses.

Evaluation Metrics

Professionalism and fair play dictate that evaluation metrics are standardized for all potential respondents. This not only "levels the playing field," rendering each vendor equal in a full and unbiased consideration, it also mitigates the likelihood of unpleasant accusations from the losing vendors once you've made your selection. ("Hey! Vendor B was chosen because their salesman plays golf with the head actuarial's brother!")

Evaluation metrics force responding vendors to go on record with their strengths and weaknesses and provide a glimpse of what you are looking for. "Ability of vendor to provide senior-level expertise in implementing our ROLAP application" is a sample evaluation metric. Another is, "Vendor's list of customer references in the insurance industry."

Staff Expertise

If the RFP requires consulting or implementation expertise, detail the desired skill sets. Be specific about individual project roles. "Consultants should all have at least five years experience, three of which involved relational database implementation," could apply just as well to a programmer as to a business analyst. This is where an open-ended question is OK, as in, "Describe the skill sets of the particular consultants slated to deliver application development and state what makes them uniquely qualified." The answer will tell you a lot about the consulting firm's ability to deliver.

Pricing

It's up to you to define how you would like the vendor to price its proposal. While an interesting exercise in gauging various approaches, leaving it up to the vendor to decide between a fixed price and a time and materials rate isn't worth much if your company insists on one or the other.

Remember to request price breakdowns, particularly when the RFP solicits prices for both product and consulting.

Projected Time Line

The RFP should contain a high-level time line that includes

- how long proposal evaluation will take
- the date a decision will be announced
- the projected project start date
- the expected project end date

If vendors are expected to deliver an in-person presentation as a follow-up to their RFPs, specify the window of time reserved for oral presentations. Be sure to elucidate that presentations will be scheduled two to three weeks in advance and that vendors will be contacted accordingly. This clarification will save you from a rash of telephone queries from eager vendors preparing their pitches.

Terms

You probably already have these in some standard corporate contracts. The terms protect you in the event that the project is canceled, or if none of the proposals submitted is accepted. Terms might also stipulate that proposals become your confidential property, or that the RFP process doesn't bind you to accepting the lowest-priced proposal. See your company's legal staff for exact wording.

Proposal Response Guidelines

Before distributing an RFP, you should understand the mechanics of proposal review. Will you be assembling a proposal review team, or is management deciding? Will there be a meeting at which everyone will vote, or an informal e-mail consensus? Knowing the answers up front will help you handle the following essential details:

- Create a proposal structure and formatting guidelines so that evaluators aren't comparing apples to oranges when evaluating responses.
- Include a proposal delivery address with the name and suite number of an actual staff member, so that respondents aren't left wondering if the proposal left in the lobby ever made it upstairs.
- State how many copies of the proposal should be submitted.
- State the proposal delivery deadline, and include a time as well as a date, so that you're not awaiting laggard proposals at 11:45 P.M.
- Establish a process and deadline for submitting questions anonymously and in writing, and explain the procedure somewhere in the RFP document. Vendors will inevitably have questions about the RFP and its contents. While many companies hold general meetings at which vendors can ask their questions in an open forum, thereby permitting all bidders to hear questions and responses, vendors are often reluctant to query the RFP in front of their rivals for fear of betraying their strategies. Thus questions remain unanswered, possibly affecting the resulting proposal.

A Sample Table of Contents

The sample RFP table of contents in table 7-1, from a financial services firm interested in developing a dependent data mart, shows how these various components can be tied together. Notice the relative length of each section.

Table 7-1: Sample RFP Table of Contents

BestBank Data Mart
Request for Proposal

Section	Page
Introduction	i
I. Company Background	1
a. Introduction to management	
b. Company profile	
c. Where we're headed	
II. Statement of Need	2
a. Business drivers for dependent data mart approach	
b. End-users and requirements	
III. Solution Description and Components	5
a. Proposed functionality: data mart	
b. Proposed functionality: analysis tools	
IV. Response Guidelines	11
V. Vendor Qualification	13
a. Technology criteria	
b. Consultant criteria	
c. Description of implementation approach	
d. Description of vendor company	
e. Resume guidelines	
f. References	
VI. Pricing and Terms	22
VII. Delivery Criteria and Question Clarifications	23
Appendix: Existing Technology Infrastructure	A-1
a. Network topology map and intranet	
b. Data warehouse database design (physical tables)	

The best and most effective RFPs are those that nimbly balance corporate strategy and technical ideas, walking the fine line between confidentiality and disclosure while leaving vendors plenty of room to showcase the best products and services they have to offer.

Some Lingering Questions

All your admonishments about hiring metrics and skill sets are fine, but I've been working with my client for over a year, and honestly, I'm doing the same job as a consultant that I'd be doing if I were a full-time employee. There's really little difference at the end of the day, right?

I once wrote an article for a high-profile IT magazine titled "Give Consultants a Break!," which was a tongue-in-cheek diatribe on how clients don't really know what to do with us consultants. It humorously described how customers often subject us to crazy deadlines and cryptic time sheets and never show us where the bathroom is.

Trouble was, in its effort to save space the magazine edited out the humor. The piece ended up sounding like an angry piece of invective about how consultants are abused and mistreated. My partners and I braced ourselves for the backlash from our clients and prospects.

A few days after the article ran, I logged on to my e-mail to find 93 new messages waiting. My career flashing before my eyes, I began scanning each message, expecting the worst.

Surprise! The vast majority of the e-mails weren't from angry customers taking me to task for my ungrateful ranting and canceling their contracts forthwith, but from consultants far and wide praising me for telling "the truth." One consultant claimed to have anonymously left copies of the article on the desks of each of her client's managers.

The point here is that consulting requires a perspective entirely different from that of working for the customer directly. Some consultants handle this well, remembering who they work for and professionally focusing on their objectives. Other consultants go native. If you're a consultant assisting a client with a data warehouse project, reread the skills section in chapter 6 to make sure your expertise is being focused correctly, and take a look at some of the books listed in the appendix.

If you're a client in need of data-warehousing expertise, remember to delineate skill sets, focus on the basics, and hold your consultants accountable for delivering. Treat them as part of the team, not as second-class citizens, but make it clear that they're expected to train your people and to render themselves dispensable over time. Oh, and please show them where the bathroom is!

PART III

Getting Ready

CHAPTER EIGHT

Data Warehousing's Business Value Proposition

Farming looks easy when your plow is a pencil and you're a thousand miles from a cornfield.

—Dwight D. Eisenhower, speaking in Peoria in 1956

So now that you know the right way to run your data-warehousing project, how do you go about starting one in the first place? This chapter discusses how to justify a data warehouse as a business solution and presents some of the steps necessary to secure funding and get going.

As part of its study "Compass International IT Strategy Census 1999," the London School of Economics polled 650 CEOs worldwide in an effort to gauge the effectiveness of IT in aligning with business goals. The CEOs' main beef with their IT counterparts? According to the study, it was their failure to provide ways to measure return on investment (ROI).

This chapter presents several tools that you can start using to tackle this challenge. While there is no one correct solution—expectations will vary across companies and management styles—we'll discuss some of the metrics with which you can justify a new data warehouse, or maintain the one you already have.

Return on Investment

ROI calculation is a much-discussed but little-practiced activity in data warehousing. With traditional operational

231

applications such as billing or reservations systems, a development team can deliver against goals that have been delineated at the outset and are relatively straightforward and measurable. It is rare for a new transaction-based system to be built devoid of any financial calculations.

But the cost of a decision support system is more difficult to justify up front. For one thing, the business areas and processes these systems aim to address are constantly in transition, with their objectives routinely changing course midstream. For another thing, even though decision support can ultimately deliver thousands or millions of dollars in direct savings or revenue growth, it isn't usually recognized as mission-critical by the business at large. Moreover, there are virtually no established metrics on which to base DSS success. Initially, it's often a lone visionary manager who can see how data warehousing can benefit his company and who appreciates that those benefits are only the tip of the iceberg.

In his best-selling book *Crossing the Chasm*, Geoffrey A. Moore paints a picture of such a visionary as not just an early adopter, but a risk taker:

> Visionaries drive the high-tech industry because they see the potential for an "order-of-magnitude" return on investment and willingly take high risks to pursue that goal. They will work with vendors who have little or no funding, with products that start life as little more than a diagram on a whiteboard. . . . They know they are going outside the mainstream, and they accept that as part of the price you pay when trying to leapfrog the competition.[1]

Moore goes on to explain that these visionaries are recognized as such and are thus often immune from the budget and approval constraints that bind their peers.

> Because they see such vast potential for the technology they have in mind, they are the least price-sensitive of any segment of the technology adoption profile. They typically have budgets that let them allocate generous amounts toward the implementation of a strategic initiative.[2]

A 1997 Forrester Research study discovered that only 16 of 50 companies polled established ROI figures prior to implementing their data warehouses. Moreover, many data warehouses begin as simple analysis reports for a finite set of users, only later evolving into corporatewide information solutions. Are these

---

1. Moore, Geoffrey A., *Crossing the Chasm,* New York: HarperCollins, 1991, 35.
2. Moore, *Crossing the Chasm.*

systems paying for themselves? Their users would contend heartily that yes, they are. But there may be no corroborating figures.

Incidentally, this is the same challenge that companies faced with office automation in the late 1970s and early 1980s. Proponents fought for word processing systems and spreadsheets, advocating their widespread adoption across the enterprise, because they discerned that these new tools, now so fundamental in the workplace, represented access to and manipulation of information.

The fact that the data warehouse and its accompanying e-data improve decision-making capabilities and deliver customer information would seem to be enough of a justification. Nevertheless, some companies are insisting on concrete proof, especially in light of frequently publicized data warehouse failures. Some executives—not visionaries, but pragmatists whose focus is rightly on the bottom line—won't spend a dime on a data warehouse unless they see promise of measurable payback. This is especially true if the data warehouse is sold internally as a technology rather than a business solution. Indeed, if the term "data warehouse" is used in lieu of the more business-friendly "decision support" or "business intelligence," even though the end result is the same it is even more likely that management will enforce ROI estimates.

However, few of these executives consider data-warehousing's opportunity cost, that is, what financial gains the investment might deliver if it were applied elsewhere, say, to a new distribution system. Or, heaven forbid, how much money would be saved—or lost—by deciding not to take on data warehousing at all?

The widespread success of data marts is in my opinion partly attributable to the fact that they are not tied to an ROI mandate. Most of the time a data mart is driven by a single organization and is developed using nontraditional resources and unauthorized technologies. In short, data marts don't fall under the rubric of those large technology initiatives—like enterprise data warehouses—that warrant executive-level sign-off. By "flying below the radar," data marts can deliver targeted decision support to business users, introducing them to self-directed data analysis while dispensing with the need for protracted business case development and hard cost-benefit justifications.

Be it a data mart or a data warehouse, any type of benefit evaluation should distinguish between "hard ROI," that is, tangible savings and increases in revenue, and "soft ROI," such as greater levels of satisfaction, increased prestige, and higher productivity (see figure 8-1). While hard ROI merely weighs costs against overall financial benefits, soft ROI, though harder to measure, is just as critical, and often has broader impact.

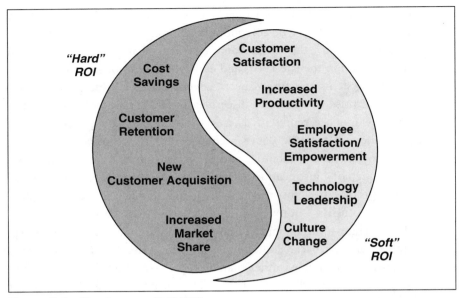

Figure 8-1: Hard versus Soft ROI

Certain executives familiar with the benefits of data warehousing might claim that soft ROI should supersede hard ROI, since the data warehouse arguably offers a company more in terms of cultural and process improvements, not to mention innovation and creativity. Nevertheless, when both are considered together, it's a powerful combination.

Hard ROI: The Tangible Benefits

Sometimes calculating hard ROI for a data warehouse is easy. The ability to project the cost of the data warehouse versus its payback can be simple in broad terms.

Whether determining ROI for a new data warehouse or for a new application on an existing data warehouse, the company's first task is to identify areas where the data warehouse might help improve business, or what might be called data-warehousing "sweet spots." These sweet spots can be business processes, new corporate initiatives, or functional areas such as campaign management or e-commerce support.

Data warehousing yields two main benefits:

- Direct savings, reflected in reduced production, distribution, staff, and supplier costs.

- Increased revenue, through cross-selling, price adjustments to increase margins, new customer acquisition, or cancellation of products or services. While this last strategy may mean decreased revenues due to lost sales of the cancelled product, it can also mean increased profits due to the cost savings associated with not having to develop or market that product. The goal here is knowing which products no longer justify their associated expense.

The cost-cutting strategy is often the first one that organizations new to data warehousing pursue. The entire premise of bottom-line improvement suggests the more efficient management of business processes such as inventory control, supplier costs, or advertising. The benefit of data warehousing is that it allows a historical look at these processes.

Example 1: Hard ROI at a Retailer

A retailer with $600 million in annual sales called us a while back for help in producing a management report containing a cost-benefit analysis of its pending data warehouse. While profitable, the company had no way of knowing which items its stores currently had on their shelves, so it had no way of analyzing whether certain items were overstocked or understocked, and which weren't moving at all.

Moreover, at any given time the retailer had $75 million worth of inventory across the entire company and averaged 12 annual inventory turns; in other words, every product in the store was replenished once a month on average. Idle merchandise, particularly perishable goods, costs retailers big money. If it could increase the number of inventory turns, the retailer could dramatically reduce its "carrying costs," resulting in significant savings.[3]

A data warehouse was acquired to track store inventories and monitor sales, surveying the rate at which merchandise entered and left the stores. Because they could finally track sales activity and product levels at the store, merchandisers were able to stop buying goods that weren't moving. This slowed the buildup of idle products, allowing the store to increase its annual inventory turns by .5. This small increase translated into a saving of over $320,000.

---

3. It was the automobile manufacturers that first recognized that it wasn't worth the space—and money—to stock inventory that wasn't being used. This drove the idea of "just-in-time" ordering. Retailers, especially those selling perishable items, adopted this model in order to streamline their inventory and sell-through process as much as possible.

The retailer was also able to streamline the supply chain, improve its ordering process, and thus reduce the cost of storing goods. The "soft" benefits included higher job satisfaction among merchandisers, as well as happier vendors.

After the first year, the retailer was able to determine a longer-term hard ROI for its data warehouse. Extrapolating from the success of its first year, the company estimated that inventory turns would slowly increase, saving $1.26 million. Since the total cost of the data warehouse was $850,000, it will have funded itself in little more than two years.

We created an ROI estimate sheet (figure 8-2) to give management a snapshot of the details.

Although far from a protracted analysis of ROI, this one-page snapshot allowed management to eyeball the extent to which the data warehouse would deliver results. The sheets are assembled for each new data warehouse application in order to help the project's sponsors internally compete for future data warehouse project funding.

Fiscal Premise:

—$600 million annual sales
—$75 million on-hand inventory
—$12 estimated store inventory turns

Justification Premise:

Inventory turns will increase due to
—timely and accessible sell-through data.
—identification of inventory plans at category, store, region, and chain levels.
—dramatically reduced out-of-stock situations.
—reduction of nonperforming items.

Operational Premise:

—Online sales reporting and merchandising will allow company to reshape overall category item mix continually.
—Exception-based reporting will support this activity.
—Management will establish inventory goals.

	Increase in Turns	Decrease of Inventory	Carrying Costs/Year	Savings/Year
Year 1	0.50	$4.2M	7.50%	$0.32M
Year 2	0.70	$6.0M	7.50%	$0.45M
Year 3	0.80	$6.6M	7.50%	$0.495M
Total				$1.26M

Figure 8-2: Retail ROI Estimate Sheet

It's important to note that despite the significant cost savings over time, increasing inventory turns with the data warehouse wasn't a "killer app," but a set of business objectives enabled with e-data and decision support.

After six months of using the data warehouse, the retailer introduced several other DSS initiatives, such as reducing the loss of perishable goods and improving seasonal ordering. Each of these new applications fine-tuned the basic inventory turn procedure, and each introduced even greater savings.

Example 2: Hard ROI at a Telecommunications Company

In the telecommunications world, some products represent free profit, since they already exist on a switch. As noted in chapter 4, voice features such as call forwarding and call waiting require no supply cost but are simply switched to "on" upon a customer's order.

One of my telephone company clients, recognizing that selling additional voice services could mean free revenue and high profits, made it a top marketing priority to stimulate voice feature sales. But the company had over 80 of these voice features in its product repertory. The challenge was how to let customers know about these products (not to mention which products to sell to which customers). Executives soon realized that in order to augment sales, they needed to target the right services to the right customers the first time.

The company's existing mass-mailing costs for vertical features averaged $50,000 a month. First, customers who already had one or two of the products were assumed to be more likely to understand their value and buy additional services. This assumption was later confirmed using data mining.

Having identified existing vertical feature users, the data warehouse could then cut the target audience in half by offering three- and-four item packages to existing customers, in effect up-selling.

The company subsequently reduced its mailing costs by roughly half, saving around $25,000 per month, but an additional benefit was the rise in mailing response rates through more targeted campaigns, which increased its total revenue yield as well.

An ROI estimate sheet for the telephone company's opportunity is shown in figure 8-3.

You'll notice that this sheet tracks revenue generation as well as cost savings. The telephone company could actually use its data warehouse to drive additional product sales, thereby increasing revenues even more.

A typical example of revenue generation using a data warehouse is the airline industry's yield management programs. As discussed in chapter 4, airlines need

Fiscal Premise:

—Monthly vertical features mass mailing costs $50,000.
—100,000 customers currently have one or more vertical features.

Operational Premise:

—Simple reports indicate names and addresses of customers with existing vertical features.
—Subsequent mailings will target only these customers.
—Increased response rate will result in sales uplift.

Justification Premise:

Cost reduction will occur due to
—fewer mailed units (decreased postage and labor fees).

Revenue will be generated due to
—increased sales of vertical features.
—increased likelihood of the purchase of two or more features.

"Soft ROI" will be realized due to
—increased customer satisfaction (fewer mailings to nontargeted customers/greater hit rate to targeted customers).

	Target Audience	Cost:	Resulting New Customers	Resulting Revenue	Investment Return
Traditional Mailings (Random)	100,000 prospects	50,000	1,000	$2500/month $30,000/year	20 months to recoup investment
Post-Data Warehouse Mailings (Qualified Customers)	100,000 prospects	$50,000	2,000	$5000/month $60,000/year	10 months to recoup investment. 20% ROI in first year, 140% cumulative ROI after second year.

Figure 8-3: Telecommunications ROI Estimate Sheet

to fill as many seats as possible, because each empty seat is a perishable commodity, representing lost revenue that can never be regained. Data warehouses that result in sales uplift for airlines thus pay for themselves very quickly.

Remember: The success of any ROI exercise rests on the availability of existing cost data and sales figures. Normally this information exists on a data warehouse. Ironically, it's difficult for a company to justify the cost of a data warehouse accurately if it doesn't have one.

Soft ROI: The Intangible Benefits

It's hard to put a dollar value on improved data quality or user empowerment. Have they rendered businesspeople more productive or operations more efficient? Have they positively or negatively impacted sales? And how are these factors actually measured?

Well, they may not need to be, especially if the data warehouse in question can prove hard ROI. But data warehouses can also result in "soft" improvements whose impact is arguably just as hard-hitting as bottom-line growth. Let's look at some of these more closely.

Improved Data Quality

A data warehouse improves the quality of operational data by enforcing data cleanup before loading. The fact that data is of higher quality once it's on the warehouse means that business users trust it more. This increased data reliability has the additional benefit of giving end-users greater confidence in their decision making.

Accessible Business Information

A data warehouse by definition consolidates disparate information from a variety of different sources into one location. In other words, it frees multiple users from having to go to multiple places to find the information they need by providing one-stop shopping for key business data. Whether the platform itself is centralized or distributed across several servers, the fact that the data is available to business users in one consistent way can result in increased productivity and untold cost savings.[4]

Streamlined Supply Chain

As we saw in the retail example above, the data warehouse can streamline the supply chain, partially or completely. Perhaps delivery personnel can enter point-of-delivery information into a hand-held device that transmits data back to corporate headquarters for eventual tracking via the data warehouse. Or maybe

---

4. Actually, "accessible business information" can be viewed as a hard benefit as well as a soft one. For example, if I have 10 different servers across the company all getting the same information from the billing system, the ongoing cost of 10 different transformation routines, 10 system administrators, 10 licenses, etc. is probably higher than consolidating the data onto one platform over time.

clickstream analysis can indicate to an e-tailer that a certain product takes too long to find and should be easier to locate on the Web site. Frito-Lay has been praised for its ability to analyze product distribution and then transfer certain items nearing expiration to higher-volume retail outlets. A by-product of supply-chain improvement is that vendors will probably become more efficient, resulting in better service and even discounts for their customers.

Employee Satisfaction

We've already talked about the cultural potential of a data warehouse. Business users who may be accustomed to waiting weeks or months for information can now retrieve it with a simple mouse-click. But beyond that, employees who may have been involved only in information delivery before the data warehouse existed—assembling reports for management or building cumbersome spread-sheets—can now take on additional tasks, and in many cases actually act on the content of that information themselves rather than having to disperse it far and wide for review.

Customer Satisfaction and Enhanced Customer Service

A call center employee able to look up information about a customer while that customer is on the line probably doesn't know that it's the data warehouse that's providing the profile. All he knows is that the customer has been ranked as a valuable small-business operator and is a good candidate for add-on services.

The customer doesn't know about the data warehouse either. All she knows is that because she's just established a line of credit over the phone, she can upgrade all the workstations in her office. Most companies acquire data warehouses to cut costs and ultimately drive revenues. Customer satisfaction is a happy by-product of data warehousing when mailings are more targeted and fewer customers are "bothered," or when companies can predict service problems or next likely purchases *before* the customer calls.[5]

Perceived Technological Leadership

This underestimated benefit can actually mean the difference between an acknowledged industry leader and a late adopter. Many companies look to their

---

5. According to the University of Michigan, a company's rating on the American Customer Satisfaction Index—a survey of consumer responses to over 200 companies—is directly related to that company's stock price. Thus, customer satisfaction might be a "hard ROI" metric after all!

industry "best practice" brethren before acquiring strategic technology, and each industry has a few acknowledged leaders that have been at the forefront of data warehousing.

State Farm Insurance tracks millions of accident records each year, analyzing the data to assess claims and track injuries. But the company does something else with the data: It releases statistics on the most dangerous U.S. intersections, thereby providing a valuable public service that has resulted in traffic and infrastructure improvements across the country. State Farm has been lauded for leveraging its data for both private and public gain. The company has thus elevated its strategic use of e-data into nothing short of a public relations coup.

People inside and outside a technology leader's industry look to these companies to promote trends. The press writes about them, the competition is afraid of them, and everyone wants to work for them. And you too could be one of them.

Budgeting for the Data Warehouse

Budgeting can eat up day after dismal day of a manager's time. The most experienced—and weary—managers try saving time by applying formulaic numerical estimations across the board, regardless of what they're budgeting for. Interestingly, data warehouses are being used more and more by companies that want to do away with budgeting altogether and instead determine a project's ongoing worth by monitoring a series of up-to-the-minute performance metrics.[6]

Developing a cost scheme for the data warehouse is more complex than simply overlaying standard IT "guesstimates" about hardware costs and database licenses. A typical budgeting exercise includes staff and ongoing infrastructure costs as well as hardware and software costs.

Of course, before you begin to cost out your data warehouse you should first answer some general questions:

- How large will this data warehouse be?
- How many people will be needed to support it?
- How many users will there be?
- What skill sets do we have in house?
- About how much short- and long-term data will there be?
- Where will the data warehouse physically reside?

---

6. Hope, Jeremy and Tony Hope, *Competing in the Third Wave: The Ten Key Management Issues of the Information Age*, Cambridge, MA: Harvard Business School Press, 1997.

Technology Costing

Table 8-1 shows a typical itemized allocation estimate. (Note that the costs are fictitious.)

The biggest mistake people make when developing their technology budgets is ignoring infrastructure costs, those mundane items such as the workstations on end-users' desktops or PC upgrades. In many cases technologies will need to be either acquired or improved prior to delivering business intelligence applications. The cost to acquire or upgrade peripheral technologies should be incorporated into the overall cost estimate in order to avoid unpleasant implementation surprises.

Table 8-1: Estimating Technology Costs

Technology	
Data warehouse hardware	
10 CPU / 2 GB memory, 400 GB RAID	800,000
Annual maintenance/upgrades @ 17%=	82,500
DBMS software license	
150 seats @ $1000/seat (concurrent users)	150,000
Annual maintenance/upgrades @ 15%=	22,500
Application tool	
150 seats @ $875/seat=	131,250
Support @ 15%=	19,688
Query gateway	50,000
Support @ 15%=	7,500
Workstation upgrades (memory)	
$250/user for 100 users=	25,000
Development tools	
Data management suite (modeling, transformation/metadata)	100,000
version control software upgrade	8,000
misc. systems mgmt. tools	50,000
Total technology:	**1,446,438**

Many of the anticipated costs can be gathered directly from hardware and software vendors. In cases where these vendors have not yet been chosen, averaging the costs from candidate vendors is a good short-term solution.

Resource Costing

The most important thing to note about resource costing is that staff resources change a lot more frequently than technology, so such an estimate should account for all planned development activities throughout the year. Every new data warehouse application will require additional staff, be they developers, business analysts, or data loaders. The following section on Data Operations Planning explains how to plan for and prioritize these applications.

The "data warehousing is a process" tag line applies very well here. Don't expect existing staff members to embrace new work as it comes down the pike, but expect to hire new staff members as new projects come up.

Table 8-2 shows a simple example of a year's worth of resource costs. Note that both internal staff members and external consultants have been budgeted for, and that requirements gathering and training activities have also been considered.

Once data warehouse costs have been estimated, the task of determining ROI can range from easy to impossible. The ease is directly proportional to the expense data that exists today. If you are looking for a broad brush formula but lack available expense information, you are in for a big surprise: You can't determine future cost savings unless you understand what you're spending today. And measuring costs against soft benefits such as "improved sales forecasts" or "more successful promotional campaigns" is also unrealistic.

For example, a food services company is painfully aware that distributing paper-based sales reports to its regional sales managers in all 137 regions costs around $14,000 per week in data collection labor, assembly, and postage, plus another $7,000 biweekly for compensation reporting. This adds up to a monthly report distribution expense of $70,000.

Let's say the total first-year cost of the data warehouse is a little over $4 million, as estimated in tables 8-1 and 8-2. It would take just under five years for the data warehouse to pay back that first-year cost. While this doesn't account for ongoing expenses, neither does it factor in the several other valuable applications developed with the data warehouse during that period that would perhaps save the company even more money. Nor does it cover the improved productivity gains and employee satisfaction that accompany on-demand reports.

Table 8-2: Estimating Resource Costs

Resources	
Internal* (internal real costs)	
Project manager @ 80/hour	128,000
1 DBA @ 75/hour	120,000
1 Data administrator @ 75/hour	120,000
System administrator@ 60/hour	96,000
Network administrator @ 60/hour for 6 weeks (sporadic)	14,400
Data modeler @ 75/hour for 4 weeks	12,000
Senior programmer @ 75/hour	120,000
Programmer @ 60/hour	96,000
Data loader @ 60/hour	96,000
Total internal resources:	802,400
External**	
Management consultant: business analysis 2 @ 250/hour for 6 weeks	120,000
Application tool vendor consulting: 185/hour for 4 weeks	29,600
Database designer: 175/hr for 3 weeks	21,000
SQL programmer: 150/hour for 4 weeks	24,000
Contract programmers: 3 @ 125/hour for 4 months	240,000
Total external resources:	434,600
Total resources:	**1,237,000**
*Internal employees based on 40 weeks/year unless otherwise noted	
**Consultants based on 42 weeks/year unless otherwise noted	
Miscellaneous	
Application training (50 users)	40,000
Total first-year costs:	**2,723,438**

The first question I ask a client who has requested help estimating data warehouse ROI is, "What current costs can you provide in order for us to determine potential savings?" When the client insists that no current cost information is available—not surprisingly, this answer comes mostly from clients who don't as yet have a data warehouse—the exercise becomes a lot more complex.

Obtaining Funding—But Not Too Much!

As important as it is for data warehouse projects to be adequately funded, we should temper our rush for budget money. Although data warehouses require capital investment, often in the millions of dollars, too much money can actually be a bad thing. For starters, it renders development organizations complacent, removing the sense of urgency. And the amount of money allocated is directly proportional to end-users' expectations.

I know of one company that has invested more than $50 million in its corporate data warehouse, an enterprisewide system supporting several dependent data marts and spanning business divisions. Because of its early DSS successes, the company automatically allocates $3 million annually in steady state funding to each of its four divisions for continued data warehouse development. Rather than using the funds to launch new applications or implement new tools, the divisions spend the money on data warehouse application maintenance plus training, seminar fees, travel to conferences, regular analyst briefings, etc. Nothing with any business impact has been delivered in over three years. And $12 million could go a long way toward implementing knowledge discovery or purchasing an integrated campaign-management tool.

Small software companies and venture capital–funded start-ups take the equity they need until they reach their delivery milestones. Then they take more money. Data warehouse projects should be run the same way.

The smart thing to do is establish an iterative planning schedule, estimate the value of each discrete project, and prioritize projects using an operating plan. This tactic will not only provide you with the long view of your data warehouse development process but also supplement your intelligence regarding budget estimates. And not to put too fine a point on it, proactive planning can help you avoid an unwelcome management inquisition later on.

Data Warehouse Operations Planning

Sometimes money isn't the issue. I work with a handful of customers with billion-dollar IT budgets for whom prioritization and execution are much bigger headaches than funding.

You may not belong to this group. In fact, your IT budget may be in the thousands, not the billions. Nevertheless, someone's going to ask the question, "How're ya gonna deliver [name of data warehouse project] by [requested delivery date]?"

An implementation roadmap and a sound project planning methodology are both valuable tools, but they won't help you prioritize data warehouse deliverables based on business need. System development lifecycles, however rigorous, aren't enough. Management wants to see a detailed implementation plan that not only gives a time line but outlines a methodical approach to implementation, staffing, and future funding—all aligning with the overarching goals of the enterprise. An operating plan shows managers and decision makers that the data warehouse isn't just an exaggerated reward at the end of a nebulous rainbow.

Furthermore, once they get a taste of the sweet elixir that is information, end-users won't stop drinking. Every sales and marketing organization, not to mention operations and logistics, understands its upcoming initiatives, and each organization has a set of financial objectives that can be translated into tactics. In short, your company's business community understands what it needs and will probably let you know. Sorting through the complex and often diverse set of business needs can be overwhelming.

To top it off, the data warehouse development team may have no formal means of gathering these requirements, let alone recording them. At worst, there's no formal process in place for business users to communicate their requirements. At best, development doesn't exactly know how to translate those needs into tactics.

A development methodology doesn't define detailed deliverables and doesn't coordinate those deliverables with business needs. Nor does it synchronize the timing of those deliverables with the corporation's most critical objectives. And all the project plans in the world won't indicate exactly when you should hire the right resources. In short, a data warehouse should be managed like a small software development company, and having an operating plan is a very good start.

Developing an Operating Plan

An operating plan is a simple method of tracking, estimating, and representing new business needs for your data mart or warehouse. It consolidates a series of forms that together help establish a data warehouse or data mart as a business program with a set of projects and deliverables that align with business needs during the year. It helps turn one or more corporate initiatives into tactical, requirements-driven applications and ensures that the data warehouse consistently provides business value.

The operating plan allows the data warehouse development team to take each new business requirement and gauge the effort involved before committing either time or resources. Each time a new requirement is defined, the team fills out prerequisite information based on its understanding of the requirement. This forces requirement deliverers—whether executives, business sponsors, or steering committees—to have thought through their needs thoroughly.

Once the requirement has been described, development experts should work together to complete a one-sheet estimation form like the one in figure 8-4.

DM029   Requirement: TopLine Measures Implementation

Summary: A TopLine Measures application would provide high-level financial perfor-mance metrics to division-level executives. The application will require data that does not exist on the Financials data mart. Implementation of this application will require sourcing the new data, which is expected to come from the billing and general ledger systems. This application will also require the acquisition of a Web-enabled EIS reporting tool.

In-Date	2/2/02	Target Delivery		Current Delivery	
Deliverable defined		TopLine Measures reports, identifying cost, cash flow, sales, and market share information			
Corroborating corporate initiative		Unknown			
Projected user community		Divisional executives, including all vice presidents and directors, as well as selected executive assistants			
Number of users		14–17			
Existing data mart data		Sales and revenue data			
Additional data sources		Internal data: general ledger data External data: none			
Existing tools		None			
New tools		EIS system (candidate identification in-process . . . see DM03)			
Skills		Legacy system expertise on G/L and billing; data loading; knowledge of existing load routines; knowledge of new EIS tool			
Resource estimates		1 data loader; 1 data modeler (part-time); 1 app. designer; 1 app. developer			
Dependency/Issue		DM014: Coordinating development effort with sales manage-ment reporting application, including identification of common data sources			
Bus. Analysis		2 staff weeks	Working with executive representatives to document data and usage requirements		
Data structure and management		6 staff weeks	Supplementing database design for financial data; extracting and loading data		
Application development		10 staff weeks	Learning new data/database structures, designing and constructing application		
Training		.5 staff week	Supplementing financial data training with new data; teaching executives		
User support		1 staff week	Training help desk staff on new application and new data structures		

Figure 8-4: Sample Estimation Form

"Who's the sickest?"

Figure 8-5: Prioritization Is Key

Note that the form has a code: DM029. This code will be used as the reference identifier for the project, identifying it in terms of other implementations that might affect it, or be affected by it.

The contents of the form are only estimates based on the development team's existing knowledge of the data and work to be done. Much of this estimation will be based on experience with other development efforts.

Once the form is filled out, it should be evaluated against the existing projects in the operating plan document. The evaluation metrics will differ depending on the priorities of the company but may include the following:

- potential ROI benefits of new requirement
- estimated staff time necessary to deliver new requirement
- skills needed prior to beginning development
- any additional costs (hardware, software, product education, specific staff, etc.)
- other applications/projects that deliver similar data/functionality

The evaluation should result in each form assuming an implementation priority based on a set of metrics such as those above. Prioritization, which can range from ease of implementation to the strategic business impact of the application, provides a starting point for long-term planning.

The form should then be inserted into the operating plan document—normally a three-ring binder for easy sheet addition and removal—according to its implementation priority.

Note also that a requirement need not result in a new application. Consider the sample operating form shown in figure 8-6.

DM06   Addition of Account Closure History

Summary: In order to determine churn rates, the new churn application requires data about account closures. This data may also be used on an ad hoc basis by field sales and headquarters marketing staff.

In-Date	9/1/00	Target Delivery		Current Delivery	
Deliverable defined		Three years' worth of account closure or lapse data loaded into the data mart			
Corroborating corporate initiative		Customer retention			
Projected user community		Sales and marketing users			
Number of users		45 (existing)			
Existing data mart data		None			
Additional data sources		Call center system			
Existing tools		N/A			
New tools		N/A			
Skills		Legacy system expertise on call center data; data loading; knowledge of existing load routines			
Resource estimates		1 data loader; 1 data steward			
Dependency/issue		DM035, customer churn prediction application, contingent on this data being loaded			
Bus. analysis	1 staff weeks	Locating and translating of source data			
Data structure and management	2 staff weeks	Mapping source data to existing data model and incorporating it into existing physical design			
		Extracting and loading data			
Application development	N/A				
Training	.5	Alerting end-users once new data is available			
User support	.5	Alerting help desk staff once new data is available; identifying impact on specific data structures			

Figure 8-6: Sample Operating Form

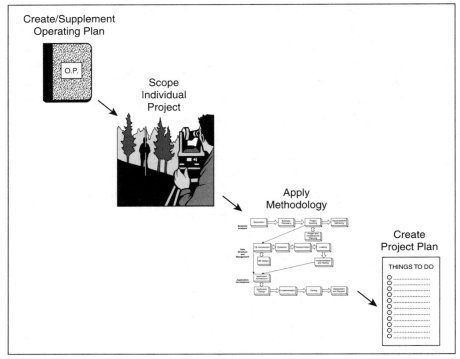

Figure 8-7: Applying the Planning Tools

By having a living document that prioritizes implementation activities as well as enforcing high-level estimates about workloads, skills, tools, and schedules, a development team can prevent "seat of the pants" project work as well as articulate its short- and long-term goals. The information can also be used to gather cost estimates for funding or end-user charge-back purposes.

The operating plan (see figure 8-7) provides centralized answers to questions about upcoming projects, data fulfillment intentions, and resource planning without requiring either end-users or developers to complete a comprehensive project plan for each activity. It can also serve as the basis for a project-scoping exercise, at which time you can check your development methodology to help define the implementation process.

Only once the operating plan is complete should you create the project plan, specifying individual development tasks and schedules. But by then, it's a lot easier.

Are You Ready for a Data Warehouse? A Quiz

You can measure costs and benefits and plan your implementation strategy until the cows come home. But there may be some pain points indicating that your company is in dire need of a data warehouse or data mart, regardless of the payback, and soon!

Answer the questions listed in table 8-3, giving yourself two points each time you answer no and zero each time you answer yes. Then turn the page to discover whether you and your company are really ready for a data warehouse:

Table 8-3: Readiness Quiz

Question	Your Score
1. Do you know which of your sales channels is the most profitable?	
2. Is it simple to find out the collection of products and services attributed to an individual customer?	
3. Are employees happy with their ability to use and respond to up-to-date information?	
4. Do staff interested in knowing how successfully the company sold this product last time get the answer quickly and easily?	
5. Can you determine why a particular division or unit didn't meet its numbers?	
6. You have 500 people in your call center, the phones are always busy. Can you characterize the top three reasons why?	
7. You're spending money on promotional ads, but you might be better off spending it elsewhere. Do you know for sure?	
8. Can you determine what your top 10 salespeople (or stores or branches) are selling that your bottom 10 aren't?	

continued

Table 8-3: Readiness Quiz (continued)

Question	Your Score
9. Is it unheard of for your company to "reassign" budgets in August in an attempt to get them under control by year-end?	
10. Are you finding out about sales or promotions problems quickly after the fact?	
11. Could you easily determine what the last three touch points with a given customer (or patient or cardholder) were?	
12. Are you avoiding runaway IT projects and stovepipe development efforts, having set up a centralized data ownership function that has established standards?	
13. When you put a product on sale and know that customers are buying other products as well, can you find out whether you're really making money on the promotion in under 10 minutes?	
14. If you spent $2.5 million in the last year on training, could you measure how this has helped increase productivity?	
15. Can you tell what your customers are doing on your Web site?	
16. Do you know for sure whether any of your company's employees who were warned about absenteeism have been promoted in the last year?	
17. You know that your customer satisfaction levels aren't up to snuff, but do you know whether it's a billing issue, a product issue, or a service issue?	

continued

Table 8-3: Readiness Quiz (continued)

Question	Your Score
18. Your company keeps investing in technology servers and adding data to them. Can your management explain why each of them needs to be distinct?	
19. Can you honestly claim never to have witnessed a business-person scan a report and exclaim, "These are the wrong numbers!"?	
20. Do you know exactly which time periods are the busiest? (For example, on Mother's Day versus the Friday before?)	
21. Were you completely unsurprised by your organization last end-of-quarter revenues?	
22. Do you know whether your customers are getting better prices on certain products during certain times of the month or year (for example, automobile purchases)?	
23. Are your firm's executive managers comfortable with information distribution and certain that there's no such thing as data that's not valuable enough or people not entitled to have access to it?	
24. Can you tell whether customers actually spend more during promotional campaigns?	
25. Are managers and executives satisfied with the formats, quality, and speed with which they are provided with information?	
26. Regardless of the type of data, are you able to get a day's worth of data in no more than a day?	
Total Score:	

Data Warehouse Readiness Score

Now tally up your points and give yourself a total score.

If your score is less than 24, you're in the "creeping readiness" category.

You've got some work to do before you begin lobbying for a data warehouse, and some of that work is probably cultural. Begin laying the groundwork of cultural acceptance and technology infrastructure before you begin watering the decision support seeds. Begin a data inventory to understand how widely the data you need is distributed across different organizations and systems. The baseline foundation must be solid before you begin building.

If your score is between 24 and 38, you're in the "sweet spot."

It's clear that your company desperately needs decision support capabilities, but your infrastructure may need some beefing up first. Review the questions to which you were unable to answer yes. Do those questions primarily touch on data availability (like questions 3, 10, or 26)? Are they more process-focused, indicating that your company needs to establish basic business functions before reporting on them (as in questions 7 and 9)? Or do they point to some basic cultural problems (like questions 12 and 23) that need to be addressed before anyone moves an inch?

If your score is between 38 and 52, you're behind the eight ball.

If you've hit this level of scoring and don't have a data warehouse, then what the heck *are* you doing? You may actually be performing some sort of decision support, but areas such as data access, report distribution, or streamlined implementation might warrant some improvement. Focus in on the specific questions where you answered no and examine why. Then consider launching a business discovery exercise to consolidate requirements.

Some Lingering Questions

My company's taken the data mart approach because it's been lauded as cost-effective. We've definitely delivered applications quickly and our users are happy. But after I completed the questionnaire, it struck me that our different data marts are generating very similar reports. Does it ever make sense to centralize?

Data marts are generally efficient, especially when they're performing specific functionality that isn't needed cross-functionally. It's when multiple marts extract the same source data and have some of the same reporting objectives that redundancy—and cost—become issues.

Question 12 in the Readiness Survey hits the nail on the head: How much of the same effort is being duplicated merely because of a multiple data mart strategy? Would it be more cost-effective to have a single DBA, a single data transformation routine, and a single group of application programmers all working against the same data—either on a centralized, enterprisewide data warehouse or on data marts linked together into a structured, consistent architecture, thereby minimizing the redundancy of both data and effort?

The latter approach of retroactively linking data marts tends to be more complex and technically challenging than simply consolidating—or in some cases, reconsolidating—data back onto a single data warehouse platform. The concept of "virtual data marts"—separately managed data marts that exist on a single platform, minimizing system management and administrative expenses—has also taken hold.[7]

Whatever approach is chosen, if the consolidation of data marts or the data itself is matched by the ability to ask additional questions that couldn't be asked when the data was in stovepipe systems, you should probably look into bringing the data back together.

---

7. See: Dyché, Jill and Evan Levy, "Beating the Data Mart Blues," *Teradata Review*, spring 1999, 46–49, for a thorough discussion of metrics for how to decide whether reconsolidating data is appropriate for your environment.

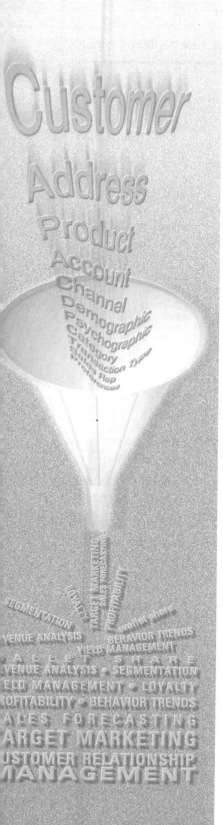

CHAPTER NINE

The Perils and Pitfalls

In the immortal words of the legendary rock band Led Zeppelin, "every now and then a little rain must fall." (Or was that Cosette in *Les Miserables*?) Anyway, whoever said it was unwittingly warning managers about to launch data-warehousing initiatives.

A lot has been written about failed data-warehousing projects and the accompanying lessons learned. Most of the failed data warehouses and data marts that I have seen were characterized by a number of bad decisions that warranted starting over again, rather than an entire misdirected development effort. While failure rates seem to be forever in dispute, with many consultants estimating huge percentages in a covert attempt to frighten prospective clients into hiring them, the process of implementing unsuccessful data warehouses has nevertheless yielded some hard-won lessons.

In an effort to condense some of these lessons, this chapter features several lists. But far from rehashing the overwrought reminiscences of data warehouse projects in peril (". . . and when they finished, they realized they never really knew what the system was supposed to do!"), I'll instead recount some new truths and present an updated perspective on some of the higher-impact, albeit lesser-known, pitfalls in data warehouse delivery and how you can avoid them—or at least prevent them from occurring more than once.

In short, the material in this chapter should prevent you from repeating the mistakes of others, while ensuring that new findings can be put into practice. After all, as the

Grateful Dead's Jerry Garcia put it, "Somebody has to do something, and it's just incredibly pathetic that it has to be us."

The New Top 10 Data-Warehousing Pitfalls

You've seen the unavoidable lists at seminars and conferences, in books, and on the Web. Alternately coined "Dos and Don'ts of Data Warehousing" and "Essential Rules of Data Warehousing," they contain the predictable staple items and hackneyed anecdotes about failed projects or idle systems. The lists invariably contain the following items:

- Design your data warehouse differently than you designed your transaction systems.
- Make sure you don't just load a bunch of data records without understanding their meaning and their business value.
- You must have a committed business sponsor.
- Don't spend months or years developing an enterprisewide data model.
- Don't set unrealistic objectives.
- If you want to fail at data warehousing, don't talk to end-users.

Recently a high-profile (and costly) report by a well-known analysts firm seeking to establish new data-warehousing success criteria was distributed to subscribers. Its top three success criteria were (1) user involvement, (2) setting clear business objectives, and (3) leveraging vendor consultants. The report admonished data warehouse adopters somewhat dramatically:

> The importance of the top three criteria cannot be overemphasized. A failure to achieve in these three critical areas, in our opinion, fatally impairs the success of the proposed data warehouse.

By now, data-warehousing success criteria have been drilled into the overflowing heads of data warehouse practitioners worldwide. They are staples in conference presentations. They have been incorporated into development methodologies. In short, most people who have heard of data-warehousing and business intelligence solutions understand that at some level their development must be requirements-driven, that end-users must participate throughout the development lifecycle, that iterative development is the order of the day, and that developers should be experienced.

So here is our list, "The New Data-Warehousing Pitfalls." The new pitfalls don't just focus on implementation; since so many companies have now delivered decision support in some form, they focus on usage as well. While by the time you read this, several of the items on the list may have become equally ubiquitous, they are nevertheless representative of more recent high-profile data-warehousing projects, in which the old pitfalls were well understood and avoided but new ones cropped up nevertheless.

Pitfall #1: The Data Warehouse as Panacea Syndrome

One of the biggest conundrums in science is rendering a new technology as good as or better than the technology it presumes to replace. The fallacy of regarding data warehouses as panaceas has affected more than a few well-meaning companies. In reality, sometimes a data warehouse is not the best solution to the problem.

A few years ago, I consulted with a telephone company whose CIO asked me to comment on a vendor's unsolicited proposal for a new data warehouse. The vendor was proposing a massive system on which CDRs would be stored. It would make CDRs available to users across the enterprise, from the call center to the R&D department. The vendor estimated that the data warehouse would end up holding five terabytes of data. The entire cost of the proposed system—including hardware, software, and services—totaled $14 million.

The vendor's account team had done its homework. It knew that the telephone company did not have call detail on its existing data warehouse and that online access to switch data was next to impossible. Furthermore, it understood the benefits of call detail data to both the networking and marketing sides of its client's business. The proposal painstakingly reviewed the range of benefits, both tactical and strategic, for providing call detail information to a cross-section of end-users.

But the CIO was unimpressed. "What's missing here?" he grilled me.

I couldn't think of anything. The vendor had made its case. "Uh, your '98 budget?" I stammered.

Testily the CIO replied, "These guys have told me why I need call detail. But they haven't explained why I need to put it on a data warehouse."

He was right. While the vendor had convincingly advocated the distributed use of call detail, it had failed to explain why online, queryable call detail would be more effective than, say, buying an optical storage machine to house and access the data at a fraction of the price, albeit with a great deal more turnaround time for data access. The vendor never justified why the company needed *online* call detail *for business users* to *access dynamically.* In effect, it had succeeded in justifying the need for data, but not the need for e-data.

While I do believe that ultimately the company would have been best served by putting call detail data onto a warehouse—serious call pattern analysis and trending are next to impossible without it—at the time end-users were barely able to call up customer names and addresses. The company's financial and cultural restrictions rendered a call detail data warehouse unrealistic.

When called into a new client to assess a data-warehousing opportunity, one of the first questions we ask is, "Can your business problem really be solved with data?" Sometimes the problem is one of business processes, or culture. If the answer is no, or even maybe, we recommend additional evaluation before the client commits money to the project. It's insurance against the hammer looking for a nail.

Pitfall #2: They Talked to End-Users—But the Wrong Ones!

This sounds like putting too fine a point on an argument, but it happens all the time. The most vocal users are usually the ones to show up in the requirements-gathering workshop. This is known of the process of "squeaky wheel end-user selection." Another problem is when the most technical subset of users is selected to participate in defining business drivers.

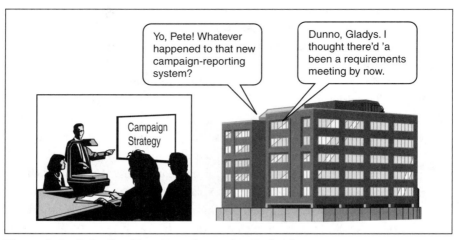

Figure 9-1: Selective User Requirements Gathering

Admittedly, selecting end-users for input into business requirements isn't easy. It's impractical to have 150 people from five different departments sitting in the company auditorium doing a round robin on their financial-reporting needs.

However, it's also a bad idea to choose a group of "subject matter experts" from the user group at large in the hope that the 80–20 rule—that is, 20 percent of the users represent 80 percent of the requirements—will win out. Often, the people who are most articulate in explaining the business problem are those who will delegate the use of the warehouse to others who have entirely different priorities.

Conversely, those who don't seem to care much might have already solved the problem themselves independently. I once attended a prototype session in which end-users were asked to provide feedback on an initial DSS application. Halfway through the prototype demo, someone piped up and said, "So what's so great about that? I can get those reports with my homegrown spreadsheet application . . . you know, the one I wrote over a weekend two years ago." With PCs able to store tens of gigabytes of information and business-people impatient for progress, it's likely that the data warehouse could end up being the right solution too late.

Overcoming disparate end-user needs isn't easy. You should require all staff even remotely likely to use the system—either in its first release or later on—to fill out a questionnaire. The questionnaire should contain both straightforward questions such as, "How would your job improve if you had point-and-click sales figures on your desktop?" and disingenuous ones such as, "If you had access to product data from other categories, how would you use it?"

Compare survey responses to personal interviews or to the findings drawn in requirements-gathering workshops or JAD sessions. Decide who the "core group" of interviewees should be. Then do a gap analysis to figure out who the "outliers" are and interview them specially. This is the surest way to avoid ugly surprises, which can rear their heads tens or hundreds of thousands of dollars into data warehouse development.

Pitfall #3: Too Much Time Spent on Research, Alienating Constituents

This is a roundabout way of saying "analysis paralysis isn't good." With apologies to all hard-working members of advanced technology groups at companies everywhere, a bunch of "assessors" frolicking in the sandbox of technology in an effort to come up with the "chosen corporate standard" for decision support is costing you money, time, potential end-users, and probably external customers.

Understanding the superset of a given technology's functions and features isn't nearly as important as understanding whether that technology meets your business requirements. Also, there are all sorts of agreements you can put in place with vendors if the technology ultimately doesn't work.

Business case development can last an eternity, especially if management has requested ROI information. Often, existing cost data must be calculated anew before determining true ROI, a process that can take months.

In the meantime, targeted end-users have given up hope of ever getting reports at the click of a button. Sometimes an "information underground" is established between end-users desperate for e-data, upping the ante for the eventual data warehouse while rendering it less urgent.

Pitfall #4: Bogging a Good Project Down by Creating Metadata

Companies that are confident in their ability to build and deploy decision support can nevertheless be very insecure about their metadata. Add to this the hype surrounding metadata, and its implementation at all costs becomes a do-or-die priority. Data stewards or technical writers may work full-time just entering data definitions and business rules into a database, while development is put on hold.

The solution? Implement metadata gradually, with the knowledge that it, like the data it describes, will evolve slowly and over time. While the first application might be targeted to power users who already understand the fundamental data elements and their descriptions, development can be preparing metadata for the next release. Iterative implementation is key. Above all, as important as metadata is, its implementation should never be given preference over the delivery of an easy-to-use application.

Pitfall #5: Being Sidetracked by "Neat-to-Know" Analysis

This pitfall goes hand in hand with pitfall number 6. Both hint at the tendency of some companies to deploy strategic technologies and use them for very banal and tactical purposes. While there's nothing wrong with tactics, many end-users simply query the data warehouse for its own sake, experimenting to see whether a given question with little business value can be answered.

The culprits are often those at the top of the pyramid, statisticians or power users trying to run linear regression on customer behavior patterns or using some arcane algorithm against useful data for some less-than-useful purpose. Why? Because they can.

The risk here is that the business value proposition erodes as processing increases. Ultimately, when someone requests a hardware upgrade or a new software tool, management asks the question, "If this data warehouse is so saturated, could you explain how it's helped increase revenues?" No one—not even a Ph.D. in statistics—knows the answer.

Pitfall #6: Adopting Decision Support Without Supporting Decisions

It happens more than we'd like to admit. An elegant, useful, and fully functional data warehouse is released. For the first time, business users can access e-data from their desktops, often discovering new information or findings that could lead to new business strategies.

Trouble is, the users aren't authorized to instigate these new business strategies. Sometimes they're not even allowed to make the decisions triggered by their decision support reports. Rather than taking the newfound knowledge gleaned via DSS and running with it, business users are forced to create formal proposals or fill out forms for management, explaining their ideas and findings in order to justify business actions. This takes time, time that could be spent actually launching a new marketing campaign or loading clickstreams from the Web server. Many users simply don't bother.

Data warehouses and the information they provide should ideally not only corroborate suspicions but also improve business processes and foster inventive business actions. In most cases, they should even incite some sort of cultural transformation within a company, empowering end-users with more data ownership and more responsibility. If your data warehouse only corroborates already accepted hypotheses, or if your end-users can look but can't touch, you're not doing all you can with it.

Pitfall #7: Greediness on the Part of Development Organizations

In the course of its evolution, the data warehouse should straddle the domain between IT and business. In other words, at some point the end-users should start footing the bill. Cross-charging for new applications or data specific to one organization has become a common practice among IT organizations that must prioritize implementation projects while dealing with ever-shrinking budgets.

The trouble with this approach is that IT development organizations start getting greedy and charge a premium for new applications. Some IT groups add as much as 75 percent to their actual costs for creating new applications. While development becomes a profit center, business units that don't pay go to the end of the queue—often irrespective of how critical their requirement is to the company at large.

But the business units are getting wise, increasingly looking to outside consultants to deliver business intelligence solutions. These solutions may require new technologies and may not adhere to the standards that corporate IT has set, but they convey the functionality for less money than a comparable internal project would.

Business organizations should be ready to pay for their DSS needs, but they should be charged at cost. This way, no one loses money, and in addition a centralized strategy can be sustained over time, thus allowing the data warehouse to mature in a single, integrated direction.

Pitfall Number 8: Lack of "Internal PR"

We've touched on it before, but it bears repeating: The most elegant and useful decision support application will fail if no one knows about it. Data warehouse sponsors from both the IT and business sides tend to forget the concept of "internal PR," that is, constantly marketing the capabilities and features of the data warehouse to key organizations and staff members. The aim here is to continually augment the functionality and data features of the warehouse, while increasing the number of end-users.

For data marts, whose functionality and end-user communities are often finite, the same principle applies. Management must understand that sales uplift depends in part on the ability of field staff to execute their own customer profiles and that improved customer satisfaction numbers stem from better customer service levels as defined by the CRM program. Otherwise, new funding for additional data-warehousing initiatives won't be forthcoming.

Staff across the organization should understand that the various new corporate initiatives, from campaign management to e-marketing to frequent-shopper programs, all touch—indeed, rely on—the data warehouse to work. Continuous socialization of the data warehouse and its benefits engenders the support you need to keep it alive and evolving.

Pitfall #9: Failing to Acknowledge That DSS Applications Are Finite

True, most useful DSS applications will be around for years, perhaps even decades. But once every quarter or so, the list of a company's decision support applications should be revisited to see what's required for ongoing support and enhancement.

Just as most software development companies examine the ongoing revenue stream and perceived value of each of their products, a data warehouse development team needs to balance the ongoing business value of a DSS application with the cost of ongoing development and enhancement.

The normal presumption here is that once such an application is built and deployed to end-users, it lasts forever. Moreover, simply because it's been deployed, it has ongoing maintenance dollars associated with it. The fact is, many applications of all sorts cease to be useful—and thus stop being used—for a variety of reasons. It's not that the application or tool is bad, it's just that it has outlived its purpose.

A large bank deployed a product profitability application in the mid-1980s that relied on the company's corporate data warehouse. A companywide activity-based costing project then usurped the data on the warehouse and changed the business processes involved in cost allocation. So the bank revised its mechanisms for determining profitability and acquired a new profitability calculation tool.

Nevertheless, the bank somehow continued to pay support fees to the vendor that had supplied the original profitability tool. Because no periodic review process was in place, no one at the company realized that the initial tool had been rendered obsolete and that no one was using it. For three more years, the bank continued to pay the annual maintenance bill for a software tool that had disappeared.

Figure 9-2: DSS Applications Sometimes Outlive Their Purpose

The bank could have prevented this by establishing a regular review process through which each discrete application is evaluated for functionality and end-user satisfaction. Users should participate in this process, and measurements should be put in place to determine the ongoing life span and features of the application. Metrics such as usage log records (indicating system usage statistics), trouble tickets, and enhancement requests should all figure into the decision to either continue supporting an application or let it die a benign death.

Pitfall #10: Overemphasizing Development and Ignoring Deployment

Perhaps you've seen an unwieldy diagram of a data warehouse implementation process, with all its boxes and arrows pointing hither and yon, and you asked yourself, *But how does the data wind up in my spreadsheet?*

This is a valid question, since many such methodologies focus on getting the data onto the data warehouse. Experienced data-warehousing practitioners understand that the hard part of data warehousing is the extraction, transformation, and loading of the data from various operational systems onto the data warehouse platform of choice.

So that's where they stop.

But a panoply of activities must occur once the data is loaded, of which building the application is only one component. Once the application is built, several decisions need to be made:

- How will we test the application? Will end-users be involved in the testing?
- Once the application is tested, how will we get it onto the desktops of end-users? Is our intranet ready?
- How will the application be maintained? By whom? How often?
- How will the application be supported? Will our help desk be involved? Is additional help desk staff required? Who will train them?
- What about end-user training? Do we know whether the users will need the training? If they do, who will train them?
- What about documentation? Should there be a handbook? Should it include data descriptions as well as how the tool works?
- What about overall system maintenance? How often should the data on the warehouse be backed up in order to protect it? What about usage logging? What about incremental loading and change data capture? Who will decide on these maintenance strategies?

While you as a manager may or may not be concerned about this level of detail, somebody should be. Ignoring postdevelopment issues, whether related to user support or to system maintenance, can result in lackluster rollout of the warehouse or, worse, lack of adoption by end-users—the kiss of death in data warehousing.

Thinking of Outsourcing?

As large consulting firms and systems integrators beef up their outsourcing services and IT infrastructures grow more complex, outsourcing becomes an attractive option for many companies looking to pare down costs and resources.

But as data warehouses begin proving benefits, financial and otherwise, they are increasingly considered to be strategic technologies. And do you really want someone else controlling one of your core competencies?

Outsourcing as a concept isn't bad. When done selectively, it does in fact allow companies to refocus on overarching business objectives such as customer satisfaction and increased wallet share, as it controls only the technologies critical to those programs. Companies that have separated their strategic technologies from their operational systems, outsourcing the latter while maintaining tight control over the former, will be the surefire winners.

The problem with outsourcing is that the large firms providing it by and large focus on technology. They understand databases and software tools and system outage procedures. They don't concentrate on how end-users need to ask and answer their questions. And they don't understand the business problems that drove the establishment of the data warehouse in the first place.

In a recent pitch for new business, a top outsourcing firm encouraged prospective customers to identify valid reasons for outsourcing:

> Are projects delivered on time and within budget? Do you feel you are in control of overall information technology expenditures? Is your internal organization up to speed on the latest technological developments? A "no" to any of these questions would merit a more detailed exploration of outsourcing as an alternative.

The argument goes on to encourage prospective clients to consider the enhanced career paths their staff will enjoy once they are transferred to the outsourcing firm, and it stresses the certain performance improvements to be gained by outsourcing. Nowhere are end-users, let alone the fulfillment of business objectives, mentioned.

Companies that decide in favor of outsourcing their data warehouses normally do so in the mistaken belief that data warehouse development costs are comparable to more traditional OLTP and data center operation expenditures. Unfortunately, this is a comparison of apples and oranges. Thriving data warehouses don't rely on commodity-oriented skills for their development and usage. Business analysis, requirements gathering, and data modeling are specialties that are neither as widely practiced nor as critical in other technologies.

If the premise of outsourcing is to relieve the burden of data center operations by releasing the responsibilities of hardware maintenance, server operations, database administration, and the like, that's fine. But data warehouses, and data marts in particular, are increasingly owned and managed in the line of business. Thus, business expertise becomes part and parcel of the development team. Outsource the data warehouse, and you've lost the accompanying knowledge base.

In fact, outsourcing companies build and maintain systems according to a set of specifications. While these specs may be rigorous, defining terms for data loading, backups, and availability, they don't account for development driven by end-users.

A large insurance company outsourced its data warehouse, along with most of its other large systems, to a major outsourcing and consulting provider. What they got was the efficient management of the data warehouse, quick release of new user IDs, and structured system maintenance procedures. But the outsourcing firm couldn't update the data model once new requirements emerged, nor could it design the applications as well as its client could. Finally, $3 million later, realizing that the outsourcing firm couldn't handle aligning business requirements to technical functionality, the insurance company ended up reassuming many of its core development tasks.

"You have to have control of your strategic technologies if you're going to innovate," said the insurance company's CIO, who, after an expensive false start, actually reclaimed his data warehouse. "We realized that we had too much at stake letting someone else own our data warehouse—and by extension, our data and our end-user relationships. It just wasn't worth it."

The entire premise of outsourcing applies general and historically proven principles of system development and maintenance. To outsource HR, payroll, or accounting systems is to shed a resource-intensive commodity skill base. However, the premise of a data warehouse is to deliver specific and evolving business benefits, frequently with specialized technologies, to aid a company in differentiating its products and services or to gain competitive advantage.

Outsourcing a data warehouse applies commodity resources to a highly specialized set of technologies and skills. Do you really want another firm—one that could also be serving your rivals—controlling online competitive assets as precious as customer names and addresses or lifetime value scores? Unless for some reason you regard your data warehouse as just another component of your technology infrastructure (and if you do, you haven't been paying attention), avoid outsourcing it.

Data Warehousing's Dirty Little Secrets

Here's another list for you. Not to encourage paranoia, but this one describes some common facts that some professionals would rather you didn't know. They're the "dirty little secrets" of data warehousing. There are technology vendors hoping their customers haven't caught on, and data-warehousing development managers praying that their executive sponsors remain in the dark about some of these truisms.

In short, while the list of pitfalls at the beginning of this chapter represents honest mistakes and lessons learned, the following list includes items that data-warehousing experts would like to keep secret. But they're true.

Dirty Little Secret #1:
The large data warehouse vendors struggle
to find good consultants to help you.

We're *all* trying to find good consultants to work on data-warehousing projects, and large vendors don't have any more pull than the rest of the industry. For companies looking to recruit experienced data warehouse talent—especially practitioners with over five years' experience—it's a jungle out there.

Dirty Little Secret #2:
Data modeling gets a disproportionate
amount of attention.

Don't get me wrong. Data modeling and database design are not only crucial to data warehousing's success, they are specialized skills that require training and practice. In the worst cases, a bad data model will result in

- slower response times
- more complex SQL generation
- heavier reliance on software metadata
- the rework of the data model

Notice I didn't say, "the inability of the business to understand fully what it's trying to do with its warehouse." The term "data modeling" is used far too often in conjunction with requirements gathering, and that's precisely why there's so much debate over the various conventions. The implication is that if the data model is badly done, a business will need to return to the very beginning and start over.

However, if requirements gathering has been done prior to data modeling—the requirements being leveraged as input to the modeling activity—there is much less risk of confusion with data modeling. Data modeling is a convention used to document the logical relationships between data elements, not as a means of gathering business requirements. If a data model is used in this fashion, it moves beyond data modeling and can become the de facto requirements

Figure 9-3: Data Modeling Is Not Requirements Gathering

document, not to mention the physical database design. This can have disastrous consequences, even resulting in functionality that's worlds away from the data warehouse's fundamental business objectives.

"The biggest mistake managers make when they hire data modelers and database designers is that they get too caught up in pedantic conventions," says Mike Schmitz, a top database design consultant who has modeled data warehouses on behalf of several vendors. "There's not enough importance attached to communication and creativity, both of which can render the database design process a lot more straightforward."

When requirements are gathered first and then published in a document that a cross-section of managers, end-users, and technical staff can review and approve, data modeling becomes what it was always meant to be: a means of representing business requirements through documenting data relationships, serving as input to the subsequent implementation of the database tables.

Dirty Little Secret #3:
Developers are responsible for significant
processing on the data warehouse.

You've probably seen it happen. An end-user submits a query and waits for the answer to come back. A minute passes. Then another. Exasperated, she calls the help desk and politely inquires, "Where is my data?" the subtext being more along the lines of, "Which idiotic user is saturating the CPU on the data warehouse at the expense of my query?"

Collective finger pointing among business users is often aimed in the direction of the poor DBA, who wields an almost mythical control over the warehouse and has more than likely given himself special access and control privileges. However, if developers are using the production data warehouse to load test data or to prototype new applications, it can cause much more damage than whatever the DBA is doing behind the scenes.

Developers need access to the data warehouse to create and test new applications that are in the works. The above user's simple OLAP query was in fact hindered by a five-table join, otherwise known as a "coma query," submitted by a well-meaning test developer. As she grills the help desk staff about CPU usage, several developers downstairs are launching multiple parallel queries to test concurrency, while end-users throughout the company wonder what's taking their simple queries so long.

The moral of this story is that a good data warehouse architecture includes a separate test environment, thereby protecting end-users from the inherent complexity and arbitrary experiments characteristic of development activities and allowing them to get on with their work.

The other moral is that it's not easy working on a help desk.

Dirty Little Secret #4:
Regardless of the number of user logon IDs enabled,
most data warehouses are used by dozens,
not hundreds or thousands of users.

This isn't necessarily a bad thing. Managers push to get users signed up, but often few need the data warehouse to do their everyday work. People are very quick to identify "quantity of users" as a success metric. But the success metric should be the ability of the data warehouse to support new and different business tactics. Given this fact, one user might be plenty. This said, the greater the number of regular data warehouse users, the more people who will lobby for additional functionality and be willing to pay for it.

Dirty Little Secret #5:
Many IT departments don't really know how
their business colleagues are using the data warehouse.

We've already discussed talking to end-users. Everybody has. Each time I hear someone admonishing data warehouse practitioners to "talk to the users" and "gather business requirements," I think to myself, *Haven't we all heard this a million times already?*

Well, maybe a million isn't enough, because there is still a vast divide between how businesspeople are really using the warehouse and what IT thinks they're doing.

There is an argument to be made, however, that IT doesn't necessarily need to understand the exact business activities and resulting decisions, as long as the IT organization can furnish the appropriate technologies, processes, and horsepower to enable them. This claim might be a valid one, depending on your culture and your end-users' expectations. I've seen many a recalcitrant end-user roll his eyes when asked a question about his business goals by a well-meaning IT representative seeking to be part of the team and to understand the endgame. At the end of the day, it's really all about delivering against requirements, no matter how well they're understood.

Dirty Little Secret #6:
Few enterprise data warehouses have technically
proved ROI. Moreover, most companies haven't required it.

In most cases, data mart users know what data they need, how they'll be using it, and the expected payback, sometimes before the hardware is even installed.

Not so for enterprisewide data warehouses. Because of the disparity among users and organizations leveraging the power of cross-functional data, it's difficult—some would say impossible—to demonstrate the overall return of such a far-reaching technology.

According to a 1999 META Group survey of two thousand large corporations worldwide, data warehouse development budgets rose 150 percent in 1998, accounting for 23 percent of IT budget dollars. These figures indicate that data warehouses have delivered demonstrable benefits, with or without ROI. Executive sponsors realize that being without the data warehouse would have a devastating effect on their business, and often that's all the justification they need.

Dirty Little Secret #7:
Most data warehouse hardware upgrades occur
because of lease-payment decrease rather than business value increase.

Most upgrades are typically tied to leased-cost decreases rather than proven benefits. Many companies don't need to upgrade their hardware platforms, but since the upgrade extends the lease—in many cases preventing the company from having to purchase the hardware outright—a company would rather upgrade its hardware to continue the lease. Beware the IT director boasting about CPU horsepower or "number of nodes." These arcane factoids have little to do with what the data warehouse is actually delivering to the business.

Dirty Little Secret #8:
Metadata isn't as prevalent as everyone says it is.

In chapter 5 we discussed three different levels of metadata. With the thought processes that have gone into different uses for metadata, it's hard to believe that there are companies out there with mature data warehouses but still no metadata.

It's a good-news, bad-news situation. While metadata is both important and useful, it is not always a critical success factor for your data warehouse. I know several data warehouses that were built long before the concept of metadata was ever introduced, and even as they retrofit metadata into their data architectures, they've been wildly successful in delivering business intelligence.

I often recommend getting quality data on the data warehouse, *sans* metadata, especially if it means that power users can begin retrieving important information quickly. Figuring out which type of metadata and metadata technologies are the best fit, whether the metadata should be distributed or centralized, and who should have access to which metadata will take time. If it takes too much time, your users may find other alternatives. In any case, trying to get metadata onto a data warehouse is not a good enough excuse to keep users from querying the underlying data to get the knowledge they've been lobbying for.

> *Dirty Little Secret #9:*
> *A project's rate of progress is inversely proportional*
> *to the number of "architects" working on it.*

The term "architect" has many and varied interpretations, which is precisely why it's a bad idea to have one or more of them on your project. The exception is when the word is preceded by an area of expertise. Your database architect, network architect, or application architect, if they are responsible for tangible deliverables, are all doing useful things.

It's the architect without a modifier who can be dangerous, because the vagueness of the title circumscribes the role. A roving linebacker has no place on a data warehouse development team. Consider the following three descriptions of an architect role from three different data warehouse projects.

> The architect defines the data warehouse architecture, including the technology components and how they work together. Candidate technologies include hardware, software, middleware, and networking functions.
>
> The project's architect researches various technology solutions as they relate to [the company's] enterprise data warehouse and selects those technologies on the basis of their conformance to requirements and [the company's] existing technological standards.
>
> The architect ensures that the application is designed to leverage the specific design of the databases on the data warehouse and instructs the modification of both the database designs and the application in order to ensure two-way communications at all times.

The first description is hopelessly nebulous and ambitious, describing a job at which any one person would fail. Few individuals have the appropriate expertise to define and lay out how the various components of a data warehouse work together. This work should be done by a team of people of various backgrounds and skill sets.

The second job description characterizes every technologist's dream job: technology evaluation with no accountability. Reading between the lines, this architect would spend her days reading brochures, seeing demos, surfing the Web, and eating free lunches supplied by eager vendors on their way to becoming the company's chosen solution. This job, too, should be performed by a committee—ideally consisting of both IT and business staff—that defines standards and guidelines, including everything from protocols to "look and feel," and evaluates any candidate technology against those measurements. The committee should then narrow down a list of technology vendors that meet the established standards and create a scoring mechanism for selecting the best of the bunch.

The final job description is a valid one, except for the fact that it misuses the term "architect." A database administrator and application designer or programmer should work together to ensure seamless integration between database and application.

Dirty Little Secret #10:
The size of the data warehouse development team
is often in inverse proportion to its delivery capabilities.

I cringe when it happens, and it happens all too frequently. Here's the scenario:

A development team deploys a data warehouse, along with the initial application, and users are thrilled. The data warehouse development manager gets more budget money and begins hiring more staff. New people join the team, but skill set delineation never took place—see chapter 6—so everyone's rather tentative about what to do.

Then comes the next layer of management: The development manager hires someone euphemistically called a program manager to buffer him from day-to-day staff and scheduling issues. The program manager, new to the team, plays catch-up, reviewing time lines with the project manager (who's not sure what the program manager's supposed to be doing, and vice versa) while trying to implement new procedures and hire new people (yes, more people!). Sometimes, a few more architects join the team (see Pitfall #9). The number of meetings increases as staff members struggle to carve out their responsibilities. In the meantime the original developers, those who successfully delivered the initial system, feel overwhelmed (what happened to the small, nimble development team who made the first iteration so successful?) and begin looking for other jobs.

Sure, the scenario smacks of empire building, and even the most successful data warehouses won't change a company's culture enough to eradicate that. More important, it suggests that the combination of new staff members with the lack of skill set delineation equals confusion, bureaucracy, and management without leadership.

While some larger organizations, particularly those with enterprise data warehouses that support multiple organizations and data subject areas, rely on a critical mass of development staff in order to cover simultaneous projects, many data warehouse development groups are overstaffed and undermanaged. In most cases, if end-users aren't experiencing incremental value—that is, if they're not seeing anything new on their desktops three months after new data is loaded or, in the case of new applications, every four months—then there's something wrong.

The Politics of Data Warehousing

Speaking of staffing overkill, I know of a data warehouse development organization composed of over 50 people that hasn't done very much in the last few years. As far as having actually received new decision support functionality goes, the company's end-users just shake their heads.

Meanwhile, the director of data warehousing has his developers repackaging existing functionality into yet another reporting tool. ("Let's call new vendor X and see a demo!") Developers no longer talk to end-users. The data warehouse development team has transformed itself from a cost recovery center into a large corporate expense. Over half of its permanent staff members are administrators. And it has delivered no new business value for a long, long time.[1]

In reality, a competent project manager, a DBA, a data administrator, a business analyst, and a few crack programmers could turn the entire project around in a matter of weeks and begin delivering real value for a fraction of the current budget.

What happened here? Many of those failed data warehouses everyone's been citing floundered for reasons having nothing to do with technology. While the

---

1. One hallmark of a data warehouse development team in trouble is when the majority of the team members spend more time talking about architecture and acquiring technology than they do discussing gathering additional data and defining new business functionality.

failure rate may have been overstated or understated, most of these projects crashed and burned because of nontechnical issues. I've seen data warehouses fail—good data warehouses with valuable data—for reasons that were strictly cultural or political.

I know, I know. Avoiding corporate politics is easier said than done. Granted, the issue is bigger than you and me. Often, politics are so entrenched in an organization that behavior simply doesn't change, regardless of the type of project. The director mentioned above almost tripled his staff and quintupled his budget allocation, while deploying *fewer applications* and *less data* over time. Inexperience? Probably. Empire building? For sure.

The danger here is widespread disenfranchisement, not only among users but also among managers and even external people. Data-warehousing practitioners are a small community, and people talk. The project described above has an unbelievable attrition rate. Other companies in the same city, having heard about the project, avoid recruiting its staff. Developers who quit expunge the project from their resumes. The end-users have launched their own decision support development projects and are calling outside consulting firms for help.

If we applied Maslow's old hierarchy of needs to today's business world, it would become apparent that the basic human need for survival is alive and well in corporate America. And in their effort to "survive," people take on interpersonal and social roles that will give them the most control over their outcomes. This need for control unfortunately often supersedes the need for the greater good—like delivering meaningful information to end-users—and can steer a data warehouse project off track in no time.

The need for control can be translated into a struggle for "ownership," and the ownership battle is bloodying the hallways and executive office suites of companies trying to deliver decision support as a business solution. While we've already touched on well-documented conflict between IT and the business community, strife within those organizations also foments data warehouse setbacks. Should the executive sponsor be from Marketing or from F&A? Should the advanced technology group select the appropriate application software, or should the development staff? Should the project manager deliver status reports to the steering committee, or should the CIO? And who owns the data?

In fact, a data warehouse project, often involving months or years of development time and millions of dollars in funding, can upset the organizational apple cart, replete with employees who are comfortable with their place in the heap. Corporate data warehouse projects poach staff members and budget money from other programs and often hang out their own shingles as separate development groups. And because these organizations do things differently—talking directly to users, often simultaneously with other IT projects, and delivering high-impact tools quickly—employees on different projects are either threatened or tempted to join the data warehouse team themselves.

Sometimes you can spot the trends, nipping them in the bud before they topple the project. This chapter's final top 10 list illustrates a few warning signs that may indicate that politics are hindering your data warehouse's progress. Look for the following indicators, take decisive action early, and you may spare your business untold cost.

The Top 10 Signs of Data Warehouse Sabotage

1. Hiring and staffing take up much more time than actual development activities do.
2. Key stakeholders come from either IT or the business side, but not both.
3. The same business users show up time and time again to articulate new requirements.[2]
4. Euphemistic job functions such as "program manager" or "architect" are established without socializing an understanding of what those functions are intended to deliver, or relating them to existing job functions.
5. One or more "skunkworks" development projects emerges that people don't know or aren't supposed to talk about.
6. Staff members are continually reassigned to other projects or different roles.
7. Executive sponsors selectively spoonfeed progress reports to other organizations or staff members.
8. Executive sponsors favor a single vendor and impose that vendor's technology or architectural tenets on the project with no due diligence and without consensus.[3]

---

2. Of course, this is also a function of the size of your company or organization. If you have only three end-users using your data mart, chances are you'll want them to show up for the next functionality go-round.

3. During a highly competitive bid process to implement a CRM application, a consultant I know was asked by the CIO about her familiarity with the company's chosen middleware product. That in the repertory of possible questions related to CRM and strategic business intelligence the executive was gauging middleware experience was not a good sign. It hinted that the competitor, a technology company specializing in three-tier architectures, and thus middleware, was a shoo-in.

9. There are no formal processes for requirements sign-off, changes to project scope, prototype review, or end-user acceptance.

10. There are no formal processes for establishing projects, priorities, time lines, or reviews.

The premise behind Occam's Razor says that the simplest solution is most likely the best. But overkill technologies, numerous staff resources, and padded budget allocations are the dicta of the day for many data-warehousing projects that should really be straightforward and easily executed.

My advice? Don't go into the light! Try the easy approach first. Identify the work, skills, people, and core requirements needed prior to selecting technology. Make your development teams small and your deliverables quick wins.

If it's an empire you want, deliver decision support right the first time, and you'll be recognized based on your merit, not your head count.

The Vanguards of Data Warehousing

The case studies in this book have been collected from a large set of candidate companies. But many other companies share the traits representing the key indicators of a "successful data warehouse."

So, since this chapter is chock-full of lists, here's one more. This list presents some of the consistent practices that have emerged among those companies that have experienced measurable success deploying and getting payback from data warehouses and decision support. Those that have incorporated most or all of the following practices represent the vanguards of data warehousing:

1. Iterative development. The days of multiyear data warehouse projects are over. Businesses change too frequently to endure such lengthy development projects, and requirements are constantly shifting. The companies with the happiest end-users are those that deliver iterative quick wins, and regularly. Often this means nothing more or less than a new data subject area going online, or a rereleased application. Nevertheless, when users see incremental progress, so does the company. Furthermore, when the data warehouse's value is questioned or the budget is up for review, these companies have a long list of allies willing to testify to the range of benefits it has delivered.

2. Skill set delineation prior to development. Yes, it's a pet peeve. And no, not enough companies do it. But those that do are most likely to meet their data

delivery and application turnaround times, not to mention job satisfaction and lower attrition rates. Assumed here are an understanding of the work that will be needed to deliver a data warehouse and the qualifications of the practitioners who will do it.

3. End-user empowerment (part 1). This is actually a two-pronged metric. On the one hand, end-users are empowered to retrieve data. While this may sound fairly obvious, it wasn't so long ago that user support personnel outnumbered end-users in most companies. The companies that make end-users stakeholders, responsible for retrieving their own data, even if doing so means extensive training and even job redefinition, achieve the greatest benefit in the long run.

4. End-user empowerment (part 2). The other side of the empowerment coin is that users are charged with making decisions based on the information they get. If decisions aren't being made, users are doing nothing more than corroborating already held suspicions about the data, thereby marginalizing the value of the data warehouse. At worst, they're simply playing at "neat to know," in which case the value of the data warehouse is less than zero.

5. Minimal vendor bigotry. Companies that have achieved success in data warehousing opt for the "best of breed" technologies to solve their business problems. Technology is selected based on its ability to address user requirements, irrespective of the bells and whistles. While implementing and maintaining a diverse product set might result in more work, it also results in consistently being able to adopt the best approach to the business problem at hand. The minimal vendor bigotry maxim also applies to consultants: choosing one company as a jack-of-all-trades regularly backfires. (See number 2, above.)

6. Admitting internal weaknesses and fixing broken processes. Companies that are most successful at deploying valuable DSS applications actually consider their organizational problems, past habits, and "corporate pathologies" implementation jeopardy. They recognize that their weak technologies need upgrading before DSS delivery, that internal politics will add meetings—and thus time—to the project time line, and even that compensation plans should be modified to encourage the use of the data warehouse. Moreover, while many of these problems are too entrenched to be solved, others can be fixed during implementation, allowing the company to "do it right the first time."

7. Willingness to modify business processes. A new data warehouse can touch many different business areas. Often, it can fundamentally change the way

an organization functions. Companies that are truly open to the innovation a data warehouse sustains understand that information isn't the only benefit. For example, a call center that previously relied on research and call-backs now leverages customer profiles generated on the data warehouse. A company's ability to transform its business processes due to increased information or more rapid data access is a key indicator that it can maximize its data warehouse potential, and indeed that of other strategic technologies.

8. Closed-loop processing. Most successful data warehouses allow for tactical and strategic decisions as part and parcel of their value proposition. But the more advanced data warehouse users are leveraging business intelligence not only to perform the analysis needed to take these actions but also to monitor the actions once they've been executed. While this development is typical of dozens of campaign-management systems—the data supports the decision to deploy a given promotion, and the results of that promotion are then loaded back onto the data warehouse and used to invent subsequent promotions—it is also useful for yield management, customer win-back, and compensation applications.

9. An understanding that customer data is only a piece of the puzzle. While this may seem like heresy at first, it ends up making sense, especially if companies realize that customer data is all they have, and it's not enough. With the onslaught of CRM and initiatives promoting customer intimacy, it's easy to forget about other data. Customer information should be used in conjunction with other business data in order to prove its true value. For instance, even if it owns its market, a company must constantly innovate. A data warehouse can be used to make decisions such as which products to discontinue, which products warrant more R&D money, and which products might differentiate the company yet again, all of them critical to future strategies. Key data areas that work in conjunction with customer data include sales and revenue data, usage, channel and distribution, sales performance, compensation, and promotion history. The *e* in e-data stands for *eclectic*!

10. Being circumspect about advanced technologies. The best and brightest companies with data warehouses understand that technology for its own sake is a costly and often dangerous proposition. These firms don't begin evaluating any new technology until they've identified the business problem that it can help solve and the specific improvements they want it to make. This saves time and resources and allows companies to focus on developing business solutions, not just technology architectures.

11. Planning "horizontal" as well as "vertical" decision support delivery. A common assumption among even senior practitioners is that the goal of any data warehouse is to move "up the pyramid," providing more complex analysis over time. While this is true of many companies, executives I spoke to while researching this book expressed plans to continue evaluating new and advanced technologies, and especially to work on deploying *existing* functionality to a broader group of users. In other words, these companies were confident that the various tools they had developed with the data warehouse were useful and beneficial, and that as much of their business as possible should be exposed to them.

12. The recognition of end-users as "internal customers." As we discussed earlier in this chapter, some companies have a culture of ownership and territory, whereas others just want to get the job done. Those who do it best understand the importance of internal customers—staff who need decision support so that the company can make a difference. As with the company's external customers, internal customers need to be kept happy so that they don't go elsewhere. Take a look at the following case study for an example of internal customer awareness.

Case Study: Charles Schwab & Co., Inc.

"It's all about getting data into the hands of business users as efficiently as possible."

While any of the companies used for this book's case studies would comfortably avow a similar goal, Nadene Re and her group are realizing it at Charles Schwab & Co., Inc. As vice president of data services for Schwab IT, Re and her colleague Maury Ostroff have devised a strategy for not only acquiring and maintaining data on the company's data warehouse but also providing that data across the business to users who might have as-yet-unanticipated uses for it. While this plan is ambitious enough on its own, the fact that it dovetails so well with the culture of the company at large is even more impressive.

Schwab's decision support architecture leverages a variety of technologies to transform operational data from transaction systems into information that's meaningful and usable. Factored into the mix are diverse platforms—including IBM, Sun, and Oracle—and data structures from simple mainframe sequential files accessible via various programs to relational database tables.

While the data warehouse is a work in progress—confirming the aforementioned tenet of process versus technology—Schwab has been delivering decision support for years. The company has made sure since the early days that even its mainframes support an "open" architecture that can provide key data across the enterprise. Indeed, Schwab's mainframe continues to be a staple in the company's DSS delivery strategy.

Thus Ostroff is naturally ambivalent about using the term "data warehouse." "One of the reasons I dislike it is that the emphasis seems to be on building a monolithic repository as opposed to a more dynamic and open data distribution and dissemination function. It is an ongoing process." And Re notes:

> Our operational systems are continually evolving. Consequently, we have new data all the time. We've learned to acquire and load these new operational data elements onto the data warehouse once they become available. This way, data on the warehouse is ready to support evolving business requirements at the outset, and we're not rushing around to furnish data after users have requested new functionality. With this approach, users can run reports and perform analysis right from the start.

Schwab's strategy is to support islands of data around a centralized system of record. This means that line-of-business organizations are empowered to build their own applications, as Re and her team ensure that a central warehouse consolidates data while offering straightforward access. "Our users have a choice of the data they need," explains Ostroff. "We just run the buffet."

Before joining Schwab, Re worked for a leading database vendor and Ostroff hailed from a Wall Street brokerage house. Both understand the trade-offs of IT data management with end-user ownership and the mythic struggles for dominion and autonomy that can be waged in corporate corridors in the name of information. Schwab business units, which include retail marketing, electronic brokerage, operations, and finance, each need data for individual business operations. Nevertheless, Re is circumspect about the role of her organization: "We're a support function. Our job isn't to control what our end-users are doing, but to free them from having to focus on how to get to their data."

This attitude of supporting the business has mitigated many of the classic organizational tensions. Re and her team meet with business users on a regular basis to understand burgeoning requirements and identify new data. They participate in planning sessions with business units. In short, they consider Schwab's business users their customers, and data provision the ultimate goal.

Despite the administrative choreography they perform, Re and Ostroff consider the data they're providing to be a basic corporate asset. "Like a desk and a chair and a PC workstation, corporate information is one of the basic tools people need in order to do their jobs," says Ostroff.

The resulting analysis is an eclectic mix of customer categories—Schwab recently used the results of customer segmentation to deploy its *Schwab Signature Services* program to high-value market segments—as well as channel analysis, customer profitability, and cost allocation optimization. Schwab's lauded Web site is one of many rich data sources, in this case supplying trading activity data, that can lead to a more refined understanding of customer behaviors and preferences. This improved understanding in turn creates better customer service and enhanced customer satisfaction.

The captivating thing about Schwab is that its focus on customer satisfaction—one of the company's core competencies—applies to internal as well as external customers. Schwab's CIO Dawn Lepore claims that customer satisfaction is nothing less than "part of Schwab's corporate DNA," and indeed Re sees her organization less as a technology supplier than a service provider. "We're constantly looking at improvements so that our end-users won't have to work as hard to get what they need," she confirms, adding, "Our ultimate goal is to make data access both cost effective and easy."

What's next for those vanguard companies that have truly achieved demonstrable benefits from their data warehouses? More of the same. Perhaps an old Buddhist saying sums it up best:

> Before enlightenment, chop wood, carry water.
> After enlightenment, chop wood, carry water.

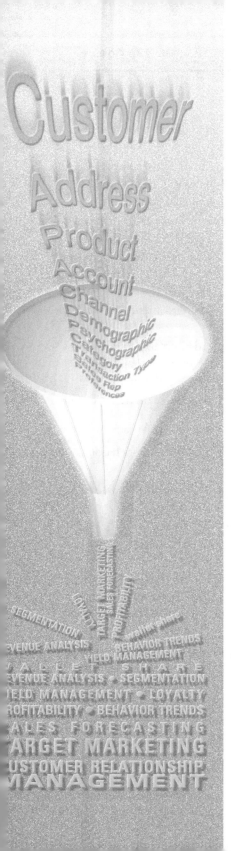

CHAPTER TEN

What to Do Now

Picture this: you've successfully loaded data onto your data mart, applications are working, your corporate intranet is in place, and your end-users are OLAPing away. You're almost finished, right?

Not exactly. To quote a previously mentioned aphorism, the data warehouse isn't just a technology, it's a process. So, the question shouldn't be how close are you to being finished, but what's the next set of business problems you can address?

Whether you're in the throes of determining your next major application, or whether you've only recently realized that decision support isn't a choice but a competitive mandate, this chapter offers some valuable tactics for moving forward.

If You Need a Data Warehouse

So your company's been grousing about the need for data quality, better information distribution, higher customer retention rates, or increased market share. You understand that strategic technologies might be the answer. Maybe you scored well in the data warehouse readiness quiz at the end of chapter 8. You think you might need a data warehouse. What do you do now?

Here are a few suggestions on how to begin preparing for the data warehouse. If you've begun the acquisition process already, use this list as a preparation checklist to make sure you've covered all the bases.

Establish Up-Front Success Metrics

No, it's not just a formality, it's a list of measurements that will tell you: (1) how important decision support is perceived to be within the company and (2) what it will take to ensure that the eventual data warehouse is considered a success.

The first point is important, because you can tell by simply eyeballing the success metrics how the eventual data warehouse will benefit people. The last point is particularly consequential. The data warehouse you build can have lots of bells and whistles and purport to satisfy every requirement, but if your business users don't *consider* it successful, it may as well be relegated to door-stop duty.

What are success metrics? They connote the "ideal state" of the data warehouse once it's been delivered. How do you define that state? Finish the sentence, "Our data warehouse will have been a smashing success if . . ."

The end of that sentence is a success metric. Asking end-users to help articulate their own success metrics forces them to align their job requirements with the uses of the data warehouse. The amalgam of responses is a good first shot at basic data warehouse requirements. Here are a few sample success metrics from actual data warehouse end-users:

- "It lets me look at a list of all the products any one of my customers has at a given point in time."
- "It lets me access last month's sales information by the third day of the following month."
- "It ensures that Finance and Marketing are looking at the same data."
- "I can submit inquiries myself, without having to call someone and endure the two-day turnaround. My time is money!"
- "It allows us to perform target marketing and allows me to measure the results in order to refine our promotions . . . before the next promotion!"
- "It serves as a single resource for sales performance. I won't have to 'gather' data from different systems and consolidate it myself."
- "Product purchasing can now compare order numbers with customer purchase numbers."

Note that these success metrics share a common trait: Each is measurable or observable. It's not enough for a success metric to express a vague goal, such as, "It's easy to use." The key to an effective success metric is describing an enhancement to an end-user's specific task.

And this is the main reason that success metrics mustn't be defined in a vacuum. The most difficult part of defining success metrics isn't coming up with them; it's getting the proper group of people—your eventual end-users—to take the time to sit down and express their own success metrics. If you can convince the right businesspeople to share their success metrics and sign off on them once they're documented, you have the seminal information on which you can build for requirements gathering and designing the data warehouse. Congratulations!

Consider Benchmarking[1]

Benchmarking is the process of studying and incorporating other companies' best practices. The overwrought and time-consuming competitive benchmarking of yore has given way to "fast cycle" benchmarking, in which a company identifies a specific "pain point," targets companies that have dealt with that particular pain, and studies what those companies are doing right. For example, a pizza delivery company might look to FedEx to uncover faster distribution tactics, while a telephone company might look to American Airlines for enlightenment about yield management.

Certain companies are renowned leaders in the data-warehousing market. Some of them appear in this book, and they might also inspire you with their decision support applications, their technology architectures, or their requirements-gathering processes. Identify some key problems you hope a data warehouse will solve, and contact companies that have solved a similar problem with theirs. Focus on processes: information distribution, technology selection, end-user satisfaction—that way you won't have to rely on competitors in your industry who may be unwilling to share their secrets—or talk to a similar company in a different country or geographic area where you don't compete. Nada Khater, director of data warehousing for National Bank of Kuwait, explains how the process worked for her company.

> Before we funded and acquired our marketing data warehouse, we checked
> out some of the leaders in the U.S. financial services. We assembled a team of
> IT and marketing staff and visited six North American banks to investigate

---

1. I'm not talking about technical-performance benchmarking, which tends to elevate systems performance as a key success metric whether or not it's actually key to end-user acceptance. Yes, your data warehouse should offer fast response times, but is relative speed—each vendor claims to have superior performance—really more important than having a fault-tolerant product that supports the optimal number of users?

the implementation plans of their customer information strategy. When we got home, we were able to confirm our intended uses for the data warehouse, as well as cement our implementation strategy. One of our key learnings was: "Products are not profitable, customers are." The trip helped us develop an approach and strategy for customer-focused relationship building, so it was definitely worth it.

Before visiting best-practice companies, understand what you're interested in discovering. If you are visiting more than one company, record a set of questions so that you can compare different answers to the same questions. Above all, don't just focus on the company's objectives and implementation strategies and payback. Focus on past and future challenges, and ask the company to share its missteps so that you can avoid the mistakes of those who went before you.

Research External Staff

Once your data warehouse is operational and you've delivered a successful application or two, you can establish an ongoing development infrastructure in which your company's staff leads the charge. If you've never implemented a data warehouse before, chances are your company's staff doesn't understand the clear distinctions involved in implementing one. Relying on existing resources to deliver your first data warehouse is unrealistic, and sometimes downright dangerous.

Refer back to chapter 6 for a thorough description of different job functions for data warehouse development, and develop a skills matrix (also described in chapter 6) to determine what your skills gaps are. Use these tools to determine whether either retaining external consultants or hiring new staff is warranted for each development phase: business analysis, data structure and management, and application development.

Focus specifically on work you've never done before, as well as once-only tasks. A consulting firm experienced in the development of business cases and seasoned in requirements-gathering processes can take you a long way toward implementing business requirements, while ultimately teaching you to become self-sufficient. Know that even if your company employs business analysts or database specialists on other development projects, data warehousing is a breed apart because success depends on end-user acceptance. This mandates specific skill sets. Watching an experienced practitioner work is the best way to apply experience to the work when you repeat it yourself.

While your data warehouse or data mart might be months away, it's best to jump the gun on staffing issues in order to secure good people by project kick-off.[2]

Prepare Your Environment

A key consideration in data warehouse preparation is ownership. Before getting started, make sure everyone knows the answers to these five questions:

1. Who owns the data warehouse platform and DBMS technology?
2. Who (which department) will own specific work tasks?
3. Who's responsible for data quality?
4. Who owns PC workstation application development?
5. Who owns the relationship with the end-users?

For example, do individual lines of business have their own internal IT functions, and if so, are they able to own application development themselves? A skills matrix like the one presented in chapter 6 might help you determine which people or organizations are best qualified to own the various technologies and processes involved in the warehouse.

It's also a good idea to inventory the various technologies that will affect or be affected by the data warehouse. Do targeted end-users have desktop PCs? How will the data warehouse be connected to the operational systems that source it? A lot has been written about taking a technology inventory. Performing such an inventory will give you a good idea of how much advance work you'll need to do to prepare for the data warehouse.

Lastly, be honest about your company's culture. Is the sharing and distribution of data anathema to management? Are employees accustomed to delegating data retrieval tasks to others? Does the IT organization insist on total control of any project that requires a technical strategy? You might have your work cut out for you, so begin socializing change early.

Classify Your Stakeholders

Before you adopt a data warehouse or data mart, it's important to consider your cultural change readiness as well as your business operations. We've discussed data-warehousing failures several times in this book. "Lack of end-user buy-in"

---

2. This is particularly important in non-U.S. companies, where new employees are often required to give their employers four to six weeks' notice prior to leaving.

continues to be a resounding refrain from those bemoaning their DSS defeats. How can you avoid this?

One effective method of socializing the benefits of DSS and educating the business at large is to profile the status quo. Nothing gets people's attention faster than showing how poorly certain work is being done. While few people are willing to go out on a political limb and point out weaknesses such as sporadic data availability or turnaround time for shipment reports, those who do can quickly provoke change. (See the discussion on visionaries in chapter 9.)

Another effective tool is called the "stakeholder classification grid." Used during a business discovery or requirements-gathering project, the grid divides data warehouse stakeholders—be they potential business users, development team members, or management—into four quadrants, as illustrated in figure 10-1.

1. *The Warrior.* The data warehouse warrior feels an urgent need for the data warehouse, and soon! Warriors are hungry for data, need it to do their job, and are willing to "do whatever it takes" to aid in the data warehouse

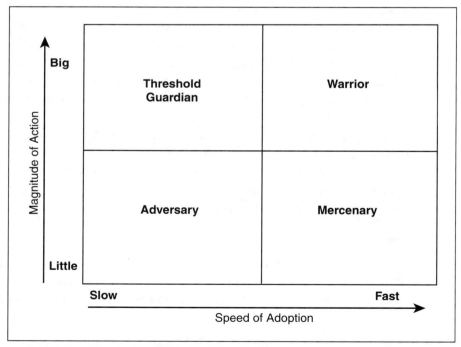

Figure 10-1: Stakeholder Classification Grid

adoption process. Warriors are most verbal during business discovery exercises, sometimes using the back page of survey forms to elaborate their myriad needs, and they are willing to go out on a limb to lobby management for the warehouse. Warriors make the best end-users and, not coincidentally, are willing to change entrenched behaviors in order to use the data warehouse.

2. *The Mercenary.* Mercenaries are also interested in data warehousing, but they maintain more of a "wait and see" attitude. They often reserve judgment—and enthusiasm—until they understand how the data warehouse will help them. Their participation in requirements gathering is as much about educating themselves as it is to see how the warehouse can help them. They are cooperative, but they won't actively sponsor the data warehouse.

3. *The Adversary.* These folks don't want a data warehouse, for whatever reason. Adversaries believe that the benefits of data warehousing, as they understand them, aren't worth the time and effort, let alone the cost. Adversaries usually have other priorities that they think should take precedence over a data warehouse, particularly if they feel that one of their projects must compete with the data warehouse for funds. In the worst case, adversaries are naysayers who go around sniping and predicting failure. But their rare sabotage efforts are usually passive and considered political.

4. *The Threshold Guardian.* Threshold guardians are the gatekeepers of the data warehouse. While not firmly "against" the data warehouse as adversaries are, threshold guardians believe that certain criteria should be met before adopting data warehousing lock, stock, and barrel. The words "only if" come up often in conversation with threshold guardians, and what's more, they have the power and funding to can the data warehouse if they sense that it won't meet the company's needs. Those who insist on the delivery of specific functionality or demand ROI figures are threshold guardians.

Whether you use interviews, surveys, or informal chats, try assigning people scores so that you can map where people "cluster" relative to one another. The grid in figure 10-2 has classified a stakeholder community of 25 people, consisting of data analysts, managers, and executives.

There are many nuances to using the grid, but be aware of some key indicators.

- If there are more threshold guardians than warriors, your organization probably needs a bit more time before embarking on a data warehouse. Bring someone in to do a day of high-level data warehouse training to ensure that people really understand how data warehousing can help.

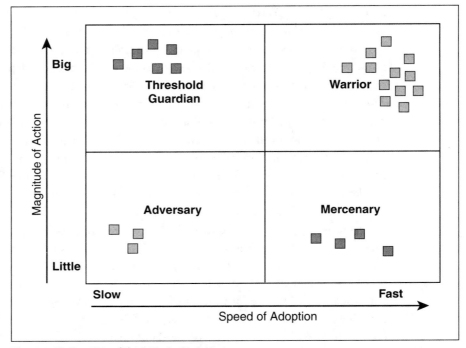

Figure 10-2: Classified Stakeholders

- If there are more mercenaries than warriors, take a look at the common denominator of need among the mercenaries. A data mart might be in order.
- Conversely, the presence of lots of warriors with lots of different requirements suggests an enterprisewide data warehouse.
- Do the adversaries or threshold guardians belong to the same organization? If so, there's a higher chance of sabotage.
- If there are several or more threshold guardians, how many of them are in management? A handful of highly placed gatekeepers will win out over an army of warriors every time.

And don't be afraid to use analyst research, magazine articles, and even this book to continue socializing decision support. Surges in data-warehousing demand have been widely reported, and new companies are constantly jumping on the business intelligence bandwagon. Some may even be your competitors. This information may be enough to turn everyone into a data warehouse warrior.

Ramp Up Support Capabilities

If, after preparing your organization for a pending data warehouse, you realize that users aren't ready, you might choose to begin slowly by having an end-user support desk run selected queries. In that case, do you have the necessary staff to do the job? And are those people adequately trained?

It's more likely that you've decided to bite the bullet and deploy applications directly to end-users. Paint the scenario about what end-user responsibilities will be relative to IT. Are there "escalation procedures" already in place, with which end-users understand the guidelines for dealing with problem queries and troubleshooting? If not, begin delineating the boundaries for end-user responsibility early.

Also, begin considering the additional training your help desk staff will need to support the data warehouse. Some companies actually create a brand-new support organization that is specific to the data warehouse (see the profile below). Either way, make sure that support staff know enough about the technology's business uses as well as the technology itself. This knowledge will enable them to "speak the same language" as the end-users who will inevitably call them for help.

Profile: Philippe Klee, Qantas Airways

Philippe Klee is a busy man. Working in Qantas's commercial systems division, Klee and his team in the decision support organization are responsible for supporting 600 users worldwide. But don't envision Klee manning phones all day long, fighting with highly strung end-users about report formats and data quality. Instead, he spends his time working with people focused on the continuous provision of information from the data warehouse, which Klee believes—despite its success so far—is still a work in progress.

Take new requirements as an example. Klee and his team are active in identifying new data usage opportunities, which result not from formal requirements gathering but from Klee's team's close work with end-users. Klee himself is conversant with the business uses of the airline's corporate data warehouse (CDW), reviewing "spillage and spoilage"—airline terminology for over- or underbooking of flights—as effortlessly as he describes electronic ticketing and cabin configuration. Klee can not only characterize the often arcane analysis on the data warehouse, he has also led the charge to justify the cost of the two-terabyte system, resulting in several rounds of additional funding.

Klee and his IT counterparts have in fact been instrumental in translating these new business requirements and business functions into a technology implementation. He understands the drawbacks and benefits of various types of DSS analysis, knows who's who in the vendor community, and can articulate which user groups will require which new functional features.

How does he so aptly straddle the fence? For one thing, Qantas's business users have become relatively self-sufficient, enabling Klee's organization to take a much broader view of the CDW's day-to-day usage. The company's WorldNet application provides a standard interface whereby end-users can submit thousands of different business questions, ranging from market profiling to bookings activities to frequent-flier itineraries (see the Qantas case study in chapter 4). "Our users are so grateful for the data warehouse that they're willing to experiment with the data and try things out for themselves," explains Klee.

To further stimulate user self-sufficiency, Qantas has formalized end-user training and systems documentation for the data warehouse, from the database to the application. Indeed, it's rare for Klee's team to get calls from users who want reports run for them. In the time it takes to make such a call, the user normally has the report on his screen. When users do need to request help for queries that exceed the boundaries of their WorldNet application, they can e-mail Klee's staff or call a central support number.

It's rare enough to see an IT manager sitting next to an end user, but in one such meeting both Klee and Steve Goudie, one of Quantas's power users, take turns describing the business value of a forward-bookings report. ("Forward bookings" represent reservation data signifying a passenger's intent to fly, regardless of whether the ticket has actually been purchased.) "Few airlines would be able to compare their forward bookings to those for the same period last year," Klee says. "We've been very self-critical, but when these reports show up and our end-users are happy, we know we're doing something right." Critical or not, this constant self-monitoring has kept Qantas's user support function humming, its business users delighted, and its CDW a state-of-the-art resource.

Look Outside Your Box

Business departments are sophisticated. They know what their problems are. Not only that, they know how to solve their problems, sometimes down to the exact software package and discrete data elements. Such organizations have the endgame in mind, be it risk management, customer profiling, or churn propensity, and want to get going.

But before you go soliciting bids, be sure that there aren't other areas in your company that are already doing what you're setting out to do. For example, if you need to perform risk management for your credit card division, are you certain your mortgage division isn't doing something similar?

Or does IT know of other systems that use the same data sources you need? Wouldn't it be practical to leverage existing technology and support infrastructures rather than creating a new platform from scratch?

The phrase "mine! mine! mine!" isn't only an admonishment to launch data mining, it's the mantra of the midlevel manager who, in her quest to own an important new business function, redefines existing problems, thereby rationalizing new responsibilities and even empires. Don't be her.

By the same token, there is probably someone somewhere in your company right now who doesn't know about your data warehouse and is scribbling up a business case for "push" technology to distribute enterprise-wide revenue reports. To prevent the dilution of effort and budget, promote your decision support applications and publicize the successes. Proselytize your data warehouse as the sacred fount of corporate information.

Solicit a Request for Information

You'll need to understand the specific feature functionality of a vendor's product set before you agree to acquire its technology; but developing an RFP directly may be premature. In order to create one that does justice to your unique requirements, you'll need to have cemented corporate sponsorship, secured a funding commitment, and gathered business requirements. These take time.

While this information gathering is in process, do some research on the various hardware and software vendors using the success metrics you created for your data warehouse. Map the cursory vendor research to your success metrics and arrive at a handful of vendors for each class (hardware, DBMS, application software, consulting).

Then draft a high-level description of your data warehouse drivers, incorporating some of your specific success metrics and including some of the following areas of specific interest:

- the vendor's experience with your business problem, and whether it offers any packaged solutions
- whether the vendor can describe three data warehouse or data mart implementations it has delivered in your industry, the user area, the top 10 business questions, and the business value of each
- the vendor's latest TPC-R and TPC-H performance benchmark results. You should be circumspect about these numbers, as your mileage may vary.

- whether the vendor offers a packaged data model for your industry—and your specific business problems
- the vendor's service and support structure
- the vendor's education courses
- a description of local technical talent, or a recommendation for local integrators
- a list of similar customers within your metro area or state
- whether the vendor sells directly to companies of your size and type, or prefers to work with resellers
- why the vendor considers its particular architectural or feature/functionality approach superior to that of its competitors

Notice that these are high-level qualification questions, as opposed to detailed questions relating to costs or specific configurations. The answers should help you gauge whether the vendor is both qualified and interested in helping your data warehouse see the light of day, and whether it is a candidate for a subsequent RFP.

If You Already Have a Data Warehouse

Perhaps while you were reading chapter 9 and pondering all the metrics for a successful data warehouse, you were thinking to yourself:

> We do all those things. We must be a data-warehousing vanguard. Wait a minute! Why aren't we in this book?

If this is the case, take a bow. You're doing things right. But don't think about resting on your laurels just yet. Somebody once said: "To live is to change, and to be perfect is to change often." So what are you going to do next?

Of course, if you've built it right, it's likely that end-users are beating down your door for more data or additional applications. Don't stop! But consider, too, some of the ideas below. They might help make a good thing even better.

Establish a Formal Postmortem Process

Do you have a project postmortem process in place? One that reviews development activities after the deployment of every data warehouse application? One that reviews what went wrong, and what went right?

Regular postmortems are the surest way of establishing continuous data warehouse improvement during implementation. They review the implementation from a project, task, staffing, and technology perspective and solicit feedback not only from developers involved, but from support personnel and end-users, who often have a more objective view of how the next implementation project could be better than the last.

Postmortems are normally conducted in a meeting or structured workshop. They are often uncomfortable because they hold people accountable. Project managers and developers are forced to go on record with the truth, which is sometimes not pretty. For this reason many data warehouse development managers avoid them like the plague. But since good postmortems focus on processes, and because they are often conducted by objective third parties, they ultimately do more good than harm.

In fact, if done correctly, postmortems can render themselves practically obsolete over time. They dissect what went wrong on a project, capturing recommendations on how to avoid missteps the next time. They refine the development process.

One of the outputs of the postmortem is a simple table that lists suggested tactical improvements, who is in charge of making them, and when they will be made. Table 10-1 is an example of such a table.

A positive by-product of regular postmortems is that staff members, mindful that at the project's conclusion they'll be asked to explain certain actions and justify decisions, are more likely to be more quality-conscious during development. The best postmortems abound with self-assessment and proactive suggestions, not finger pointing. If you're lucky enough to have an internal quality assurance organization, great. If not, find a good consultant experienced in delivering structured postmortems and give it a try. The first one's always the hardest.

Inventory Existing Applications

It's the third year of your data warehouse . . . do you know where your applications are? We have touched on the reality that end-user DSS applications have a finite life span. By regularly taking stock of each application in your data warehouse repertory, you'll have a good idea of which applications warrant revision or updating, which should be replaced, which are underused or not used at all, and which overlap with new or in-process development efforts.

Also evaluate how much each application is costing, considering not only tools but developer costs, space usage, and maintenance expense. Compare the overall cost to the business value that the application is delivering. Determine the answers to the following questions:

Table 10-1: Sample Postmortem Improvement Report

Improvement/Action	Department Responsible	Team Member Responsible	Due Date
Create standard agenda for end-user prototype demos and distribute to subject matter experts along with prototype invitation.	User requirements	B. Newell	3/15/00 (sample document)
Hire administrative project manager.	Project management	S. Smith	3/31/00
Define requirements for a database change control process.	Database administration	J. Ho	3/31/00
Distribute space usage report every week.	Database administration	J. Ho	4/15/00 (first report)
Define process for copying data from test machine to production system.	Testing	S. Mays	4/30/00
Document end-user feedback during prototype session.	User requirements	M. McIntire	4/30/00
Document and distribute revised schedules and slippage to development team weekly.	Project management	S. Smith (pending new hire)	4/30/00 (sample document)

- Is there data that users are no longer accessing? Is everyone really using all those summary tables on the data warehouse? Is all that historical data being queried?
- Has the business problem changed, rendering a given application less practical?
- If the application leverages external data sources, do the costs correspond to the business value of the resulting data?

Once you've inventoried your applications, consider whether the number of applications can be whittled down to make way for new ones. Also, if you haven't done so already, have an application brief written up for each of the applications in your inventory. As noted in chapter 6, application briefs are one-page descriptions profiling an application that can be used to educate IT, future end-users, management, new development staff, and consultants on the suite of applications being used with the data warehouse.

Spring for an Audit

Like postmortems, data warehouse audits or assessments can be scary. After all, who wants some self-proclaimed expert poking around at the data warehouse, reading internal documentation and interviewing management and end-users?

The purpose of a data warehouse audit is to provide an assessment of the effectiveness and efficiency of an existing data warehouse. But like many painful experiences, data warehouse audits have their rewards. Often, the consultants conducting the audit can quickly hone in on critical problems you may have missed, ultimately saving you bigger headaches later on. More likely, if you've delivered successful applications and have an operating plan in place that maps out the development horizon, an audit can deliver some simple fine-tuning recommendations.

Data warehouse audits can concentrate on a wide variety of areas. For example, some are design reviews, in which a design expert inspects the data model and/or physical design in order to determine whether it is flexible and able to support queries. Some audits might include an assessment of the following elements:

- data and database design
- application requirements gathering
- end-user satisfaction
- business alignment
- education and training
- support

The classic audit focuses on a range of data warehouse components and how they work together to meet business goals. Whatever its focus, an audit should always bear in mind the data warehouse's business drivers, and the goals of its end-users.

Audits normally call for outside staff, and that's a good thing. Not only can an experienced consultant provide a fresh and unbiased view of your data warehouse technology, its operating environment, and its overall value proposition, she'll normally tell you hard truths you might not be hearing from your DBA or project manager. She might also be able to diplomatically point out some cultural or team problems that might have been awkward for an internal resource to mention. Moreover, an effective data warehouse auditor can compare your data warehouse with others in your industry, offering ideas for additional vendor tools, external data sources, or new uses.

When retaining a consultant to perform an audit, make sure that the firm in question uses a structured approach with predefined evaluation metrics, checklists, and customizable questionnaires to ensure objectivity and shorten the amount of time involved. With rare exceptions, most data warehouse audits should last no more than six to eight weeks, typically involve three or four people, and require experience—unequivocally "hands-on"—in the area being audited.

Improve Customer-Facing Business Processes

Your marketing data warehouse has been a smashing success: Marketing staff can profile an existing customer on demand; your product planning organization can research and deploy new packages, and optimally price them; your distribution center has consolidated its operations; and your target-marketing campaigns are generating 12 percent returns.

But your customers are still ticked off.

With all that juicy data and your newfound customer intimacy, how could customers be angry? Because, with all the expenses poured into technology, no one bothered to check whether the improvements were trickling down to the actual customer touch points. The data warehouse and the accompanying business benefits aren't worth much if your tellers are testy, your call center operators brusque, and your sales force frazzled.

Consider Egghead, the former brick-and-mortar computer retailer that has reengineered itself into a computer cyberseller. A company with Egghead's history is certain to know a lot about applying technology to solve business problems. But realizing that technology could only go so far, the company recently revamped its customer service organization by beefing up the number of telephone representatives, with measurable results. Calls to Egghead's customer service center are now answered within five seconds—a measurable success—and e-mails are answered in three to ten hours. The company claims that management's top priority is to provide a "positive customer service experience."[3]

---

3. Wood, Christina, "On Your Side: Heads Up," *PC World*, July 1999, 35.

If your company gathers customer satisfaction statistics, how are you doing? Has customer satisfaction improved since your data warehouse began delivering business intelligence about your customers? It might be a good time to enhance training for customer-facing staff or streamline some outdated business processes.

If your company has recently launched a CRM initiative, changing its accompanying business processes is even more critical. Far from offering improved customer data and broader information access, CRM programs mandate changes to customer-based business processes (see figure 10-3). This process may be as simple as retraining field sales staff or as significant as reorganizing company departments away from product lines and toward customer segments.

Simply put, for CRM to truly benefit the business, its results should be measured and the program continually refined.

First Union, the sixth largest U.S. bank, recently announced that it was hiring two thousand additional bank tellers, admitting it had misjudged the extent to

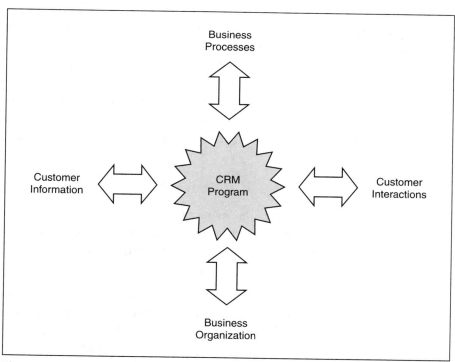

Figure 10-3: CRM Transcends Data

which its customers desired "face time" when doing their banking. While knowledge of its customer base aided First Union in its decision to augment branch staff, it's interesting to note that hiring more people flies in the face of most banks' goals to automate their customer interactions. First Union's bold move in the other direction illustrates the importance of the new mantra, "It's the customer, stupid."

Establish a Closed-Loop Process

Maybe you're justifying the cost of every new data warehouse application. Maybe you're proving ROI at the back end. Maybe management wants to know why the new customer retention program cost so much. Or maybe users are so tickled with being able to run their own reports that nobody's even asking you to rejustify the data warehouse.

As valuable as your data warehouse is, it's often a helpful exercise to measure the benefits of specific programs or initiatives that may have been launched with its data. For example, the increased inventory turns of our retailer in chapter 8 resulted in a significant first-year payback. Entering that data onto the warehouse, along with measuring subsequent months or years, allows the retailer to track ongoing benefits, monitor whether they're growing or shrinking, and register a running total of the data warehouse's return over time.

This exercise does more than protect you in the event that management reorganizes and some new executive wants to know if the data warehouse has paid for itself. It also lets you refine new marketing campaigns based on the successes of old ones, monitor the sales of new products and tweak their features to maximize their benefits, and improve a host of different business processes based on outcomes analysis.

Go Web, Young Man!

If you've been successful in deploying a range of applications, examine migrating them to the Web. Data warehouse tool vendors like Microstrategy, Cognos, and Hummingbird have Web-enabled their base products. Below we list some of the advantages of Web-based decision support.

- Business users are more accustomed to browser interfaces. This makes for easier end-user training and acceptance. Browser-based applications have a uniform look and feel, rendering business users more comfortable with new functionality. With the right bandwidth, Web-enabled tools can leverage better documentation, audio, and video to facilitate tutorials and online demos.

- There are few distribution or transportation costs for the application and data.
- The incremental cost of adding new users is negligible. This makes it much easier to get new people online quickly, thereby introducing the data warehouse to a broader business audience. For example, e-commerce companies like Amazon.com incur infinitesimal costs each time they add a new customer to their site: It's literally just another record on a disk drive.
- The days of installing a new or revised application on each workstation are over. Desktop deployment via the Web is automatic.
- Because of the three-tier architecture involved (remember chapter 5?), Web-based DSS applications lower the total cost of ownership on the desktop by putting processing power on an application server. This means that the desktop workstation requires fewer features. In addition, Web browsers are more flexible, allowing developers to focus on GUI implementation instead of being forced to conform to the limitations of desktop hardware.
- Web-based applications remove the need for complex, multiplatform support because browsers are so ubiquitous. This prevents having to troubleshoot different platforms and Windows configurations. Browsers look and behave the same way on PCs, Macs, and UNIX workstations.
- Decision support can be distributed over a wide geographic area. If end-users want to work at home, they don't have to fiddle with modems or proprietary security procedures in order to dial into their data marts. The Internet is everywhere.

This doesn't mean you should plan on Web-enabling every one of your applications. For one thing, browser-based decision support absolutely requires a higher-bandwidth communications infrastructure to support the higher amount of data traffic over the network. Furthermore, some of the most important decision support technologies, including most true data-mining tools and many proprietary or industry tools, are not Web-enabled but may nevertheless be very, very useful.

Case Study: Allsport

You may not have heard of Allsport, one of the world's leading sports photography providers. But you've probably heard of its parent company, Getty Images (yes, *that* Getty). Allsport, based in London and Santa Monica, California, distributes sports images to a high-profile client base. From advertising agencies to magazines to shoe companies to the NBA, Allsport is the acknowledged source for high-quality sports images.

In the early 1990s, the company's legacy accounting and reporting system began running out of steam, and information provision was woefully inadequate. For an organization with a 30% annual growth rate, business data was critical and flexibility key.

Rather than continuing with its proprietary system, Allsport opted for the clean-slate approach. "Management was willing to basically start over," says Greg Walker, Allsport's CEO. "We identified the key legacy data and business needs, and basically just began again."

Building a new system from scratch was a leap of faith, and a risky one. But it allowed Allsport to furnish a solid infrastructure to support continued double-digit growth while responding to the evolving needs of its business users. Sales staff needed data about which types of images were selling and which clients were requesting them. Executives were lobbying for flexible sales and revenue reports, and not just by specific clients or dates. The company had no way of tracking photographers' commissions in real time. Allsport needed customer information so that it could target specific markets, while increasing its understanding of how and where its products—sports photographs—were actually being used.

"With our old system, we would have never been able to get the variety of information we needed," says Matt Schoen, Allsport's vice president of information systems. With the authority to start anew and the wherewithal to design a more nimble system, Schoen and his team elected to go with Web-based decision support.

"We didn't want to go with a client/server solution because of the platform issues involved," Schoen says. "For one thing, we were opening so many new offices, we didn't want to have to worry about different desktop technologies. We have some die-hard Mac users here, including executives. We weren't about to change what they were comfortable using." Allsport selected an HP-Oracle data mart on Windows NT with a Netscape browser at the front end.

The gamble has paid off. Allsport has now delivered Web-based decision support reporting to a cross-section of users from London to Santa Monica to Sydney. The browser front end has reduced training time and provided a common "look and feel" across the company, which has been able to open additional offices without having to increase support staff. Moreover, the resulting reports have become both more elaborate and more useful.

For one thing, the company can now profile the images its customers are buying, from the type of sport most in demand to various regional trends. Account executives can discover that, for example, images of extreme sports seem to be selling well among European magazine publishers, and they can even drill down to specific photographic criteria such as wide-angle live-action shots. In addition to their bread-and-butter profit and loss reports, managers can request daily sales breakdowns and revenues via a variety of dimensions, from photographer to sport code. "With this information, we can now aggressively attack specific markets," claims Walker.

Understanding who is buying what also lets Allsport enhance its "Concepts" line, photographs the company actually stages itself. Understanding sales trends can pinpoint emerging sports, allowing the company to plan photo shoots according to anticipated demand and thereby supplement its library with the optimal set of images.

Allsport is gradually barcoding its stock photographs so that it can track each of its 6 million physical and half-million digital images. Eventually, it will offer its extensive image library over the Web.

Indeed, Schoen's vision is for a complete Web-enabled order-processing and fulfillment environment, made even more efficient by the elimination of the sales and research efforts that are now involved in order provisioning. This will not only cut costs but also maintain the customer knowledge so integral to the company's market leadership. "We've seen the industry actually modify its deadline structure because of our ability to deliver over the Web," he claims.

While Schoen and Walker are thrilled with the business improvements engendered by decision support, they go one step further, implying that their innovative technology strategy may have actually been a factor in the company's purchase by Getty in 1998. Whatever the reason, Allsport and Getty are now teammates fortified by customer knowledge and sprinting into the millennium.

Consider Branching Out Vertically

Perhaps you're ready for additional tools. Let's take another look at the pyramid in figure 10-4.

How high is your most "advanced" decision support tool on the pyramid? Are your users still using query and reporting tools, yet yearning to slice and dice with OLAP? Or are they using OLAP and calling it data mining? Or are you beginning to see the true benefits of undirected knowledge discovery, in which the data warehouse answers questions before you ask them?

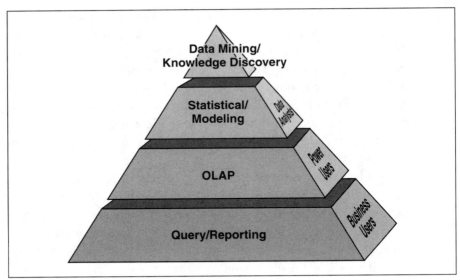

Figure 10-4: The Vertical Evolution of the Warehouse

The historian Herbert Butterfield proclaimed that scientific revolutions are nothing more than "handling the same bundle of data as before, but placing them [sic] in a new system of relations with one another." Maybe you're ready to revolutionize your information analysis capabilities and step up to the next level, whatever it may be.

But before you begin calling those vendors, make sure that you have a business driver for whatever new tool you're considering. If you have functional needs that can't be addressed by your existing suite of application software, then by all means begin looking into more specialized tools or those with more complex algorithms.

Don't succumb to the pressure and hype of the marketplace: If you really don't NEED data mining—and many companies don't—then don't buy a data mining tool.

Consider Branching Out Horizontally

As we saw in the last chapter, many of the most experienced companies are looking into how to distribute existing applications to more and more end-users. This is a different type of evolution, and one that arguably has just as much value as adopting a new technology. If we spin the pyramid (see figure 10-6), we can once again illustrate the various end-user classifications.

"It's a poor craftsman, son, who blames his tools."

Figure 10-5: Are Your Current Tools Adequate?

Perhaps a greater number of business users could benefit from a certain reporting application. Or perhaps someone could train a group of those business users on a new application or analysis method, helping them grow into power users and giving them more freedom with e-data, and more of it. Likewise with the data analysts: While teaching a power user about linear regression analysis might be impractical, introducing him to SAS or SPSS could result in increased data intimacy, and thus knowledge.

A word here about using data-mining technology: Although much has been written about data mining, past efforts to socialize data mining by putting it in the hands of the average businessperson have failed. In fact, few data-mining tools are actually useful to business users and power users who are accustomed to point-and-click desktop tools. While some companies, including SPSS and Business Objects, market their tools to business users, most data-mining tools concentrate on complex algorithms to churn through large data volumes and are only secondarily concerned about their ease of use.

Moreover, business users simply don't care whether their information needs warrant neural networks or memory-based reasoning or genetic algorithms. What they want is the information that such analysis methods yield. While end-user

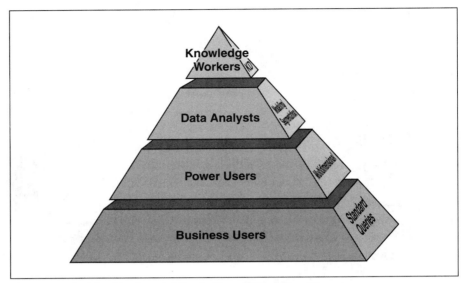

Figure 10-6: The Horizontal Evolution of the Warehouse

desktop deployment should be the rule for your data warehouse applications, there is a clear place for specialist data analysts who do understand the various analysis tools and methods and can deploy them in the right circumstances. Use these experts to run the most complex tools, ensuring that the data that results is available to everyone via easy-to-use canned reports and ad hoc queries.

If You Already Have a Data Mart or Marketing Analysis System

If you already have a data mart, all the above points apply. However, there are two other recommendations specific to data marts or single marketing analysis systems also worth considering.

Share Your Toys

Simply put, could your data mart be making more of an impact if it were available to additional user organizations? Or are there multiple DSS initiatives across your company that may be competing for funding or management attention? Many valuable data marts are used by a mere handful of people, for a variety of reasons: Some store specialized or proprietary data that only highly trained data analysts can understand. In other cases it would require significant rework or updating to link the data mart to other corporate systems. Some data marts are designed to answer only a core set of business questions; others may have valuable data that's being used for only one purpose. And many data marts aren't directly available to end-users, are dedicated to data mining, or are controlled by someone else's budget.

In each of these instances, an independent data mart is providing business value but could be providing even more "bang for the buck" by either being more visible across the business, storing additional data, or supporting a more diverse set of application tools. By sharing your data and data mart infrastructure and broadening it to support a greater variety of uses, you increase its business value and thus its funding potential, as well as preventing dangerous stovepipe development efforts that, by their very nature, discourage the sharing of information.

Migrate to Enterprisewide

If sharing your data mart seems appropriate for your organization, and other organizations have turned their heads in your direction because of the valuable work it is delivering, you might consider transforming it into a cross-functional data warehouse.

While most independent data marts[4] should probably stay that way, it sometimes makes sense to consolidate homogeneous data. For example, if your company has been relying on more than one data mart, say, one in finance and one dedicated to risk management, users often wind up consolidating data from both.

One bank I know realized quite quickly the disadvantages of maintaining call center data on a stand-alone data mart. Customers who called the bank to lodge a complaint or make an inquiry had their feedback entered into a transactional system by a call center service rep. Feedback data was then loaded onto an independent data mart owned by the call center, where it was matched with the customer's name and address. That way, once the problem was resolved, the bank could send out a "thanks for the feedback" letter, explaining the resolution.

The trouble was, since the marketing analysis system—another independent data mart—stored comprehensive information about individual customers, the bank's call center couldn't easily link customer input to more comprehensive customer behaviors (see figure 10-7). This capability could have allowed complaint analysis by customer segment, revealing how customers in the same segment who did not complain might feel.

---

4. Chapter 3 defines the differences between an independent and a dependent data mart.

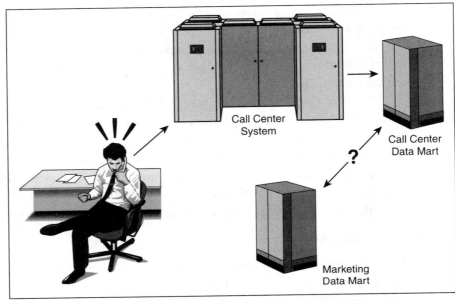

Call Center
System

Call Center
Data Mart

?

Marketing
Data Mart

Figure 10-7: The Marts Aren't Talking (But the Customer Is!)

Moreover, if an improvement was made to a product or service, salespeople and product managers with access to only the marketing data mart had no choice but to specifically request reports from the call center data mart to find out whether product or service improvements had been made. And they had no way of discovering why the improvement was initiated in the first place.

By combining both data marts and centralizing the data on a single platform fed by the billing, call center, and usage transaction systems, the bank combined system administration and data management efforts and reduced costs. Power users from different organizations could profile customers, examine trouble tickets, and even predict which customers might be averse to service changes.

This consolidation made decision making a whole lot easier. Users could now find out which customers had received new services, which products or services had been modified based on customer complaints, and which products caused the most frequent complaints without having to access multiple systems. Product improvements were made. A new follow-up process was implemented. This ease of use made everyone happier, most of all the support staff, who no longer had to maintain two separate systems.

An Insider's Crystal Ball

I don't purport to be a technology soothsayer, nor am I a futurist. But I've worked with over 40 companies in the last two years alone, and there are some definite trends in their strategies and visions for data warehousing. Below I've briefly outlined a few of those trends, explaining the issues and concerns that many data-warehousing leaders are in the midst of evaluating. They could save you some duplicate research and perhaps spark some new ideas.

It's worth mentioning that one of the most pervasive trends in data warehousing is the evolution of the term itself. The greater the degree to which a company's data warehouse touches new technology, the more likely it is that the data warehouse becomes synonymous with that technology. Thus, decision support, business intelligence, database marketing, CRM, knowledge management, and a host of other "systems" may in fact be synonymous with a really useful data warehouse providing key knowledge to the business.

Clickstream Storage

Everybody has a Web site. Whether the site is a core sales channel or simply brochure-ware, recording visits to your Web site establishes an interesting registry of record and provides a new window into the behavior of existing customers and imminent prospects.

The ability to store visitors' every mouse click as they go from screen to screen around your Web site is an invaluable tool with which to determine the content that best contributes to successful outcomes or purchases. And where better to store the succession and volume of those mouse clicks than on the data warehouse?

Clickstream analysis allows companies to track what visitors are looking at and also monitor how long they dwell on each screen. This information can indicate that certain screens are more interesting than others, that specific keywords are frequent search criteria, or that a site visitor might have abandoned his search for a given product due to wait times or poor information.

Clickstream analysis can contribute to enhanced product development, facilitate more robust customer profiling, and even raise customer satisfaction levels. It can help companies with e-commerce Web sites track which pages are key stepping stones to sales.

For example, United Airlines, discouraged by less than flattering quality surveys in the late 1990s, now captures customer profile data from its Web site in order to better tailor service to individual fliers. Clickstream data records can reveal which customers have visited the site multiple times, how regularly they have done so, and whether they have bought or not.

A retailer I work with has recently begun gathering and analyzing clickstream data to identify e-shoppers who may leave the company's Web site prematurely. An abandoned shopping cart can not only mean lost revenue, but may in fact suggest a dissatisfied customer. By analyzing a shopper's clickstreams, the retailer can surmise the point at which shopper left the site. The company can then modify its e-commerce Web site to make it easier for future shoppers to find what they're looking for and proceed to checkout. Clickstream analysis also allows the retailer to motivate a valuable customer to return to the site by e-mailing him coupons and discounts on items that he may have left in his cart during the prior shopping trip.

In short, clickstream information gives a company yet another end-user touch point that can be monitored and ultimately melded into a customer's overall profile, thereby enabling more detailed understanding of customer behaviors, both past and future.

Enterprise Resource Planning

When enterprise resource planning (ERP) software arrived on the scene in the early 1990s, many customers began centralizing their corporate data for the first time. It was only a matter of time before ERP and data warehousing collided. After all, ERP systems such as Peoplesoft, SAP, and Baan rely on data to help companies streamline their business operations, capturing the data and consolidating it onto a single platform.

Concerned with peaking sales, ERP vendors have begun searching for alternative ways to leverage their systems. In addition, their current tool offerings don't support the variety and depth of analysis that many DSS tools currently offer. Their collective head has thus turned toward data warehousing.

In an attempt at greater market share, some ERP vendors want to *become* the data warehouse. Most ERP systems are transaction-based and thus don't lend themselves well to decision support. ERP wasn't designed to support the ad hoc queries many businesspeople need to submit in order to analyze the human resources, general ledger, fixed-asset, or accounts payable data that populates their ERP systems.

So ERP vendors are busily creating separate data models in order to offer new reporting capabilities. With cross-functional data already sitting on an ERP system, the putative logic is that an ERP tool can be reengineered to accommodate decision support in addition to operational transactions, and *voilà*: a data warehouse!

ERP software products are part of a larger collective known as "packaged applications." Packaged applications are by and large process-oriented, dealing with common business functions such as human resources administration or product distribution. This data is by itself marginally useful for decision support. But when combined with additional corporate data, it can become a valuable addition.

Instead of the ERP platform supporting query and analysis, the data should be extracted and loaded onto a data warehouse, where it can coexist with non-ERP data, offering an even richer set of reporting capabilities. ERP packages offer data to support examination of human resource allocations, forecasting of demand for goods and services, and tax record analysis, all legitimate uses for DSS. Granted, ERP systems offer their own data-sourcing challenges—most comprise hundreds or even thousands of proprietary files that must be translated into a relational data model before being loaded onto the data warehouse. Moreover, ERP systems aren't designed to support the large volumes of historical information that are key to advanced decision support analysis.

Data warehouse data models are much easier to interpret and modify than most ERP data structures. The payoff is ultimately greater flexibility and ease of use. By focusing its data warehouse on a range of corporatewide data, of which ERP data is a subset, a company can adopt ERP as simply another data warehouse data source, enhancing its reporting capabilities even further via a unified e-data standard.

Extending the Data Warehouse to External Vendors

The concept of opening up a data warehouse to external suppliers has been around for years. Rather than managing the cumbersome order and stocking process, large retailers gave manufacturers secure access to their data warehouses. In return, a given manufacturer could determine when a certain product warranted restocking, prevent costly out-of-stock situations, save the retailer the hassle of reordering, and forge a closer partnership into the bargain.

But security, data quality, and infrastructure issues have deterred the majority of data warehouse users from handing out logon IDs to external third parties. Companies have been having enough trouble just keeping their own end-users happy.

Enhanced data quality, combined with trends in end-user ownership of applications, has freed companies to build the infrastructure necessary to allow suppliers to see their own data. A supplier can now remotely log on to his customer's data warehouse and gauge sales of his product, evaluate product performance, review stock levels, and plan production schedules accordingly.

For example, a supplier to a construction firm can track his tools not only through development but also through sales and usage. By tracking the product through the supply chain, the supplier can even monitor complaints by builders or home buyers, resulting in refinements that can ultimately improve customer satisfaction.

In fact, many retailers have now transferred responsibility for stock levels from their own employees to the suppliers themselves, offering them financial incentives to maintain optimal stock levels and penalizing them for failing. In fact, releasing selected data to suppliers and vendors can allow companies to offload certain logistics and focus more on marketing and efforts to increase customer satisfaction.

Some companies are guarded about their data, considering it top secret and thus releasing it only to select internal users. Data security for its own sake can quickly become a de facto corporate policy.

These companies don't understand, however, that allowing business partners to view data on the warehouse isn't an all-or-nothing proposition, but rather a strategy that involves careful planning and control procedures. These companies need to learn that they can maintain customer ownership—and prevent the access of proprietary information—while fostering all-around improvements.

One of my clients, a brokerage firm, resells mutual funds and allows fund managers to monitor fund sales while never actually seeing the customers who have purchased them. Smart companies provide vendors with canned reports specific to their products, maintaining control of the information while defining the information the vendor sees. When customers reap the rewards via refined products and more effective product placement, seller-vendor data sharing becomes a win-win-win situation.

Customized Web Portals

When I asked the president of my company to describe the future of data warehousing, here's what he said:

> The future of data warehousing is a lot like the cruise ship industry: the captain knows more about troubleshooting than about management,

customers grouse about the price, workers go from one place to the next, the boat's so slow you can't tell if it's even moving, the most exciting thing is the next meal, and in order to see what's ahead, you need a port hole.

The next wave in data warehousing is the customization of data presentation, and portals are showing the way. While traditional implementation efforts have concentrated on customizing information content, for the first time the focus is shifting toward customizing end-user access methods.

Internet portals allow end-users both to see their data via standard Web browser technology and to personalize their browsers so that they have a unique window into the data. In effect, it's the same principle that companies like Yahoo! (with My Yahoo!) and Netscape (with My Netscape) have adopted: allowing users to view information according to their own specifications. But the portal concept is being taken one step further: The data warehouse application can now present answers to the individual user based on who she is and the types of formats she prefers.

By allowing end-users to create their own personal interfaces instead of requiring programmers to create the user interface, as with other application tools, Web portals provide users with a unique look and feel. They can actually encourage users to log on. When a user arrives at the office, he can call up his own welcome screen with a diverse array of information—from automatically executed canned revenue reports to company Web broadcasts to stock prices to his daily horoscope.

But the truly exciting feature of DSS portals is that they can offer up information based on the end-user's specific needs. For example, a grocery store manager isn't interested in global shipping reports, any more than a merchandiser wants to see daily sales for one specific store. Web portals offer the right person the optimal set of information. Since this information is likely to be critical to that employee's daily job performance, it is considered highly valuable. Portals can also be customized to specific business circumstances, for instance: "When profits drop, generate Reports 1 and 2"; or "When inventories drop, run Reports 8, 9, and 10."

Some companies are going beyond the portal idea by deploying portals directly to their customers. For instance, Bank of America allows customers to view account-specific information via portals and generate their own personal DSS reports. Some portal development projects are retrieving information from a company's Web site, or from elsewhere on the Web, and storing it on the data warehouse for later analysis. This information could include pop-up survey data from Web content providers, or even data from a competitor's Web site.

Real-Time E-Marketing

You've probably already logged on to at least one retailer's Web site and purchased something. But have you noticed that some of those retailers seem to know you better than others? And have you ever received e-mail from that vendor confirming an order or telling you about a special new offer? Many retailers, having already mastered the one-to-one marketing initiatives described in chapter 3, are looking for accelerated ways to build customer relationships through their marketing messages.

New technologies allow these retailers to use customer profile data stored on the data warehouse and access this information each time the customer visits the Web site, creating a customized welcome each time. The welcome might include a new product offer based on propensity-to-buy data, or a discount based on the retailer's knowledge of that customer's likelihood of purchasing that product. E-commerce programs across industries are increasingly relying on customer scores and other characteristics to personalize real-time interactions.

The strategy of combining e-commerce and CRM in order to examine customer data and automatically execute campaigns for specific customers or segments is emerging to a lot of fanfare. Some new technologies can actually customize an entire Web site, from "look and feel" to product set, for an individual visitor at the time of access. Customer profiles, past purchase history, demographic and household information, risk or propensity scores, and clickstream analysis can go a long way to refining the understanding of customers' specific interests and behaviors.

The most ingenious Web sites can combine this data, usually originating from a data warehouse, with products being purchased in real time, offering immediate discounts or promoting additional products. Web site users can be profiled during a Web site visit and offered purchase incentives or other custom perks on the spot. This type of ability not only requires sophisticated data mining tools in order to capture and predict customer preferences, but also data warehouses that can serve up that information with transaction processing–type speeds. The trend toward the so-called active data warehouse is in its seminal stages.

The resulting point-of-purchase information can then be fed back into the data warehouse and used to improve in-store sales or to create more traditional marketing campaigns, providing true closed-loop processing and with it a state of the art customer experience.

The name of the game is "personalization," and the companies that have meaningful customer information on their data warehouses are those best positioned to leverage these cutting-edge capabilities.

Privacy

In 1999 the state of Idaho ranked forty-ninth in the immunization rate of its children. Idaho's governor proposed creating an immunization registry, in which an immunization record—including immunization dates, birth dates, and social security numbers—would be maintained for each child in the state. Idaho could then use the registry to pinpoint children who were not immunized before they entered school, or to provide lower-cost immunization clinics for poorer children.

The outcry from the potato state's citizens was loud and large. "They're gonna have my kids' social security numbers stored on an Internet database!" cried one Idaho woman, sounding more like a systems engineer than a mother of three. "Who knows who could look at that stuff?"

The governor and his aides scrambled to ease parents' concerns. Unfortunately, their tactic was to try explaining how passwords and data encryption would solve the problem. Needless to say, this information coming from the mouths of public officials did little to assuage public fears.

The fact is that organizations in both the public and private sector routinely collect data about people in order to perform a variety of strategies described in this book, from target marketing to product refinements to purchase propensity. And this makes some people very nervous.

Privacy litigation has already forced telephone companies and banks to curtail their use of consumer information without explicit customer approval. This litigation, which among other things forces companies to request permission to use customer data for marketing and other purposes, has dramatically blunted the use of data as a strategic weapon.

Recently, Amazon.com came under fire for using customer information for its "purchase circles," which it created by mining its customer data in order to segment similar shoppers for more effective product positioning. Critics cited Amazon's use of customers' e-mail addresses, which often indicate a shopper's employer and could thus imply that company's endorsement of certain published or recorded material.[5]

---

5. As reported by David F. Gallagher in the *New York Times,* September 7, 1999.

And it's getting worse. Consumers will increasingly demand value from the use of their data, claiming ownership of their personal information and divulging it for nothing less than a *quid pro quo*. As a result, negotiating with customers on the use of their data will become prevalent. A prime example is frequent-shopper cards at grocery stores. After several industry false starts, the retail business realized that the only way it could motivate customers to sign up for the cards, and thereby share personal data, was by providing price breaks.

The privacy issue represents both good news and bad news for data warehousing. The bad news is that the information many companies take for granted today might be in jeopardy tomorrow. And organizations such as the Electronic Frontier Foundation and the Federal Trade Commission (FTC) are watching, ready to sound the siren whenever technology threatens to impinge on individual privacy. A July 1999 report left no doubt that the FTC is ready to pounce on commercial companies that abandon prudence when it comes to collecting consumer data.[6]

The good news is that because the use of customer data is still on shaky ground, companies need to become even more intelligent about each discrete customer interaction in order to continue to motivate the customer to share information. Every customer's privacy preference should be a key component of his individual profile. The first time his stated privacy preference is breached, that customer's attrition likelihood increases—often by 100 percent.

In other words, the more deliberate the handling of a given customer, the less threatened that customer is, and the greater the likelihood that he will continue to participate in information sharing and bidirectional marketing programs. The best way to make customers feel special, to keep them coming back, is to understand them. And the best way to do that is with decision support and data warehousing.

The Whole Truth

It's important to reiterate that data warehouses aren't just about customer data, integral though that may be. Data warehouses worldwide are maintaining an extraordinary panoply of data, from diabetes research results to custom shoe measurements to terrorist travel itineraries to human gene sequences to poetry. Text, audio, and video are intermixed, yielding a potent cocktail of information.

---

6. Federal Trade Commission, "Self-Regulation and Privacy Online," see *http://www.ftc.gov/os/ 1999/9907/privacy99.pdf.*

This book has touched on data-warehousing successes and failures, citing the vanguard companies that have raised the implementation standard and offering authentic case studies so that you can judge the success criteria for yourself. The truth about the successes is that each company has its own set of metrics.

But the truth about the failures is this: Many are due to mistakes of conservatism, not mistakes of excess. Whether due to budget constraints, politics, or insurgent technologies—and despite the waning "big bang" approach to implementation—many companies whose data-warehousing projects have failed haven't thought big enough.

The passing of time and, hopefully, some of the information you've read here, have let much of the hot air out of the inflated rhetoric surrounding data warehousing. Increasingly the "experts" aren't those who stand behind podiums or circulate contiguous research papers, but those who have actually delivered real, working systems resulting in tangible benefits for their end-users.

So what are you waiting for?

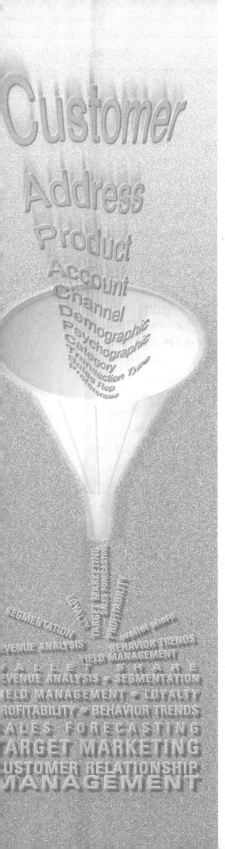

Appendix:
Haven't Had Enough?
Suggested Reading

In case this book has piqued your interest about how data warehouses are used in business, this appendix offers some additional published material on topics specific to information and how it's being used in business today.

Even though this book is for managers, I've broken down suggested reading material into three sections: business books, technology books, and Web sites. Of course, the books mentioned below are just a smattering in a vast library of works that are either pointed or tangential to data warehousing. All of them discuss business information as a competitive weapon, and all are on my bookshelf. The Web sites too are wonderful resources that feature a host of data warehouse research and key learnings.

Happy reading!

Business Books

I've cited the Peppers and Rogers œuvre, *Enterprise One to One: Tools for Competing in the Interactive Age* (Doubleday, 1997), several times in the book. They are great advocates of how treating customers differently is a competitive mandate. I particularly like their discussions of mass customization and ways to anticipate customer needs. See also their Web site: *www.marketing1to1.com*.

Arthur M. Hughes has a painstakingly thorough book on marketing concepts titled *Strategic Database Marketing: The Masterplan for Starting and Managing a Profitable,*

Customer-Based Marketing Program (McGraw-Hill, 1994). Building on his earlier books, Mr. Hughes presents a complete picture of current marketing initiatives and how they leverage data. While somewhat slanted toward the retail industry, the book offers an interesting glimpse of how marketing programs are deployed.

I really like Regis McKenna's books, and *Real Time* (Harvard Business School Press, 1997) is a front-runner. The book takes its concepts from McKenna's previous works, among them *Relationship Marketing: Successful Strategies for the Age of the Consumer* (Perseus Books, 1993), and argues persuasively that companies can't ignore technological advancements, including databases. Mr. McKenna also captures the often elusive difference between customer knowledge and customer treatment.

I like the way Ian H. Gordon describes the data warehouse as the "engine that enables Relationship Marketing" in his book *Relationship Marketing: New Strategies, Techniques and Technologies to Win the Customers You Want and Keep Them Forever* (John Wiley & Sons, 1998). For a marketing book, it's refreshingly accurate in its differentiation of data warehouses, data mining, and database technologies, and the section on justifying a new relationship marketing program could be effective ammunition for the acquisition of a data warehouse.

There are also a few worthwhile books on the emergence of the Internet that focus on e-data, particularly customer information. Jim Sterne's *Customer Service on the Internet: Building Relationships, Increasing Loyalty and Staying Competitive* (John Wiley & Sons, 1996) includes some interesting points about how the Web and customer service go hand in hand and discusses some real-world Web sites and why they work.

Also worth a read is *Net Future* (McGraw-Hill, 1999) by Chuck Martin. Like Mr. Sterne, Mr. Martin features some real-world snippets to prove his case that products are fast becoming commodities and that the Web can aid in understanding customers better. While Martin applies the term "data mining" with a liberal brush, his points about the capture and use of customer data make for interesting reading.

Crossing the Chasm: Marketing and Selling High-Tech Products to Mainstream Customers (HarperCollins, 1991) is Geoffrey A. Moore's contribution to positioning advanced technologies both within and outside an organization. While ideal for data warehouse vendors looking for new ways to peddle their wares, the book includes some more general topics that are valuable for any type of firm. I found Moore's description of the Technology Adoption Life Cycle as fresh as ever, and his characterizations of people most open to new technology developments make captivating reading.

Mobilizing the Organization: Bringing Strategy to Life (Prentice Hall International, 1996) puts an organizational twist on innovation that can be applied to the adoption of strategic technologies such as data warehouses. The authors—Litwin, Bray, and Brooke—present a refreshingly tactical perspective on socializing change within an organization and encouraging the participation of workers, leaders, and consultants to ensure successful transitions.

In *Permission Marketing: Turning Strangers into Friends, and Friends into Customers* (Simon & Schuster, 1999), Seth Godin, Yahoo's vice president of direct marketing, provides an engaging spin on targeting consumers via Web marketing and outlines what it takes to convert anonymous consumers into loyal customers.

As anyone who has read it will tell you, *The Effective Executive* (Harper & Row, 1966) is as germane to management today as it was when Peter F. Drucker wrote it. While the examples are slightly dated, many consider this book their management bible.

Technology Books

There is no shortage of technology-oriented books that discuss the architecture, planning, and implementation of data warehouse–related technologies. Here are some that I consider well balanced and organized:

The books of Dr. Bill Inmon, data warehousing's father figure, deserve a read. Although he publishes regularly, his *Building the Data Warehouse* (John Wiley & Sons, 1996) is probably his best-known work.

Ralph Kimball's books certainly bear mention as data warehouse implementation guides. His first book, the best-seller *The Data Warehouse Toolkit* (John Wiley & Sons, 1996), focuses on dimensional modeling concepts and examples. A collaborative sequel, *The Data Warehouse Lifecycle Toolkit: Expert Methods for Designing, Developing, and Deploying Data Warehouses* (John Wiley & Sons, 1998), is a compendium of tactical implementation advice, including a comprehensive discussion of dimensional design, Kimball's leitmotif.

Likewise, I admire Christopher Adamson and Michael Venerable's *Data Warehousing Design Solutions* (John Wiley & Sons, 1998). The book leverages dimensional modeling concepts by way of a systematic presentation of various dimensional designs. While it concentrates on a stovepipe approach to development, the book invites database practitioners to overcome the often turgid debates around data modeling and get on with the work.

Doug Hackney's *Understanding and Implementing Successful Data Marts* (Addison-Wesley Developers Press, 1997) applies a similar "from the trenches" perspective to implementing data marts. Hackney aptly straddles both high-level planning and low-level implementation topics, transcending technology discussion with a thorough look at data marts and their implementation lifecycle.

Barry Devlin's *Data Warehouse: From Architecture to Implementation* (Addison-Wesley, 1997) should be on the reading list of every technical project manager and data warehouse architect. Devlin has managed to render complex topics simple in this data warehouse development guide, and he is not shy about taking on some of data warehousing's modern myths. His discussions of data—its quality, its translation, and its loading—are especially skilled.

A few data-mining books are also worth a closer look, particularly for readers interested in a breakdown of the various data-mining applications. Adriaans and Zantinge's *Data Mining* (Addison-Wesley, 1996) contains an effective introduction to the various data-mining algorithms and their uses, as well as some good examples.

Likewise, *Data Mining Techniques: For Marketing, Sales, and Customer Support* by Michael Berry and Gordon Linoff (John Wiley & Sons, 1997) provides a user-friendly look at how data mining is used in marketing and how its results are measured and leveraged. In addition to discussing different data-mining types, Robert Groth's *Data Mining: A Hands-On Approach for Business Professionals* (Prentice Hall, 1997) presents a thorough list of data-mining technologies and includes usage scenarios from actual products.

And pulling back from the data warehouse space a bit more, Jeri Edwards's excellent *3-Tier Client/Server at Work* (John Wiley & Sons, 1999) is an ultra-friendly guide to client/server architectures that should be on every system integrator's reading list.

Web Sites

No data-warehousing book worth the paper it's printed on could get away without mentioning Larry Greenfield's Web site, *www.starnetinc.com/larryg*. Greenfield offers a laundry list of data-warehousing vendors and consultants and includes a series of white papers on a variety of data warehouse topics as well as links to a host of different vendor and analyst sites. This is the sine qua non of data warehouse Web sites.

DSstar is a subscription service that offers regular columns and timely industry press releases. While it targets the data-mining crowd, it's my preferred way of staying current with the tidal wave of vendor developments and new product announcements. Check out *www.tgc.com/dsstar*.

Another good site is *www.datawarehousing.com*, published by Data Mirror Corporation. This site offers an even-handed account of current data-warehousing vendors, includes white papers on a variety of topics, and is a credible and up-to-date data warehouse information clearinghouse.

Also worth mentioning is *www.datawarehouse.com*. This Web site features articles from *DM Review* magazine, as well as industry news. It boasts a discussion group on data warehousing in which experts weigh in on everything from arrogant vendors to canonical aggregates. (There are also other sites that include data warehouse discussion groups. Check out *www.remarq.com*.)

If you're interested in one of the regular data-warehousing conferences offered throughout the year, see *www.idwa.org*, the International Data Warehouse Association's reference point for data warehousing. And *www.dw-institute.com* offers research and free white papers as part of its repertory. (Note that there are membership fees for both these sites.) Likewise, *www.dci.com* lists updated conference schedules and intermingles a regular cast of speakers with presentations on emerging trends. I particularly like NCR Corp.'s annual Partners conference, *www.ncrpartners.com*, run by NCR's customers. Notwithstanding some of the more visible data warehouse conferences, some of which have seen waning attendance of late, thousands of data-warehousing practitioners continue to flock to Partners for real user testimonials and implementation experiences.

The Web site for Baseline Consulting Group, *www.baseline-consulting.com*, offers online white papers and conference presentations on various data-warehousing, database-marketing, and other industry-based topics. Current articles include scoping your data mart project, a DSS primer for the telecommunications industry, and a collection of data-mining case studies.

Also check out the sites of various analyst companies, including *gartner5.gartnerweb.com* (Gartner Group); *www.metagroup.com* (META Group); *www.pamg.com* (Palo Alto Management Group); *www.gigaweb.com* (Giga Information Group); *www.forrester.com* (Forrester Research); *www.psgroup.com*

(Patricia Seybold Group); and *www.survey.com* (survey.com). They're all good sources of market research and industry trends and often provide free snippets of their research.

The various trade publications that pertain to data warehousing and ancillary technologies often have Web sites that include up-to-date product announcements, case studies, and the occasional research poll. Check out the following:

CIO magazine: *www.cio.com*
(*CIO* has an online research center specific to data warehousing that includes articles pertaining both to data warehouse technologies and their use in business. See *www.cio.com/forums/data*)
Computerworld: www.computerworld.com/home
Information Week: www.informationweek.com
Data Management Review: www.dmreview.com
Fast Company: www.fastcompany.com
Computer Reseller News: www.crn.com
Wired: www.wired.com
San Jose Mercury News: www.sjmercury.com

And don't forget the vendor Web sites, which occasionally offer tidbits unrelated to the company's product for the technically curious.

Index

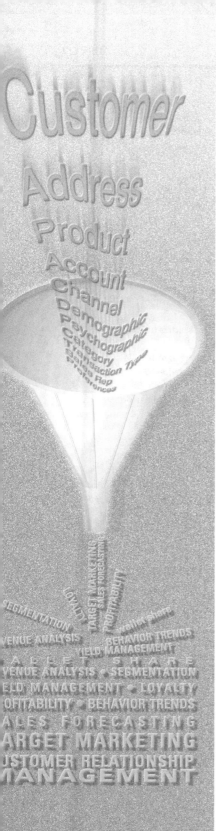

Addison-Wesley Professional

How to Register Your Book

Register this Book

Visit: **http://www.aw.com/cseng/register**

Enter the ISBN*

Then you will receive:

- Notices and reminders about upcoming author appearances, tradeshows, and online chats with special guests
- Advanced notice of forthcoming editions of your book
- Book recommendations
- Notification about special contests and promotions throughout the year

*The ISBN can be found on the copyright page of the book

Visit our Web site

http://www.aw.com/cseng

When you think you've read enough, there's always more content for you at Addison-Wesley's web site. Our web site contains a directory of complete product information including:

- Chapters
- Exclusive author interviews
- Links to authors' pages
- Tables of contents
- Source code

You can also discover what tradeshows and conferences Addison-Wesley will be attending, read what others are saying about our titles, and find out where and when you can meet our authors and have them sign your book.

We encourage you to patronize the many fine retailers who stock Addison-Wesley titles. Visit our online directory to find stores near you.

Contact Us via Email

cepubprof@awl.com
Ask general questions about our books.
Sign up for our electronic mailing lists.
Submit corrections for our web site.

mikeh@awl.com
Submit a book proposal.
Send errata for a book.

cepubpublicity@awl.com
Request a review copy for a member of the media interested in reviewing new titles.

registration@awl.com
Request information about book registration.

Addison-Wesley Professional
One Jacob Way, Reading, Massachusetts 01867 USA
TEL 781-944-3700 • FAX 781-942-3076